CASEBOOK SERIES

Wordsworth: *The Prelude*

Casebook Series

GENERAL EDITOR: A. E. Dyson

Jane Austen: *Emma* DAVID LODGE
William Blake: *Songs of Innocence and Experience*
  MARGARET BOTTRALL
Emily Brontë: *Wuthering Heights* MIRIAM ALLOTT
Dickens: *Bleak House* A. E. DYSON
T. S. Eliot: *Four Quartets* BERNARD BERGONZI
T. S. Eliot: *The Waste Land* C. B. COX AND
  ARNOLD P. HINCHLIFFE
Henry Fielding: *Tom Jones* NEIL COMPTON
E. M. Forster: *A Passage to India* MALCOLM BRADBURY
Jonson: *Volpone* JONAS A. BARISH
John Keats: *Odes* G. S. FRASER
D. H. Lawrence: *Sons and Lovers* GĀMINI SALGĀDO
D. H. Lawrence: *'The Rainbow' and 'Women in Love'* COLIN CLARKE
Marlowe: *Doctor Faustus* JOHN JUMP
John Osborne: *Look Back in Anger* J. RUSSELL TAYLOR
Pope: *The Rape of the Lock* JOHN DIXON HUNT
Shakespeare: *Antony and Cleopatra* JOHN RUSSELL BROWN
Shakespeare: *Hamlet* JOHN JUMP
Shakespeare: *Henry IV Parts I and II* G. K. HUNTER
Shakespeare: *Henry V* MICHAEL QUINN
Shakespeare: *Julius Caesar* PETER URE
Shakespeare: *King Lear* FRANK KERMODE
Shakespeare: *Macbeth* JOHN WAIN
Shakespeare: *Measure for Measure* C. K. STEAD
Shakespeare: *The Merchant of Venice* JOHN WILDERS
Shakespeare: *Othello* JOHN WAIN
Shakespeare: *The Tempest* D. J. PALMER
Shakespeare: *Twelfth Night* D. J. PALMER
Shakespeare: *The Winter's Tale* KENNETH MUIR
Tennyson: *In Memoriam* JOHN DIXON HUNT
Virginia Woolf: *To the Lighthouse* MORRIS BEJA
Wordsworth: *Lyrical Ballads* ALUN R. JONES AND
  WILLIAM TYDEMAN
Wordsworth: *The Prelude* W. J. HARVEY AND RICHARD GRAVIL
Yeats: *Last Poems* JON STALLWORTHY

IN PREPARATION

Charlotte Brontë: *'Jane Eyre' and 'Villette'* MIRIAM ALLOTT
Coleridge: *The Ancient Mariner and Other Poems* ALUN R. JONES
  AND WILLIAM TYDEMAN
Conrad: *The Secret Agent* IAN WATT
Donne: *Songs and Sonnets* JULIAN LOVELOCK
George Eliot: *Middlemarch* PATRICK SWINDEN
James Joyce: *Portrait of the Artist as a Young Man* MORRIS BEJA
Milton: *Paradise Lost* A. E. DYSON
Milton: *Samson Agonistes* STANLEY FISH
Shakespeare: *Richard II* NICHOLAS BROOKE

Wordsworth

The Prelude

A CASEBOOK

EDITED BY

W. J. HARVEY

and

RICHARD GRAVIL

MACMILLAN

40488

First published 1972 by
THE MACMILLAN PRESS LTD
London and Basingstoke
Associated companies in New York Toronto
Dublin Melbourne Johannesburg and Madras

SBN 333 04846 6 (hard cover)
      333 08565 5 (paper cover)

Printed in Great Britain by
THE ANCHOR PRESS LTD
Tiptree, Essex

CONTENTS

Acknowledgements   7

General Editor's Preface   9

Introduction   11

References to Wordsworth's Works   31

Part 1: *Waiting for 'The Recluse', 1798–1841*

Brief Chronology of the Unfinished 'Recluse'   35

Correspondence and Comment within the
    Wordsworth Circle   37

Part 2: *Victorian Assessments, 1852–1897*

WALTER BAGEHOT, p. 55 – RICHARD HOLT
HUTTON, p. 58 – WALTER HORATIO PATER,
p. 66 – ÉMILE LEGOUIS, p. 73

Part 3: *Modern Studies, 1926–1967*

HELEN DARBISHIRE: Wordsworth's *Prelude*   81

J. R. MACGILLIVRAY: The Three Forms of *The
Prelude*, 1798–1805   99

ELLEN DOUGLASS LEYBURN: Recurrent Words in
The Prelude   116

JONATHAN BISHOP: Wordsworth and the 'Spots
of Time'   134

COLIN CLARKE: From *Romantic Paradox*   155

GEOFFREY H. HARTMAN: A Poet's Progress:
Wordsworth and the *Via Naturaliter Negativa*   175

W. J. HARVEY: Vision and Medium in *The Prelude*   195

MORSE PECKHAM: A Post-Enlightenment
Imagination   212

ROBERT LANGBAUM: The Evolution of Soul
in Wordsworth's Poetry   218

W. J. HARVEY: Retrospect and Prospect   237

Select Bibliography   245

Notes on Contributors   249

Index   251

ACKNOWLEDGEMENTS

The editor and publishers wish to thank the following, who have kindly given permission for the use of copyright material: The Twentieth Century Press for 'Wordsworth's *Prelude*' by Helen Darbishire, from *The Nineteenth Century*, XCIX (May 1926); University of Toronto Press for J. R. MacGillivray, 'The Three Forms of *The Prelude*, 1798–1805', in *Essays in English Literature from the Renaissance to the Victorian Age, Presented to A. S. P. Woodhouse*, ed. M. MacLure and F. W. Watt (1964); The Johns Hopkins Press for 'Recurrent Words in *The Prelude*' by Ellen Douglass Leyburn, from *English Literary History*, XVI (1949), and 'Wordsworth and the "Spots of Time" ' by Jonathan Bishop, from *English Literary History*, XXVI (1959); Routledge & Kegan Paul Ltd and Barnes & Noble Inc. for extracts from *Romantic Paradox* (1962) by Colin Clarke; Chicago University Press for Geoffrey H. Hartman, 'A Poet's Progress: Wordsworth and the *Via Naturaliter Negativa*', from *Modern Philology*, LIX (Feb 1962), revised in expanded form as a chapter in *Wordsworth's Poetry, 1787–1814* (Yale University Press, 1964); The Library, The Queen's University of Belfast, for 'Vision and Medium in *The Prelude*' by W. J. Harvey, a revised version of *Poetic Vision in the World of Prose*, the Queen's University New Lecture Series, No. 29 (1966); George Braziller Inc. for the extract from *Beyond the Tragic Vision: The Quest for Identity in the Nineteenth Century* (1962) by Morse Peckham; Modern Language Association of America for the essay 'The Evolution of Soul in Wordsworth's Poetry' by Robert Langbaum, from *PMLA*, LXXXII (May 1967), collected in *The Modern Spirit* (New York: Oxford University Press, 1970).

GENERAL EDITOR'S PREFACE

The critical forum is a place of vigorous conflict and disagreement, but there is nothing in this to cause dismay. What is attested is the complexity of human experience and the richness of literature, not any chaos or relativity of taste. A critic is better seen, no doubt, as an explorer than as an 'authority'; but explorers ought to be, and usually are, well equipped. The effect of good criticism is to convince us of what C. S. Lewis called 'the enormous extension of our being which we owe to authors'. This Casebook will be justified only if it helps to promote the same end.

A single volume can represent no more than a small selection of critical opinions. Some critics have been excluded for reasons of space, and it is hoped that readers will follow up the further suggestions in the Select Bibliography. Other contributors have been severed from their original context, to which some readers may wish to return. Indeed, if they take a hint from the critics represented here, they certainly will.

The sudden death of W. J. Harvey was a great loss to English criticism. He was working at the time on this Casebook, but the text was not completed. I am most grateful to Richard Gravil for taking over the volume. The Introduction and the first two parts are Dr Gravil's while the selection of modern criticism is partly his, and partly Professor Harvey's. The article which Professor Harvey had prepared for an Introduction is included now as the final item. Also included is a version of Professor Harvey's Inaugural Lecture at the Queen's University, Belfast.

A. E. DYSON

INTRODUCTION

I brought home, and read, the Prelude. It is a poorer Excursion; the same sort of faults and beauties, but the faults greater, and the beauties fainter, both in themselves, and because faults are always made more oppressive, and beauties less pleasing, by repetition. The story is the old story. There are the old raptures about mountains and cataracts; the old flimsy philosophy about the effect of scenery on the mind; the old crazy mystical metaphysics, the endless wildernesses of dull, flat prosaic twaddle; and here and there fine descriptions and energetic declamations interspersed.[1]

Perhaps if we had not come to underrate *The Excursion* we should be less surprised by Macaulay's sense of *déjà vu*. For whatever reason, it requires an effort of imagination to appreciate this estimate of *The Prelude*; and for that we should be grateful. But I do not quote Lord Macaulay in order to mock egregious impercipience : only the greater colour and freedom of a private diary distinguishes his judgement from the general critical response in 1850–1. *The Prelude* was, on the whole, politely received by those reviews which condescended to notice it at all. Most were in agreement with the critic in *Graham's Magazine* who felt it would have been improved by a greater measure of Wordsworth's 'Trances of thought and mountings of the mind', and correspondingly less of the filling.

The Prelude was given, posthumously, to an age which knew its Wordsworth all too well, and which assessed the poem according to criteria divided from the poem by fifty years – in which the English had come to like their philosophy utilitarian and practical, their poetry ardent and lyrical. The greatest poem of the age was overshadowed by the publication of *In Memoriam* at the same time, and was kept in the shadows for

the rest of the century by a taste in verse set by Edgar Allan
Poe and Robert Browning. It was overshadowed, too, by
Wordsworth himself – that unloved eminence, the poet
laureate, who was known more by an image of him circulated
by the fashionable wits of London than for himself. To read
Thomas Cooper's account of his meeting with Wordsworth in
1846 or J. S. Mill's of the poet's society in the 1830s,[2] is to
meet with the astonishment of intelligent and well-informed
men at finding themselves in the company of a flexible and
generous mind and of great vitality, and not with the bigoted
and compromised fiction of Browning's 'The Lost Leader' or
Hazlitt's talk. At its publication, not only was the poem some
half-century old, but it missed the poet's brief and belated
blaze of celebrity by nearly half that time. In 1850 Wordsworth was at best a pastor figure. 'I class Wordsworth', wrote
John Ruskin in 1851, 'as a thoroughly religious book':[3] to
such a book *The Prelude* could only be a footnote.

The Prelude thus came to light as a curiosity, and as a rather
heavy duty. Thomas Chase, who reviewed the poem together
with Christopher Wordsworth's *Memoirs of William Wordsworth* in the *North American Review*, is not untypical in
taking the two together as having the same kind of interest
for Wordsworthian background. Several journals joined in
approaching the poem with the detached respect due to an
antiquarian curiosity. The *Examiner*'s article, printed in three
journals, began : 'This is a voice that speaks to us across a gulf
of nearly fifty years.' The *Gentleman's Magazine* agreed :

Historically, it carries us back to the very threshold of the nineteenth century. . . . It speaks to us across a gulf of fifty years. . . .
For the Prelude is elder than the meridian products of Goethe's
genius . . . anterior to the greatest war and to the most appalling
catastrophe the world has ever seen. It is elder, too, than all the
mechanical strides of science, and all the political and social
developments which have rendered the nineteenth century an
epoch far more momentous and marvellous than any epoch of
equal duration 'in ancient or in modern books enrolled'. . . . The
octogenarian bard may be fitly regarded as representative of the
acts and thoughts of the last half-century.

In such tones, cocky and sonorous, and comically antique
beside the poem they were reviewing, most of the reviewers
seized the chance to write a review and an obituary in one. The
Eclectic Review bequeathed Wordsworth to posterity with the
most grandiose obsequies of them all : three paragraphs of
sustained parallelisms on the theme that Wordsworth was for
an age, Milton for all time.

On a level of greater particularity the reviews indulged
greatly in analogy – in an attempt to decide what sort of
object the poem was. *Tait's* compared Wordsworth here with
Petrarch; the *British Quarterly* made several invidious com-
parisons with Goethe's *Dichtung und Wahrheit*, lamenting
Wordsworth's inattention to biographical detail and feeling
that he might have been more forthcoming in prose; the
Eclectic saw it as a sort of poetic *Sartor Resartus*; the *Prospective Review* lamented that it had not the 'rapture' of Lamar-
tine's *Confidences*. There is nothing wrong with such analogies, and modern criticism has used them widely – it *is* like
Carlyle's *Sartor Resartus*, for example, in that each belongs to
the same archetypal pattern, the myth of rebirth – but in 1850
the reviewers used them not to illuminate the qualities of *The
Prelude* but to suggest that it would have been better as something else.

The reviews were not without perceptive remarks. But these
are almost all concerned with the nature of Wordsworth's limitations, and they serve to remind us that we enthusiastic
Wordsworthians are somewhat deficient in our sense of what
constitutes poetry. In general *The Prelude* was seen by its
reviewers as a kind of rehearsal for *The Excursion*, to which,
it was assumed, it added nothing of philosophical or poetic
value. What was of much greater interest was the poem's
political revelations. Lord Macaulay is again representative :
his entry continued, 'The poem is to the last degree Jacobinical,
indeed Socialist. I understand perfectly why Wordsworth did
not choose to publish it in his lifetime.' Of the generous quotations in the reviews much the greatest space (apart from the
mountings of the mind) is given to (i) Wordsworth's stric-
tures on education, and (ii) his account of the French

Revolution. The Simplon Pass and Snowdon passages were scarce noticed in 1850 – St John's College is repeatedly discussed. From the *Prospective Review* came this cryptic message : Wordsworth, it decided, 'was an illustrious Johnian, but not illustrious *as* a Johnian'. The *British Quarterly* was carping about Wordsworth's ingratitude to Cambridge, but the *Gentleman's Magazine* thundered : '. . . we trust that the Royal Commission will inaugurate its enquiries into the studies of the university by pondering upon Wordsworth's experiences as narrated in his Prelude'. This scandal, Crabb Robinson thought, robbed Wordsworth's memorial statue of many professorial subscribers.[4]

The first reviewers, then, either delighted in finding a liberal ally in a most unexpected quarter, or looked for a didactic poem and found a rather long, rather unusual, specimen of what they were looking for. But they did not, any more than did the great Victorians, consider it as a poem, in any way remarkable as poetry. The Victorians knew what to do with Wordsworth's output. 'Reduce his seven volumes to one', Clough advised,[5] and Arnold set out to comply by jettisoning the 'illusory' philosophy, and saving the best fruits of the 'great decade'. Not that Wordsworth was denigrated by his critics. Rather they thought they had placed him rather well, in a dignified setting somewhere on the periphery of what could really be called poetry :

We cannot help feeling that the material of his nature was essentially prose. . . . The normal condition of many poets would seem to approach that temperature to which Wordsworth's mind could be raised only by the white heat of profoundly inward passion.[6]

Lowell here is saying the same as Mill, that Wordsworth is 'the poet of unpoetical natures'. Compared with Shelley – the nineteenth century's idea of what a poet is supposed to be like – Wordsworth is not really quite a poet. An age nourished on the scarlet and azure of Byron and Shelley, the gorgeous Pre-Raphaelites, the crimson agonies and purple doubts of poets from Beddoes to Tennyson, was not propitious for *The Prelude*'s visionary dreariness.

It is not, I think, that *The Prelude* was too late for its time. To be sure, Lamb and Montgomery on *The Excursion* show that there were minds well capable of loving *The Prelude*, but these, like Coleridge, were the poet's friends. 'To William Wordsworth', Coleridge's poem on *The Prelude*, remains the best nineteenth-century criticism of the poem : alone in giving a sense of its shape and concerns, and, above all, its effect on the one 'reader' to whom at that time Wordsworth addressed it. There is no reason to think, however, that the poem would have fared better in 1806 than in 1850. When Francis Jeffrey reviewed *The Excursion* in 1814 his starkest incomprehension was reserved for precisely those passages which attain to the level of *The Prelude*, indeed are a proto-Prelude.[7] Nor is one's confidence improved by Lord Jeffrey's opinion that of the *Poems in Two Volumes*, published in 1807, the 'Immortality Ode' was 'the most illegible and unintelligible part of the publication'.[8]

Had it been published in 1806 it would not, of course, have been the same poem as the one reviewed in 1850. Not the least part of *The Prelude*'s fascination is that here we have a poem with two voices, the intimate, ingenuous voice of the poem to Coleridge, and the more literary voice of the '1850' version. There is no need for us to look closely here at the difference between these texts. Professor de Selincourt's edition of 1926, revised by Helen Darbishire in 1959, has a wealth of scholarly, critical and interpretative notes. Helen Darbishire's classic review of the 1926 edition is included here, and readers may wish to compare with it Barbara Everett's review of the 1959 edition. Opinion has changed as to which version is the better poem. De Selincourt thought that the ideal text lay somewhere in between, but that 'no one would doubt that the 1850 version is a better composition', which, in the formal sense, is true. Miss Darbishire's 1926 review, however, exemplifies the interest aroused by the publication of both texts in Wordsworth's changes of emphasis on matters political and religious, and Miss Everett's 1959 review expresses the contemporary position that the 1805–50 variations show Wordsworth's 'habit of changing a rather vague phrase instinct with feeling and aspiration into something more precise and complex in design, and more intellectual . . . in tone'.[9] Neither the '1805' nor the '1850' text, of course, belongs strictly to those dates. Some of the changes between 1806 and 1850 are noted by Helen Darbishire in this volume. Less well documented is the development of the 1805 text itself. So we have included Professor MacGillivray's very useful application of the Biblical 'higher criticism' to Wordsworth's 1805 text, 'The Three Forms of *The Prelude*'.

My suggestion that a version of *The Prelude* published in 1805–6 would not have met with critical acclaim does not mean that it would not have been influential. What Francis Jeffrey might have made of it is unimportant. What it might have meant to Shelley and to John Keats is a very different matter. We know that Keats accounted *The Excursion* one of 'three things to rejoice at in this age', and we know, too well perhaps, his reference to Wordsworth's 'palpable design' and his phrase 'the Wordsworthian or *egotistical* sublime'. But on the comparatively slender basis of 'Tintern Abbey' Keats constructed his equally famous comparison of Milton with Wordsworth's greater depth, and his talk of the 'chambers of the mind' and its dark passages, which Wordsworth's genius had explored and where we may follow. It is in *The Prelude*, after all, and not in *The Excursion*, that Wordsworth, unknown to Keats and Shelley, had used his most sublime blank verse not to expound a dogma but to explore the most numinous areas of a life-experience. The guidance which this poem might have exerted on the Romantic achievement, as Morse Peckham has implied in *Beyond the Tragic Vision* (1962), is what we may most regret about Wordsworth's long secret.

Wordsworth, of course, regarded his work on the model of a Gothic cathedral, suggesting that his shorter poems were related to the longer works as the chapels to a choir and nave. And we may observe how, despite their failure to recognise *The Prelude* for what it is, the Victorian critics were able, through 'Tintern Abbey', the ballads, and the shorter lyrics, to attain to a sense of Wordsworth's 'healing power' which somehow suggests that they intuited the larger frame. We have a feeling that for Arnold and the Victorians – Mill, Pater, Swinburne, Stephen and Hutton are all in their ways eminent Wordsworthians – Wordsworth had a primordial psychic value. Their picture of Wordsworth is partial and emasculated, but Arnold's 'Memorial Verses', for example, betray a sense of the poet's enormous presence in the age.

> Wordsworth has gone from us – and ye,
> Ah, may ye feel his voice as we !
> He too upon a wintry clime
> Had fallen – on this iron time
> Of doubts, disputes, distractions, fears.
> He found us when the age had bound
> Our souls in its benumbing round ;
> He spoke, and loosed our heart in tears.
> He laid us as we lay at birth
> On the cool flowery lap of earth ;
> Smiles broke from us and we had ease.
> The hills were round us, and the breeze
> Went o'er the sunlit fields again ;
> Our foreheads felt the wind and rain.
> Our youth returned : for there was shed
> On spirits that had long been dead,
> Spirits dried up and closely furled,
> The freshness of the early world.

And Mill, resolute as he was to keep poetry and philosophy apart, had cause to agree with Arnold's question :

> But where will Europe's latter hour
> Again find Wordsworth's healing power?

For Mill, in the midst of a crisis like that of the poet in books x and xi of *The Prelude*, had turned to Wordsworth's shorter poems – poems written, we remember, to 'co-operate with the benign tendencies in human nature' and 'be efficacious in making men wiser, better and happier'.[10] Mill writes :

What made Wordsworth's poems a medicine for my state of mind, was that they expressed, not outward beauty, but states of feeling, and of thought coloured by feeling, under the excitement of beauty. They seemed to be the very culture of the feelings, which I was in quest of. In them I seemed to draw from a source of inward joy, of sympathetic and imaginative pleasure, which could be shared in by all human beings.[11]

Yet *The Prelude* remained in comparative obscurity until the closing years of the nineteenth century.

It was from France that the poem was given to the world for the second time. In 1896 Émile Legouis published his *La Jeunesse de William Wordsworth*, the first full-length study of *The Prelude*. This fresh start, like the reviews, is biographical in approach, but it established the central importance of *The Prelude* to any study of Wordsworth's poetry, and the centrality, and originality, of Wordsworth in the Romantic movement. It is to Legouis, too, that we owe the earliest work on Wordsworth's relations with Michel Beaupuy and Annette Vallon.[12] *The Prelude* is not, of course, an authoritative factual autobiography, and Legouis has been criticised – rather too strenuously – for encouraging a tendency to treat it as such. The work which owes most to Legouis's researches on William and Annette has naturally been criticised in the same way: this is Sir Herbert Read's *Wordsworth* (1930), which uses the evidence concerning Annette Vallon to suggest that Wordsworth's 'decline' after the so-called 'great decade' was due to remorse over his affair, and over his enforced abandonment of his lover and their child. Like most new evidence, the revelations concerning Annette are perhaps overvalued in Read's study, but his theory – which is more subtle than it is usually represented to be – is still the best (and effectively the only) one we have. The point I wish to make, however, is that curiously Legouis and Read between them used their biographical and psychological studies to distinguish for the first time between this poem and autobiography. Sir Herbert distinguishes Wordsworth from the 'I' of *The Prelude*, claiming that the poem is the story of 'an ideal character progressing towards a state of blessedness in which he shall be fit to write that great philosophical poem'.[13] To Legouis *The Prelude* is primarily a philosophy of mind in which the poet chooses himself as hero 'simply because he can fathom no other soul so deeply'.[14] The second view is more inclusive, allowing for a process of selectivity without imputing censorship – and is probably closer to the truth. *The Prelude* is clearly a very personal poem, yet its readers may speak of its 'mysterious' lack of vanity or of its status as an 'idealisation' without being in essential conflict. We have come to view the life of Wordsworth and the poem itself independently, yet with a gain, not a loss, in our sense of the poem as a living document. This is perhaps because we can now see it not as an inert deposition but as itself an experience in Wordsworth's life : not the record of a life, but an act of exploration and discovery. It is the act of a man who proposes to himself to write a great philosophical poem and asks himself what, if anything, fits him to do so. If he can understand aught of his own development, what better qualification? What indeed is needful, as Rilke said, 'if only we are on the track of the law of our own growth'? The poem's first critics saw it as a statement of belief or of fact; we see it as celebration, as restoration, as an immensely complex tissue of memory and feelings, thought and dreams : a poem which recollects past feeling into the present act of writing for the sake of future life and thought – a poem which has its own composition as its story, and in which the activity of memory so enriches the past as to become part of the story it unfolds.

This living poem has been opened to us through a number of approaches : the detailed exegesis of R. D. Havens, the philosophical studies of Beatty, Rader and Stallknecht, and the critical theses of Jones, Ferry and Hartman. But the main lines of modern criticism were set by A. C. Bradley in three of his consummate lectures at the turn of the century.[15] In the 1903 lecture on 'Wordsworth', Bradley called attention – as had Pater before him – to how Wordsworth often means what he says in disconcerting ways, so that what appears as metaphor is often meant literally, and what seems slight bears primordial meanings. What struck Pater, Swinburne and Bradley has become a major theme of *Prelude* criticism in the work of Helen Darbishire, William Empson and Ellen Douglas Leyburn. Empson's essay on 'Sense in *The Prelude*' (*The*

Structure of Complex Words, 1951) is essential reading as a sometimes polemical but painstaking study of the manifold meanings of the word 'sense' in this poem, and of Wordsworth's ambivalent attitudes towards those meanings. The same term is discussed in Helen Darbishire's article, and we include Professor Leyburn's broader semantic argument on 'Recurrent Words in *The Prelude*'.

The profundity of such words in their contexts was one factor which led Bradley to consider Wordsworth as a philosophical poet, in the sense of one whose awareness brought him close to the deepest metaphysical questions of his age – or, as A. N. Whitehead shows, the perennial concerns of any age.[16] Coleridge, of course, thought that Wordsworth might produce the 'first and only' philosophical poem in English, meaning that the great poem would not merely be a versification of current moral philosophy but would rather be the record of the most subtle introspections of a mind which habitually turned on the questions of the real and the ideal, the relation of man with God and the world, the powers of imagination and insight. But even Coleridge counselled a dogmatic philosophical argument, and in the Victorian age Wordsworth's real claims to have written a philosophical poem were lost in the argument as to what the dogma was. Leslie Stephen was in the main a sensitive critic of Wordsworth, but in an essay on 'Wordsworth's Ethics' he volunteered what may have been a quite deliberate overstatement that Wordsworth offered an 'ethical system . . . as distinctive and capable of systematic exposition as that of Bishop Butler'.[17] Wordsworth, too, had suggested that the reader of *The Excursion* 'will have no difficulty in extracting the system for himself'. As a result, Arnold (in *Essays in Criticism*) and Swinburne (in *Miscellanies*), who experienced considerable difficulty in doing any such thing, fell into a species of over-reaction and did their best by Wordsworth in recommending the reader to forgive the philosophy, hold to the poetry. The only systematic exposition remained that of Stopford Brooke, whose lectures in St James's Chapel in 1872 subjugated many genuine insights into the poem to an attempt to resolve the ambiguities of Wordsworth's religious experience into a theologically sound continuum. Perhaps Wordsworth's sense of God does veer towards Pantheist immanence at times, but it is right and proper, Brooke concluded, that 'Natural religion should go before Spiritual'.[18] Wordsworth himself was only interested in whether or not he was a Pantheist when called upon to justify himself before the orthodox. Schelling, in the freer speculative spirit of contemporary Germany, was luckier, and could say 'whoever wishes to call this system pantheism should have this privilege too. We gladly grant everyone his own means of *making intelligible to himself* the age. . . .'[19] But in England the tradition of testing thought only by established categories – and thereby forcing it into the very dichotomies it may seek to transcend, of immanence or transcendence, materialism or idealism – has always been inimical to progress in thought. If thought is conducted in the wrong categories it is improper thought, and if it avoids those categories it is not thought at all.

An essay by W. B. Gallie, 'Is *The Prelude* a Philosophical Poem?' (1947), poses the question definitively. Professor Gallie argues that in his poem Wordsworth was wrestling with genuine philosophical problems and that – over and above some impressive arguments in verse – what he achieves is a highly personal encounter with the inadequacies of certain metaphysical and moral categories, which resolves not in a new system, but in poetry which embodies philosophical thinking. The poetry of *The Prelude* 'focusses the struggle of thought, and advances it to original conclusions' : it shows us 'the mind "on the move" '.[20] For a long time, however, the problem of Wordsworth's philosophy remained one of how far the poet was influenced by Hartley's associationism, and how far by transcendentalist ideas. A dispassionate and erudite commentary on this and other problems will be found in R. D. Havens's *The Mind of a Poet* (1941). Havens preserves an Olympian detachment at times, holding that 'Any study of Wordsworth's religion must inevitably come to the conclusion that no formulation of his beliefs is possible' – and it is this detachment that makes his work an invaluable supplement to other commentaries.[21] Nevertheless, Havens has his own biases and readers may prefer books where these are frankly exposed : as they are, for example, in *William Wordsworth: His Doctrine and Art in their Historical Relations* (1922) where Professor Beatty calls Wordsworth 'the poet of the English philosophy of Locke and his school in general, and of the English associationistic philosophy in particular'.[22] Very few critics would now accept that claim entire – perhaps because we remember too well Bradley's comment that when we pass from Wordsworth to Locke or Hartley 'We find ourselves in the presence, not merely of an inferior degree of genius, but of a view of the world incongruous with the substance of poetry'[23] – but Professor Beatty's argument establishes more of a connection than can be quite undone. The most balanced assessments of Wordsworth's intrinsic associationism are given by Colin Clarke in 'Nature's Education of Man' (*Philosophy*, XXIII, 1948) and by Basil Willey in his chapter 'David Hartley and Nature's Education' in *The Eighteenth Century Background* (1940).

It is worth noting in this context that the question of Wordsworth's Hartleyanism is a distinctly modern one. Wordsworth's contemporaries, if they complained of the philosophy of his poetry, had in mind much more exotic strains, and Byron's exasperation is typical : 'Jacob Behmen, Swedenborg and Joanna Southcote', he says, were 'mere types of this arch apostle of mystery and mysticism.'[24] To Byron this may have been cause for complaint, but precisely this transcendental element in Wordsworth's poetry began to interest critics in the late twenties. The 'Hartleyan' critics, after all, establish simply that traces of philosophical ideas are to be found in Wordsworth; or that, to put it another way, Hartley had accurately described an area of man's experience. It is indeed plausible to argue, as Beatty does, that Wordsworth's experiences of the transcendental are based on sensation, not on mysticism, but as Melvyn Rader soon pointed out (in 1928), not all of Wordsworth's experience can be accounted for in this way.[25] Wordsworth's sense of his own subconscious life, and of the 'presences' in things, takes us far beyond the constraints of domestic philosophy. When Stallknecht, in 1929 and 1945, supported Rader's view that Wordsworth's mature poetry expresses doctrines quite opposed to Hartley, he found it necessary to turn, as Bradley had done, to the Germans, and in particular to Boehme, Spinoza and Kant.[26] His book *Strange Seas of Thought* (1945) is therefore a much more comprehensive study of Wordsworth's world-view than had hitherto been attempted, and effected a shift in the centre of gravity of Wordsworth studies. Stallknecht's approach is inclusive, recognising Wordsworth's power to synthesise views which appear to academic philosophers to be incompatible; and, himself an academic philosopher, brings to his reading of Wordsworth a range of categories and terminology capable of subtly illuminating Wordsworth's developing experience, through the 'Tintern Abbey' lines, *The Prelude*, the 'Ode to Duty' and *The Excursion*. Before Stallknecht, criticism had tended to relate Wordsworth's thought solely to prevailing moral philosophy, or to the English school, or, as J. A. Stewart did, in G. S. Gordon's *English Literature and the Classics* (1912), to Platonism. After Stallknecht the radical dimensions of Wordsworth's thought came into prominence. Wordsworth's name has become linked with contemporary and later philosophers whose work seems to be within his own tradition, not merely compatible with the poetic mind, but devoted to it : philosophers who show us, not where Wordsworth collected his finished notions, but where he was tending with his new ones. In 1960, for example, E. D. Hirsch produced his 'typological study of Romanticism', *Wordsworth and Schelling,* a thorough and exciting analysis of the extent to which Wordsworth's theory and practice overlap with the doctrine of his great German contemporary. Sir Herbert Read, in *The True Voice of Feeling* (1947), had already placed Wordsworth in

that stream which first became defined in Kant's philosophy, and continued to flow however irregularly through the minds of Schelling, Coleridge, Kierkegaard, Hegel, Nietzsche, Husserl, Heidegger, divided by a watershed from the contrary stream ... of Locke, Condillac, Hartley, Bentham, Marx and Lenin – that first stream to which we give the fashionable name of Existentialism, but which is really the main tradition of philosophy itself. ...[27]

Whether one sees Wordsworth's philosophy in such terms, or merely as the enviable power to 'generalise about human nature subtly and consistently', as Josephine Miles has said,[28] the twentieth century has come to accept that *The Prelude* and its 'philosophy' have to be taken together. In the present volume this much is common ground; and whether in Helen Darbishire's and Colin Clarke's criticism, or in Robert Langbaum's demonstration of how Wordsworth used associationism to transcend the associationists, there is a willingness to account Wordsworth as indeed a philosophical poet – a poet who philosophises and makes poetry in the selfsame act. But whether he is a prophetic one, as recent studies have held, or is still working in eighteenth-century categories, as Professor Beatty's lucid and erudite volume so nearly establishes, remains an open question.

The 'formal' equivalent of this philosophical problem is the question of Wordsworth's status as a 'nature poet'. His early poems, 'An Evening Walk' and 'Descriptive Sketches', are cast in a distinctly eighteenth-century mode, that of the loco-descriptive poem – to which *The Excursion*, formally at least, returns. Here, as in the poetry of Thomson and Akenside, the poet, as sensitive observer, introduces his meditations against a setting of natural scenes. But criticism has taken pains to suggest how Wordsworth's poetry achieves a more active unity between the observer and the world : how indeed the poetry is made in their interaction. Wordsworth's narratives provide much of the evidence for Robert Langbaum's thesis in *The Poetry of Experience* (1957), the best discussion of Romantic practice yet written. Langbaum's argument is that Romantic poetry is the poet's attempt to salvage his sense of the world, after the 'enlightenment' had reduced it to abstractions. Poetry is thus a reconstruction : each poem is a rediscovery of the self through its imprint on nature, and vice versa. How it can be so, how indeed it is possible for the forms of nature – through immediate experience and through memory – to be accounted 'powers', is the subject of another book which also straddles the aesthetic and philosophical approaches : Colin Clarke's *Romantic Paradox* (1962), which has had an immense impact

on Wordsworth studies by exploring lucidly the double meaning, mental and spatial, which the word 'image' always has for
Wordsworth. Nature can teach, or heal, chasten and subdue,
because rocks and stones and trees are of the same stuff as the
mind. Since John Morley, in 1888, found it necessary to call
'The Tables Turned' a 'half-playful sally',[29] criticism has had
to establish two major points about Wordsworth's naturalism :
first, in the work of John Danby and Colin Clarke and others,
how seriously Wordsworth meant, and in what way he meant,
that 'One impulse from a vernal wood' can teach us more 'Of
moral evil and of good, Than all the sages can'; and secondly,
how wrong it is to assume that nature is therefore the dominant partner in this process. That *The Prelude* is the story of
the humanising of the imagination, and a record of how the
mature mind, under the guidance of Nature's self, is liberated
from nature, is Geoffrey Hartman's theme in the essay on
Wordsworth's *via naturaliter negativa*. This essay, and Colin
Clarke's, taken together – both appeared in 1962 – represent
the most sophisticated breakthrough in our understanding of
Wordsworth's experience of nature. Wordsworth, Arnold said,
laid us on the 'cool flowery lap of earth'. Both Bradley and
Danby found this a curiously inadequate description of Wordsworth's effect. In *Wordsworth's Poetry, 1787–1814*, Hartman
expressed these doubts in his provoking assertion that for
Wordsworth in *The Prelude* 'Nature and Poetry matter only
as they quicken regeneration. The most enthralling impression
should still be a middle term, a thoroughfare to a new birth of
power and liberty'.[30] Hartman is referring to the Simplon and
Snowdon episodes of the poem, but his brief expression has
two implications for any overall view of the work. It establishes
the theme of the poem more clearly than before as a humanist
dynamic, and it implies a great deal about the relation between
The Prelude's 'purple passages' and its labyrinthine form – the
third great concern of modern criticism.

The last person in the nineteenth century to find in *The
Prelude* a unitary phenomenon was probably Coleridge :
Arnold soon inaugurated, and Eliot compounded, the tradi-
tion that Wordsworth – and thereby *The Prelude* – was not to

be read entire. But with the critical endeavours of the sixties
that tradition has been severely shaken. For a time it seemed
that Wordsworth's evocation of the 'spots of time' would per-
manently justify the tendency to read the poetic spots alone,
but a number of critics have drawn attention to the way in
which the 'spots' resonate within the overall context of memory
and resolve. Jonathan Bishop's psychological study (1959)
comments on the methodology of the 'spots' in such a way as
to make them a way into the methodology of the entire poem.

Professor Harvey's first essay in this volume is a justification
of the medium of the poem, and its method, in the light of
modern understanding of its real dynamic : his second points
to ways in which *The Prelude,* as poem, has yet to be
considered. Both take up the implied question in Lord
Macaulay's bemused reaction to the poem, and the question
Bradley articulated in 1905 as to the fate of 'The Long Poem
in the Age of Wordsworth'. In other words we have come to
tackle again the question which vexed the poem's reviewers :
what exactly *is The Prelude*? Three excellent studies of this
problem should be noted : Karl Kroeber's *Romantic Narrative
Art* (1960); Herbert Lindenberger's *On Wordsworth's Prelude* (1963) and Abbie Potts's *Wordsworth's Prelude: A
Study of its Literary Form* (1953). Professor Potts surveys the
whole range of formal questions, from an indispensable study
of the poem's literary analogues, 'What is it like?', to the prag-
matic question, 'What is it for?' Kroeber's book has an excellent essay on *The Prelude*, which he sees as an authentic epic :
the form of a personal epic being devised as a vehicle for the
modern myth – that of an individual in manifold revolt
against a prevailing culture. Lindenberger studies *The Prelude*
primarily as a 'time poem' – his chapters on the 'spots of time'
should be read along with Bishop's essay – and regards it as
prophetic not merely in its grasp of the modern obsession with
temporality, but in its convoluted structure. Lindenberger's
chapter on 'The Possibility of a Long Poem' is the fullest
debate of this topic to date. All of these studies, apart from
their intrinsic value, are notable for raising the same issue that
the philosophical and practical criticism approaches do : they

see *The Prelude* no longer as an isolated and inexplicable
phenomenon – a sort of literary ugly duckling – but as the ful-
filment of one tradition and the inauguration of a new one.

In many ways we are more sure of ourselves than were the
poem's first critics : we can approach it more confidently as a
literary artefact, or as an act of personal growth, or as the ideal
poetic expression of the philosophic mind. But in other ways
our Wordsworth is more elusive than theirs. We no longer
take the poem naïvely (if it is naïve) as unambivalent statement or as artless autobiography. And the question as to what
kind of meanings the poem may bear is much less simple.
Bradley, in full possession of his faculties, claimed Wordsworth
as 'pre-eminently, the poet of solitude', and 'emphatically the
poet of community'. He did not ask which was true : he let
Wordsworth speak, and heard a complex voice which must be
listened to entire. For Wordsworth's positives contain within
them, simple as they seem, powerful oppositions. There is, for
example, the paradox of self-consciousness, and Wordsworth's
disconcerting treatment of 'self-possession' and 'self-forgetful-
ness' as equally of the highest good. There is the curious matter
of Wordsworth's attitudes to nature : how naturalism is shown
to lead naturally to anti-naturalism which is then shown to be
the highest achievement of nature. And there is the paradoxical element in Wordsworth's approach to cognition, by which,
it would appear, the path to godlike perception lies through
self-effacement, and the 'mind's excursive power' is liberated
in 'wise passiveness'. Whether these are paradoxes, or ambi-
valences, or simple confusions, the reader will decide for himself. Modern criticism, with its taste for the complex, has taken
all three positions.

Is Wordsworth the poet of the egotistical sublime or, as he
and Professor Potts maintain, a connector, a teacher of love?
Despite its title, H. J. F. Jones's *The Egotistical Sublime*
(1954) follows Bradley in giving us both : the history of
Wordsworth's imaginative life was a development of modes of
solitude in relationship. David Ferry, whose *The Limits of
Mortality* (1959) claims the former to be exclusively true, for
all Wordsworth's protestations to the contrary, points to

another opposition which touches at the heart of *The Prelude*. Does Wordsworth ever resolve the tension which grows in the last three books between his optimistic 'sacramental' view of life and his pessimistic 'mystical' view? Are we – and Geoffrey Hartman's book leaves us with a similar question – are we left exulting in the spousal consummation of mind and world, or lamenting how inaccessible are the hiding-places of our power?

RICHARD GRAVIL

NOTES

1. G. O. Trevelyan, *The Life and Letters of Lord Macaulay* (Longmans, 1876) IV 45.

2. *Cooper's Journal.* vol. I; and *The Letters of John Stuart Mill*, ed. Hugh S. R. Elliot (Longmans, 1910) I 10–13.

3. John Lewis Bradley, *Ruskin's Letters from Venice 1851–2* (New Haven : Yale U.P., 1955) p. 92.

4. H. Crabb Robinson, *Books and Their Writers*, ed. Edith J. Morley (Dent, 1938) II 778.

5. Arthur Hugh Clough, *Prose Remains* (Macmillan, 1869) p. 318.

6. James Russell Lowell, 'Wordsworth' (1875), in *Selections from Wordsworth*, ed. H. B. Cotterill (Macmillan, 1904) p. xxxiv.

7. *Edinburgh Review*, XXIV (Nov 1814) and *Contributions to the Edinburgh Review* (London, 1844) III. I refer of course to those which stem from 'The Ruined Cottage' and its addendum of 1798, which passed into books I, II, IV, and VIII of *The Prelude* before returning to *The Excursion*, books I and IV.

8. *Edinburgh Review*, XI (Oct 1807) 214 f.

9. Barbara Everett, 'The Prelude', *Critical Quarterly*, I (1959).

10. E. de Selincourt, *The Letters of William and Dorothy Wordsworth: The Middle Years* (Oxford, 1937) I 131.

11. J. S. Mill, *Autobiography* (London, 1873) p. 148.

12. *William Wordsworth and Annette Vallon* (Dent, 1922).

13. *Wordsworth* (Faber, 1930) p. 42.

14. É. Legouis, *The Early Life of William Wordsworth, 1770–1798* (Dent, 1897) p. 14.

15. Two chapters of the *Oxford Lectures on Poetry* (Mac-

millan, 1909) and *English Poetry and German Philosophy in the Age of Wordsworth*, Adamson Lecture (Manchester, 1909).

16. A. N. Whitehead, *Science and the Modern World* (Penguin Books, 1938).

17. Leslie Stephen, *Hours in a Library*, 2nd ed. (Smith, Elder, 1892) II 297.

18. Stopford A. Brooke, *Theology in the English Poets* (H. S. King, 1874) p. 135.

19. F. W. J. von Schelling, *Of Human Freedom*, trans. James Gutmann (Chicago : Open Court Publishing Co., 1936) p. 91.

20. *Philosophy*, XXII (1947) 138.

21. R. D. Havens, *The Mind of a Poet* (Baltimore : Johns Hopkins Press, 1941) p. 197. Havens has been rightly criticised for hair-splitting, however. His claim, for example, that Wordsworth nowhere 'affirms or implies' that the Imagination apprehends truth (p. 253) is a classic of misplaced legalism. Wordsworth implies this insistently and repeatedly, though he nowhere *explicitly* makes such a claim.

22. Arthur Beatty, *William Wordsworth: His Doctrine and Art in their Historical Relations,* cited from the paperback edition (Madison : Univ. of Wisconsin Press, 1960) p. 285.

23. Bradley, *English Poetry and German Philosophy*, p. 10.

24. R. E. Prothero (ed.), *Lord Byron's Letters and Journals,* 6 vols (John Murray, 1898–1901) III 239.

25. Melvyn Rader, 'The Transcendentalism of Wordsworth', *Modern Philology*, XXVI (1928); *Presiding Ideas in Wordsworth's Poetry* (Seattle : Univ. of Washington Publications in Language and Literature, 1931); and *Wordsworth: A Philosophical Approach* (Oxford U.P., 1967).

26. Newton P. Stallknecht, *Strange Seas of Thought* (Durham, N.C. : Duke U.P., 1945; 2nd ed., 1958); cf. 'Wordsworth and Philosophy', *PMLA*, XLIV (1929) 1116–43.

27. *The True Voice of Feeling* (Faber, 1965) p. 210.

28. Josephine Miles, 'Wordsworth and the Mind's Excursive Power', in *Major English Romantic Poets: A Symposium in Reappraisal*, ed. C. D. Thorpe, Carlos Baker and Bennett Weaver (Carbondale : Southern Illinois U.P., 1957) p. 35.

29. John Morley, *The Complete Poetical Works of William Wordsworth* (Macmillan, 1888) p. lxii.

30. G. H. Hartman, *Wordsworth's Poetry, 1787–1814* (New Haven : Yale U.P., 1964) p. 68.

REFERENCES TO
WORDSWORTH'S WORKS

The dual nature of *The Prelude* creates problems in foot-noting since critics may cite from either version or from both. The first reference in each essay therefore explains which version is normally followed, and references to the alternate version are then prefixed by its date.

Since the later version divides book x into two, the reader should remember that in references to the 1805 version any citation from book x later than line 567, or from books xi, xii and xiii, will correspond to passages in books xi, xii, xiii and xiv, respectively, of the 1850 text.

References to others of Wordsworth's poems are to *The Poetical Works of William Wordsworth*, ed. E. de Selincourt and Helen Darbishire, 5 vols (vols ii and iii in the 2nd edition). References are usually abbreviated to *P.W.*, i–v.

References to manuscripts are sometimes given as page references, in *The Prelude*, ed. E. de Selincourt, 2nd ed., revised by Helen Darbishire (Oxford U.P., 1959), or in volumes of the *Poetical Works*.

PART ONE

Waiting for 'The Recluse',
1798–1841

BRIEF CHRONOLOGY OF THE UNFINISHED 'RECLUSE'

1797–8   Wordsworth completes 'The Ruined Cottage', narrated by the Pedlar, and adds to it an account of its narrator's mind. This Addendum to MS.B is in effect a sketch for the philosophy of *The Prelude*. Wordsworth and Coleridge conceive a great philosophical poem, 'The Recluse'.

1799   Wintering in Germany, Wordsworth begins to draft passages of childhood autobiography, which later appear in *The Prelude*.

1800   'Home at Grasmere' written. This is the first and only book of 'The Recluse' proper. Its closing argument is published in 1814 as a 'prospectus' to *The Excursion*. The rest remains in MS. until 1888.

1800–2   The story of 'The Pedlar' continues to grow.

1804   By now Wordsworth sees his future work in three parts : (i) an autobiographical poem, taking his life up to the time of 'Home at Grasmere'; (ii) a philosophical poem by 'a poet living in retirement'; (iii) a narrative poem.

1804–5   The '1805' version of the 'autobiographical poem' is completed.

1814   *The Excursion* published. This 'narrative poem' incorporates 'The Pedlar' and describes an 'excursion' undertaken by the 'recluse' and the 'pedlar' – as narrative relief from the recluse's speculations in the unwritten 'philosophical' poem.

1839   The last of many revisions of the still untitled 'Prelude'.

1841   Wordsworth appears to have abandoned 'The Recluse'.

1850   The 'portico to the Recluse' is published posthumously as *The Prelude*.

For further data see J. R. MacGillivray's essay below; Helen Darbishire's notes in the revised editions of *The Prelude* and *P.W.*, v; Mary Moorman, *William Wordsworth: A Biography*.

NOTE:
THE DATING OF WORDSWORTH'S MANUSCRIPTS

The dates given in this chronology are those assumed by contributors to this volume. John Alban Finch's controversial essay 'On the Dating of "Home at Grasmere"' in Jonathan Wordsworth's *Bicentenary Wordsworth Studies* argues that although parts of this poem may be early, the first full version belongs to 1805–7. On this view, the 'one book' of 'The Recluse' which Wordsworth refers to on 6 March 1804 (see p. 40 and my note) must still be 'The Ruined Cottage'. Yet Wordsworth speaks of 'also' having 'arranged the plan of a narrative poem'. Since 'The Ruined Cottage' is clearly part of that narrative poem, it still seems likely that the 'one book' of the 'longer poem' is a version of 'Home at Grasmere'. The tragic death of John Finch, who discovered a wealth of scholarly data about Wordsworth's early work, means that we are still without a full assessment of those data in relation to older evidence. As yet, the meaning of the new evidence is still uncertain. When Mark Reed publishes his sequel to *The Chronology of the Early Years* (Cambridge, Mass.: Harvard U.P., 1967), more of Finch's brilliantly researched material may fall into place. Until then the date of 'Home at Grasmere' is one open question among many others.

CORRESPONDENCE AND COMMENT WITHIN THE WORDSWORTH CIRCLE

WORDSWORTH TO JAMES TOBIN, 6 MARCH 1798

I have written 1300 lines of a poem in which I contrive to convey most of the knowledge of which I am possessed. My object is to give pictures of Nature, Man, and Society.[1] Indeed I know not any thing which will not come within the scope of my plan. If I ever attempt another drama,[2] it shall be written either purposely for the closet, or purposely for the stage. There is no middle way. But the work of composition is carved out for me, for at least a year and a half to come.

NOTES

1. i.e. *The Recluse*. The 1300 lines may include 'The Ruined Cottage' and its Addendum (these became book 1 of *The Excursion*); early draft lines for the 'glad preamble' of *The Prelude*, 1, or the Prospectus to the *The Excursion*, or both; and the earliest draft of the Discharged Soldier lines of *Prelude*, IV see Mary Moorman, *The Early Years*, p. 365). The Addendum and the Prospectus do in fact summarise a great deal of Wordsworth's 'knowledge' – which might explain the apparently curious syntax. [Ed.]

2. The reference is to *The Borderers*, which Wordsworth had finished four months before in its shortened 'stage version'. It was not published until 1842. *The Excursion* of course attempts a degree of dramatic interest 'purposely for the closet'. [Ed.]

COLERIDGE TO WORDSWORTH, *c.* 10 SEPTEMBER 1799

My dear friend, I do entreat you to go on with 'The Recluse'; and I wish you would write a poem, in blank verse, addressed to those, who in consequence of the complete failure of the

French Revolution, have thrown up all hopes of the ameliora-
tion of mankind, and are sinking into an almost epicurean
selfishness, disguising the same under the soft titles of domestic
attachment and contempt for visionary *philosophes*. It would
do great good, and might form a part of 'The Recluse', for in
my present mood I am wholly against the publication of any
small poems. . . .

COLERIDGE TO WORDSWORTH, 12 OCTOBER 1799

I long to see what you have been doing. O let it be the tail-
piece of 'The Recluse'! for of nothing but 'The Recluse' can I
hear patiently. That it is to be addressed to me makes me more
desirous that it should not be a poem of itself. To be addressed
as a beloved man, by a thinker, at the close of such a poem as
'The Recluse' is the only event, I believe, capable of inciting in
me an hour's vanity – vanity, nay, it is too good a feeling to be
so called; it would indeed be a self-elevation produced *ab extra*.

COLERIDGE TO THOMAS POOLE, 14 OCTOBER 1803

. . . I rejoice therefore with a deep and true Joy, that he has at
length yielded to my urgent & repeated – almost unremitting
– requests & remonstrances – & will go on with the Recluse
exclusively. – A Great Work, in which he will sail; on an open
Ocean, & a steady wind; unfretted by short tacks, reefing, &
hawling & disentangling the ropes – – great work necessarily
comprehending his attention & Feelings within the circle of
great objects & elevated Conceptions – this is his natural Element – the having been out of it has been his Disease. . . . & I
really consider it as a misfortune that Wordsworth ever
deserted his former mountain Track to wander in Lanes &
allies; tho' in the event it may prove to have been a great Bene-
fit to him. He will steer, I trust, the middle course.

COLERIDGE TO RICHARD SHARP,[1] 15 JANUARY 1804

Wordsworth is a poet, a most original poet. He no more
resembles Milton than Milton resembles Shakespeare – no

more resembles Shakespeare than Shakespeare resembles Milton. He is himself and, I dare affirm that, he will hereafter be admitted as the first and greatest philosophical poet, the only man who has effected a complete and constant synthesis of thought and feeling and combined them with poetic forms, with the music of pleasurable passion, and with Imagination or the *modifying* power in that highest sense of the word, in which I have ventured to oppose it to Fancy, or the *aggregating* power – in that sense in which it is a dim analogue of creation – not all that we can *believe*, but all that we can *conceive* of creation. – Wordsworth is a poet, and I feel myself a better poet, in knowing how to honour *him* than in all my own poetic compositions, all I have done or hope to do; and I prophesy immortality to his 'Recluse', as the first and finest philosophical poem, if only it be (as it undoubtedly will be) a faithful transcript of his own most august and innocent life, of his own habitual feelings and modes of seeing and hearing.

NOTE

1. 'Conversation' Sharp, the M.P. [Ed.]

WORDSWORTH TO THOMAS DE QUINCEY, 6 MARCH 1804

I am now writing a poem on my own earlier life; and have just finished that part in which I speak of my residence at the University; it would give me great pleasure to read this work to you at this time, as I am sure, from the interest you have taken in the L[yrical] B[allads], that it would please you, and might also be of service to you. This Poem will not be published these many years, and never during my lifetime, till I have finished a larger and more important work to which it is tributary. Of this larger work I have written one Book[1] and several scattered fragments: it is a moral and philosophical Poem; the subject whatever I find most interesting in Nature, Man, and Society, and most adapted to poetic illustration. To this work I mean to devote the prime of my life, and the chief force of my mind. I have also arranged the plan of a narrative Poem; and if I live to finish these three principal works I shall be content.

That on my own life, the least important of the three, is better [than] half complete, viz., 4 books, amounting to about 2500 lines.[2]

NOTES

1. 'Home at Grasmere' (*P.W.*, v, appendix A), described as The Recluse, Part One, Book One. [Ed.]

2. J. R. MacGillivray, below, explains how the poem continually outgrew Wordsworth's estimates. [Ed.]

WORDSWORTH TO RICHARD SHARP, 29 APRIL 1804

I have been very busy these last ten weeks, having written between two and three thousand lines, accurately near three thousand, in that time; namely, 4 books, and a third of another, of the Poem which I believe I mentioned to you on my own early life. I am at present in the 7th book of this work, which will turn out far longer than I ever dreamt of; it seems a frightful deal to say about one's self; and, of course, will never be published (during my lifetime, I mean) till another work has been written and published, of sufficient importance to justify me in giving my own history to the world. I pray God to give me life to finish these works, which, I trust, will live, and do good; especially the one to which that, which I have been speaking of as far advanced, is only supplementary.

WORDSWORTH TO SIR GEORGE BEAUMONT, 25 DECEMBER 1804

You will be pleased to hear that I have been advancing with my work : I have written upwards of 2,000 verses during the last ten weeks. I do not know if you are exactly acquainted with the plan of my poetical labour : it is twofold; first, a Poem, to be called *The Recluse*; in which it will be my object to express in verse my most interesting feelings concerning Man, Nature, and society; and next, a Poem (in which I am at present chiefly engaged) on my earlier life or the growth of my own mind taken up upon a large scale. This latter work I expect to have finished before the month of May; and then I purpose to fall with all my might on the former, which is the chief object upon which my thoughts have been fixed these many years. Of this poem, that of 'The Pedlar', which Coleridge read you, is part, and I may have written of it altogether about 2000 lines. It will consist, I hope, of about 10 or 12 thousand.

WORDSWORTH TO SIR GEORGE BEAUMONT,
1 MAY 1805

My dear Sir George,

I have wished to write to you every day this long time, but I have also had another wish which has interfered to prevent me – I mean the wish to resume my poetical labours; time was stealing away fast from me and nothing done and my mind still seeming unfit to do anything. At first I had a strong impulse to write a poem that should record my Brother's virtues, and be worthy of his memory. I began to give vent to my feelings, with this view, but I was overpowered by my subject and could not proceed. . . .

Unable to proceed with this work, I turned my thoughts again to the Poem on my own life, and you will be glad to hear that I have added 300 lines to it in the course of last week. Two books more will conclude it. It will be not much less than 9000 lines, – not hundred but thousand lines long, – an alarming length ! and a thing unprecedented in literary history that a man should talk so much about himself. It is not self-conceit, as you will know well, that has induced me to do this, but real humility; I began the work because I was unprepared to treat any more arduous subject, and diffident of my own powers. Here, at least, I hoped that to a certain degree I should be sure of succeeding, as I had nothing to do but describe what I had felt and thought; therefore could not easily be bewildered. This might certainly have been done in narrower compass by a man of more address, but I have done my best. If, when the work shall be finished, it appears to the judicious to have redundancies, they shall be lopped off, if possible; but this is very difficult to do, when a man has written with thought; and this defect, whenever I have suspected it or found it to exist in any writings of mine, I have always found incurable. The fault lies too deep, and is in the first conception. If you see Coleridge before I do, do not speak of this to him, as I should like to have his judgment unpreoccupied by such an apprehension.

WORDSWORTH TO SIR GEORGE BEAUMONT,
3 JUNE 1805

I have the pleasure to say that I finished my poem about a fortnight ago. I had looked forward to the day as a most happy one; and I was indeed grateful to God for giving me life to complete the work, such as it is; but it was not a happy day for me; I was dejected on many accounts; when I looked back upon the performance it seemed to have a dead weight about it, the reality so far short of the expectation; it was the first long labour that I had finished, and the doubt whether I should ever live to write *The Recluse*, and the sense which I had of this poem being so far below what I seemed capable of executing, depressed me much; above all, many heavy thoughts of my poor departed Brother hung upon me, the joy which I should have had in showing him the Manuscript, and a thousand other vain fancies and dreams. I have spoken of this because it was a state of feeling new to me, the occasion being new. This work may be considered as a sort of *portico* to *The Recluse*, part of the same building, which I hope to be able, ere long, to begin with in earnest; and if I am permitted to bring it to a conclusion, and to write, further, a narrative Poem of the Epic kind, I shall consider the *task* of my life as over. I ougnt to add that I have the satisfaction of finding the present Poem not quite of so alarming a length as I apprehended.

SAMUEL TAYLOR COLERIDGE

TO WILLIAM WORDSWORTH

COMPOSED ON THE NIGHT AFTER HIS RECITATION OF A POEM ON THE GROWTH OF AN INDIVIDUAL MIND

Friend of the wise! and teacher of the good!
Into my heart have I received that lay
More than historic, that prophetic lay
Wherein (high theme by thee first sung aright)
Of the foundations and the building up
Of a Human Spirit thou hast dared to tell
What may be told, to the understanding mind
Revealable; and what within the mind
By vital breathings secret as the soul!
Of venal growth, oft quickens in the heart
Thoughts all too deep for words! —

                          Theme hard as high!
Of smiles spontaneous, and mysterious fears,
(The first-born they of Reason and twin-birth)
Of tides obedient to external force,
And currents self-determined, as might seem,
Or by some inner power; of moments awful,
Now in thy inner life, and now abroad,
When power streamed from thee, and thy soul received
The light reflected, as a light bestowed —
Of fancies fair, and milder hours of youth,
Hyblean murmurs of poetic thought
Industrious in its joy, in vales and glens
Native or outland, lakes and famous hills!
Or on the lonely high-road, when the stars
Were rising; or by secret mountain-streams,
The guides and the companions of thy way!

Of more than Fancy, of the Social Sense
Distending wide, and man beloved as man,
Where France in all her towns lay vibrating
Like some becalmed bark beneath the burst
Of Heaven's immediate thunder, when no cloud
Is visible, or shadow on the main.
For thou wert there, thine own brows garlanded,
Amid the tremor of a realm aglow,
Amid a mighty nation jubilant,
When from the general heart of human kind
Hope sprang forth like a full-born Deity !
– Of that dear Hope afflicted and struck down,
So summoned homeward, thenceforth calm and sure
From the dread watch-tower of man's absolute self,
With light unwaning on her eyes, to look
Far on – herself a glory to behold,
The Angel of the vision ! Then (last strain)
Of Duty, chosen laws controlling choice,
Action and joy ! – An Orphic song indeed,
A song divine of high and passionate thoughts
To their own music chanted ! ...

                              Eve following eve,
Dear tranquil time, when the sweet sense of Home
Is sweetest ! moments for their own sake hailed
And more desired, more precious for thy song,
In silence listening, like a devout child,
My soul lay passive, by thy various strain
Driven as in surges now beneath the stars,
With momentary stars of my own birth,
Fair constellated foam, still darting off
Into the darkness; now a tranquil sea,
Outspread and bright, yet swelling to the moon.

And when – O Friend ! my comforter and guide !
Strong in thyself, and powerful to give strength ! –
Thy long sustained Song finally closed,

And thy deep voice had ceased – yet thou thyself
Wert still before my eyes, and round us both
That happy vision of beloved faces –
Scarce conscious, and yet conscious of its close
I sate, my being blended in one thought
(Thought was it? or aspiration? or resolve?)
Absorbed, yet hanging still upon the sound –
And when I rose, I found myself in prayer.

[1807]

WORDSWORTH TO SIR GEORGE BEAUMONT, 8 SEPTEMBER 1806

I have been busily employed lately; I wrote one book of *The Recluse* nearly 1000 lines [i.e. *Excursion,* II – Ed.], then had a rest, last week began again, and have written 300 more: I hope all tolerably well, and certainly with good views.

WORDSWORTH TO WALTER SCOTT, 10 NOVEMBER 1806

I am going to the press with a volume . . . of small pieces . . . with great reluctance; but the day when my long work will be finished seems farther and farther off.

HENRY CRABB ROBINSON, 3 JANUARY 1815

My visit to Witham was made partly that I might have the pleasure of reading *The Excursion* to Mrs W. Pattisson. The second perusal of this poem has gratified me still more than the first, and my own impressions were not removed by the various criticisms I became acquainted with. I also read to Mrs Pattisson the *Eclectic Review*. It is a highly encomiastic article, rendering ample justice to the poetical talents of the author, but raising a doubt as to the religious character of the poem. It is insinuated that Nature is a sort of God throughout, and consistently with the Calvinistic orthodoxy of the reviewer, the lamentable error of representing a love of Nature as a sort of

purifying state of mind, and the study of Nature as a sanctify-
ing process is emphatically pointed out.[1]

Mrs Pattisson further objected that, in Wordsworth, there
is a want of sensibility, or rather passion; and she even main-
tained that one of the reasons why I admire him so much is
that I never was in love. We disputed on this head, and it was
at last agreed between us that Wordsworth has no power
because he has no inclination to describe the passion of an
unsuccessful lover, but that he is eminently happy in his
description of connubial felicity. We read also the *Edinburgh*
review of the poem.[2] It is a very severe and contemptuous
article. Wordsworth is treated as incurable, and the changes
are rung on the old keys with great vivacity – affectation, bad
taste, mysticism, &c. He is reproached with having written
more feebly than before. A ludicrous statement of the story is
given, which will not impose on many, for Homer or the Bible
might be so represented. But though the attack on Wordsworth will do little mischief among those who are already
acquainted with *Edinburgh Review* articles, it will close up
the eyes of many who might otherwise have recovered their
sight.

Perhaps, after all, *The Excursion* will leave Mr Wordsworth's admirers and contemners where they were. Each will
be furnished with instances to strengthen his own persuasions.

SOURCE : *Diary,* 3 January 1815.

NOTES

1. In fact James Montgomery's review makes two important
points. First, it explains Wordsworth's 'natural religion' very
subtly as a faith in the soul's capacity for self-amelioration in
communion with natural forms. Second, it suggests that Wordsworth's mode is neither fictional nor autobiographical : the poet
uses idealised personae. *Eclectic Review,* n.s., XIII (Jan 1815).
[Ed.]

2. Francis Jeffrey's review, *Edinburgh Review,* XXIV (Nov
1814). The best review of *The Excursion* was Charles Lamb's, in
the *Quarterly Review,* XII (Oct 1814). [Ed.]

DOROTHY WORDSWORTH TO SARA HUTCHINSON,
18 FEBRUARY 1815

William has had one of his weeks of rest and we now begin to
wish that he was at work again, but as he intends completely
to plan the first part of *The Recluse* before he begins the composition, he must read many Books before he will fairly set to
labour again.

COLERIDGE TO WORDSWORTH, 30 MAY 1815

[Coleridge had written to Lady Beaumont in April, volunteer-
ing a judgement of disappointment on *The Excursion*. Discovering this, in May, Wordsworth wrote, with some hurt, to
ask 'where I have failed'. This is part of Coleridge's reply.]

Secondly, for *The Excursion*, I feared that had I been silent
concerning *The Excursion*, Lady Beaumont would have
drawn some strange inference; and yet I had scarcely sent off
the letter before I repented that I had not run that risk rather
than have approach to dispraise communicated to you by a
third person. But what did my criticism amount to, reduced to
its full and naked sense? This, that *comparatively* with the
former poem, *The Excursion*, as far as it was new to me, had
disappointed my expectations; that the excellencies were so
many and of so high a class that it was impossible to attribute
the inferiority, if any such really existed, to any flagging of the
writer's own genius – and that I conjectured that it might
have been occasioned by the influence of self-established con-
victions having given to certain thoughts and expressions a
depth and force which they had not for readers in general. In
order, therefore, to explain the *disappointment*, I must recall
to your mind what my *expectations* were: and, as these again
were founded on the supposition that (in whatever order it
might be published) the poem on the growth of your own
mind was as the ground plot and the roots, out of which 'The
Recluse' was to have sprung up as the tree, as far as [there was]
the same sap in both, I expected them, doubtless, to have

formed one complete whole; but in matter, form, and product to be different, each not only a distinct but a different work. In the first I had found 'themes by thee first sung aright', . . . [Coleridge quotes part of his own poem on *The Prelude*, which he claims to have taken as *The Excursion*, and says that he expected the new poem to be 'The Recluse' itself, which he had] . . . anticipated as commencing with you set down and settled in an abiding home, and that with the description of that home you were to begin a *philosophical poem*, the *result* and fruits of a spirit so framed and so disciplined as had been told in the former.

Whatever in Lucretius is poetry is not philosophical, whatever is philosophical is not poetry; and in the very pride of confident hope I looked forward to 'The Recluse' as the *first* and *only* true philosophical poem in existence. Of course, I expected the colours, music, imaginative life, and passion of *poetry*; but the matter and arrangement of *philosophy*; not doubting from the advantages of the subject that the totality of a system was not only capable of being harmonised with, but even calculated to aid, the unity (beginning, middle, and end) of a poem. Thus, whatever the length of the work might be, still it was a *determinate* length; of the subjects announced, each would have its own appointed place, and, excluding repetitions, each would relieve and rise in interest above the other.

CHARLES LAMB TO WORDSWORTH, 7 JUNE 1819

If, as you say, The Waggoner in some sort came at my call, Oh for a potent voice to call forth *The Recluse* from his profound dormitory, where he sleeps forgetful of his foolish charge – the world!

WORDSWORTH TO W. S. LANDOR, 20 APRIL 1822

The Recluse has had a long sleep, save in my thoughts; my mss. are so ill-penned and blurred that they are useless to all but myself; and at present I cannot face them.

DOROTHY TO H. CRABB ROBINSON, 13 DECEMBER 1824

My Brother has not yet looked at *The Recluse*; he seems to feel the task so weighty that he shrinks from beginning with it ... yet knows that he has now no time to loiter if another great work is to be accomplished by him ...

CHARLES LAMB TO WORDSWORTH, 22 JANUARY 1830

For your head (I do not flatter) is not a nob or the end of a ninepin – unless a Vulcanian hammer could fairly batter a Recluse out of it, then would I bid the smirch'd God knock and knock lustily, the two-handed skinker.

DORA WORDSWORTH TO MISS KINNAIRD, 17 FEBRUARY 1832

Father is particularly well and busier than 1000 bees. Mother and he work like slaves from morning to night – an arduous work – correcting a long Poem written thirty years back and which is not to be published during his life – The Growth of his own Mind – the Ante-chapel as he calls it to The Recluse ...

S. T. COLERIDGE, 21 JULY 1832

I have often wished that the first two books of *The Excursion* had been published separately, under the name of 'The Deserted Cottage'. They would have formed, what indeed they are, one of the most beautiful poems in the language.

Can dialogues in verse be defended? I cannot but think that a great philosophical poet ought always to teach the reader himself as from himself. A poem does not admit argumentation, though it does admit development of thought. In prose there may be a difference; though I must confess that, even in Plato and Cicero, I am always vexed that the authors do not say what they have to say at once in their own persons. The introductions and little urbanities are, to be sure, very delightful in their way; I would not lose them : but I have no admiration for the practice of ventriloquizing through another man's mouth.

I cannot help regretting that Wordsworth did not first publish his thirteen books on the growth of an individual mind – superior, as I used to think, upon the whole, to *The Excursion*. You may judge how I felt about them by my own poem upon the occasion. Then the plan laid out, and, I believe, partly suggested by me, was, that Wordsworth should assume the station of a man in mental repose, one whose principles were made up, and so prepared to deliver upon authority a system of philosophy. He was to treat man as man, – a subject of eye, ear, touch, and taste, in contact with external nature, and informing the senses from the mind, and not compounding a mind out of the senses; then he was to describe the pastoral and other states of society, assuming something of the Juvenalian spirit as he approached the high civilization of cities and towns, and opening a melancholy picture of the present state of degeneracy and vice; thence he was to infer and reveal the proof of, and necessity for, the whole state of man and society being subject to, and illustrative of, a redemptive process in operation, showing how this idea reconciled all the anomalies, and promised future glory and restoration. Something of this sort was, I think, agreed on. It is, in substance, what I have been all my life doing in my system of philosophy.[1]

I think Wordsworth possessed more of the genius of a great philosophic poet than any man I ever knew, or, as I believe, has existed in England since Milton; but it seems to me that he ought never to have abandoned the contemplative position which is peculiarly – perhaps I might say exclusively – fitted for him. His proper title is *Spectator ab extra*.

SOURCE : *Table Talk,* 21 July 1832.

NOTE

1. The reader may judge for himself how great was the gulf between Coleridge's expectations and Wordsworth's intentions (and indeed his own earliest hopes) as described in the letters of

1804. Had Coleridge supplied Wordsworth with the philosophical notes for *The Recluse* (which W. W. inquires about in a letter of 6 March 1804), Wordsworth's achievement might of course have been very different in kind. Coleridge's specimen 'argument' is given in much greater scholastic and dogmatic detail in his letter to Wordsworth in May 1815 (*Letters of Samuel Taylor Coleridge*, ed. E. L. Griggs (Oxford, 1956–9) IV 570). [Ed.]

WORDSWORTH TO DORA WORDSWORTH, MAY 1839

Now let me thank you and Elizabeth C[ookson] for the labours you have gone through in transcribing that long Poem; pray, when it is done, let it be sealed, and deposited with Mr Carter,[1] to provide against any unlucky accident befalling the other.

NOTE

1. Wordsworth's secretary and part-time gardener, who ultimately supervised the publication of *The Prelude*. [Ed.]

AUBREY DE VERE TO HIS SISTER, 25 JUNE 1841

Wordsworth says that the 'Recluse' has never been written except a few passages – and probably never will. . . .

PART TWO

Victorian Assessments, 1852–1897

Walter Bagehot

Now it came to pass in those days that William Wordsworth went up into the hills. It has been attempted in recent years to establish that the object of his life was to teach Anglicanism. A whole life of him has been written by an official gentleman, with the apparent view of establishing that the great poet was a believer in rood-lofts, an idolator of piscinæ. But this is not capable of rational demonstration. Wordsworth, like Coleridge, began life as a heretic, and as the shrewd Pope unfallaciously said, 'once a heretic, always a heretic'. Sound men are sound from the first; safe men are safe from the beginning, and Wordsworth began wrong. His real reason for going to live in the mountains was certainly in part sacred, but it was not in the least Tractarian:

> For he with many feelings, many thoughts,
> Made up a meditative joy, and found
> Religious meanings in the forms of nature.

His whole soul was absorbed in the one idea, the one feeling, the one thought of the sacredness of hills.

> Early had he learned
> To reverence the volume that displays
> The mystery, the life which cannot die;
> But in the mountains did he *feel* his faith.
> All things responsive to the writing, there
> Breathed immortality, revolving life,
> And greatness still revolving; infinite;
> There littleness was not. (*Excursion,* I 223–30)

> He sate, and e'en in their fixed lineaments
> Or from the power of a peculiar eye,
> Or by creative feeling overborne,

Or by predominance of thought oppressed,
E'en in their fixed lineaments
He traced an ebbing and flowing mind,
Expression ever varying ! (1 156–62)

            A sense sublime
Of something far more deeply interfused,
Whose dwelling is the light of setting suns,
And the round ocean and the living air
And the blue sky, and in the mind of man.
A motion and a spirit that impels
All thinking things, all objects of all thought,
And rolls through all things. ('Tintern Abbey', 95–102)

The defect of this religion is, that it is too abstract for the practical, and too bare for the musing. What active men require is personality; the meditative require beauty. But Wordsworth gives us neither. The worship of sensuous beauty – the southern religion – is of all sentiments the one most deficient in his writings. His poetry hardly even gives the charm, the entire charm, of the scenery in which he lived. The lighter parts are little noticed : the rugged parts protrude. The bare waste, the folding hill, the rough lake, Helvellyn with a brooding mist, Ullswater in a grey day, these are his subjects. He took a personal interest in the corners of the universe. There is a print of Rembrandt said to represent a piece of the Campagna, a mere waste, with a stump and a man, and under is written 'Tacet et loquitur'; and thousands will pass the old print-shop where it hangs, and yet have a taste for paintings and colours, and oils : but some fanciful students, some lonely stragglers, some long-haired enthusiasts, by chance will come, one by one, and look, and look, and be hardly able to take their eyes from the fascination, so massive is the shade, so still the conception, so firm the execution. Thus is it with Wordsworth and his poetry. *Tacet et loquitur*. Fashion apart, the million won't read it. Why should they? – they could not understand it, – don't put them out, – let them buy, and sell, and die, – but idle students, and enthusiastic wanderers, and solitary thinkers will read, and read, and read, while their lives and their occupations hold. In truth, his works are the Scriptures of the intellectual life; for that same searching, and finding, and penetrating power which the real Scripture exercises on those engaged, as are the mass of men, in practical occupations and domestic ties, do his works exercise on the meditative, the solitary, and the young.

> His daily teachers had been woods and rills,
> The silence that is in the starry sky,
> The sleep that is among the lonely hills.

> And he had more than others,

>   that blessed mood,
> In which the burthen of the mystery,
> In which the heavy and the weary weight
> Of all this unintelligible world
> Is lightened : that serene and blessed mood
> In which the affections gently lead us on,
> Until the breath of this corporeal frame,
> And even the motion of our human blood
> Almost suspended, we are laid asleep
> In body, and become a living soul;
> While with an eye, made quiet by the power
> Of harmony, and the deep power of joy,
> We see into the life of things. ('Tintern Abbey', 37–49)

And therefore he has had a whole host of sacred imitators. Mr Keble, for example, has translated him for women. He has himself told us that he owed to Wordsworth the tendency *ad sanctiora*, which is the mark of his own writings; and in fact he has but adapted the tone and habit of reverence, which his master applied to common objects and the course of the seasons, to sacred objects and the course of the ecclesiastical year, – diffusing a mist of sentiment and devotion altogether delicious to a gentle and timid devotee.

SOURCE : 'Hartley Coleridge' (1852),
Literary Studies, pp. 60–3.

Richard Holt Hutton

The commonplace modern criticism on Wordsworth is that he is too transcendental. On the other hand, the criticism with which he was first assailed, which Coleridge indignantly repelled, and which is reflected in the admirable parody published among the 'Rejected Addresses', was that he was ridiculously simple, that he made an unintelligible fuss about common feelings and common things. The reconciliation of these opposite criticisms is not difficult. He drew uncommon delights from very common things. His circle of interests was, for a poet, singularly narrow. He was a hardy Cumbrian mountaineer, with the temperament of a thoroughly frugal peasant, and a unique personal gift for discovering the deepest secondary springs of joy in what ordinary men either took as matter of course, or found uninteresting, or even full of pain. The same sort of power which scientific men have of studiously fixing their minds on natural phenomena, till they make these phenomena yield lessons and laws of which no understanding, destitute of this capacity for detaching itself entirely from the commonplace train of intellectual associations, would have dreamt, Wordsworth had in relation to objects of the imagination. He could detach his mind from the commonplace series of impressions which are generated by commonplace objects or events, resist and often reverse the current of emotion to which ordinary minds are liable, and triumphantly justify the strain of rapture with which he celebrated what excites either no feeling, or weary feeling, or painful feeling, in the mass of unreflecting men. Two distinct peculiarities, and rare peculiarities of character, chiefly assisted him in this – his keen spiritual courage, and his stern spiritual frugality. Though his poetry reads so transcendental, and is so meditative, there never was a poet who was so little of a dreamer as Wordsworth. There is volition and self-government in every line of his poetry, and his best thoughts come from the steady resistance he opposes to the ebb and flow of ordinary desires and regrets. He contests the ground inch by inch with all despondent and indolent humours, and often, too, with movements of inconsiderate and wasteful joy – turning defeat into victory, and victory into defeat. He transmutes sorrows into food for lonely rapture, as he dwells upon the evidence they bear of the depth and fortitude of human nature; he transmutes the periodic joy of conventional social occasions into melancholy as he recalls how 'the wiser mind'

> Mourns less for what age takes away
> Than what it leaves behind.

No poet ever contrived by dint of 'plain living and high thinking' to get nearer to the reality of such life as he understood, and to dispel more thoroughly the illusions of superficial impression.

To this same result again the rare spiritual frugality of Wordsworth greatly contributed. Poets, as a rule, lust for emotion; some of the most unique poets – like Shelley and Byron in their very different ways – pant for an unbroken succession of ardent feelings. Wordsworth, as I shall try to show, was almost a miser in his reluctance to trench upon the spiritual capital at his disposal. He hoarded his joys, and lived upon the interest which they paid in the form of hope and expectation. This is one of the most original parts of his poetic character. It was only the windfalls, as one may say, of his imagination, the accidents on which he had never counted beforehand, the delight of which he dared thoroughly to exhaust. He paused almost in awe at the threshold of any promised enjoyment, as if it were a spendthrift policy to exchange the hope for the reality. A delight once over, he multiplied it a thousandfold through the vision of 'that inward eye which is the bliss of solitude'. Spiritual thrift was at the very root of his soul, and this was one of his most remarkable distinctions among a race who, in spiritual things, are too often prodigals and spendthrifts. In these two characteristics lies sufficient explanation of

the opposite views as to his simplicity as a poet. No poet ever
drew from simpler *sources* than Wordsworth, but none ever
made so much out of so little. He stemmed the commonplace
currents of emotion, and often succeeded in so reversing them,
that men were puzzled when they saw weakness transformed
into power and sorrow into rapture. He used up successfully
the waifs and strays of his imaginative life, reaped so much
from opportunity, hope, and memory, that men were as
puzzled at the simplicity of his delights as they are when they
watch the occasions of a child's laughter.

Thus there is no poet who gives to his theme so perfectly
new a birth as Wordsworth. He does not discern and revivify
the *natural* life which is in it; he creates a new thing altogether,
namely, the life of thought which it has the power to generate
in his own brooding imagination. I have already said that he
uses human sorrow, for example, as an influence to stir up his
own meditative spirit, till it loses its own nature and becomes

> Sorrow, that is not sorrow, but delight;
> And miserable love, that is not pain
> To hear of, for the glory that redounds
> Therefrom to human kind, and what we are.
>
> > (*Prelude*, XIII 246–9)

And it is this strange transmuting power, which his meditative
spirit exercises over all earthly and human themes, that gives
to Wordsworth's poems the intense air of solitude which everywhere pervades them. He is the most solitary of poets. Of him,
with far more point than of Milton, may it be said, in Wordsworth's own words, that 'his soul was like a star, and dwelt
apart'. Of all English poems, his works are the most completely outside the sphere of Shakespeare's universal genius. In
solitude only could they have originated, and in solitude only
can they be perfectly enjoyed. It is impossible not to feel the
loneliness of a mind which never surrenders itself to the natural
and obvious currents of thought or feeling in the theme taken,
but changes their direction by cool sidewinds from his own
spiritual nature. Natural rays of feeling are refracted the
moment they enter Wordsworth's imagination. It is not the

theme acting on the man that you see, but the man acting on the theme. He himself consciously brings to it the spiritual forces which determine the lines of meditation; he evades, or, as I have insisted, even resists the inherent tendencies of emotion belonging to his subject; catches it up into his high spiritual imagination, and makes it yield a totally different fruit of contemplation to any which it seemed naturally likely to bear. It is in this that he differs so completely in manner from other self-conscious poets – Goethe, for instance, who in like manner always left the shadow of himself on the field of his vision. But with Goethe it is a shadow of self in quite a different sense. Goethe watches himself drifting along the tide of feeling, and keeps an eye open outside his heart. But though he overhears himself, he does not interfere with himself; he listens breathlessly, and notes it down. Wordsworth, on the other hand, refuses to listen to this natural self at all. He knows another world of pure and buoyant meditation; and he knows that all which is transplanted into it bears there a new and nobler fruit. With fixed visionary purpose he snatches away his subject from the influence of the lower currents it is beginning to obey, and compels it to breathe its life into that silent sky of conscious freedom and immortal hope in which his own spirit lives.

. . . In reverie the mind wholly loses the boundaries of its own life, and wanders away unconsciously to the world's end. Wordsworth's musings are never reveries. He neither loses himself nor the centre of his thought. He carries his own spiritual world with him, draws the thing or thought or feeling on which he intends to write, from its common orbit, fixes it, like a new star, in his own higher firmament, and there contemplates it beneath the gleaming lights and mysterious shadows of its new sphere. It is in this respect that he differs so widely in habit of thought from Coleridge, who was also a muser in his way. All his thoughts in any one poem flow as surely from a distinct centre as the fragrance from a flower. With Coleridge they flit away down every new avenue of vague suggestion, till we are lost in the inextricable labyrinth of tangled associations. The same spiritual freedom which set Wordsworth's imagination in motion, also controlled and fixed it on a single focus. And this he himself noted in contrasting his own early mental life with his friend's abstract and vagrant habits of fancy:

> I had forms distinct
> To steady me; each airy thought revolved
> Round a substantial centre, which at once
> Incited it to motion, and controlled.
> I did not pine like one in cities bred,
> As was thy melancholy lot, dear Friend!
> Great spirit as thou art, in endless dreams
> Of sickliness, disjoining, joining, things
> Without the light of knowledge. (VIII 429–37)

That this hardy spiritual freedom, acting through the imagination, and drawing the object of the poet's contemplation voluntarily and purposely into his own world of thought, is the most distinguishing characteristic of Wordsworth's poetry, may be best verified by comparing him with any other of our great poets. Most other poets create their poetry, and even their meditative poetry, in the act of throwing themselves *into* the life of the scene or train of thought or feeling they are contemplating: Wordsworth deliberately withdraws his imagination from the heart of his picture to contemplate it in its spiritual relations. Thus, for instance, Tennyson and Wordsworth start from the same mood, the one in the song 'Tears, idle tears', the other in the poem called 'The Fountain'. [Hutton quotes both poems in full.]

Tennyson continues in the same strain of emotion with which he begins, picturing the profound unspeakable sadness with which we survey the irrecoverable past; Wordsworth no sooner touches the same theme than he checks the current of emotion, and, to use his own words, 'instead of being restlessly propelled' by it, he makes it the object of contemplation, and, 'with no unconquerable sighs, yet with a melancholy in the soul, sinks inward into himself, from thought to thought, to a steady remonstrance and a high resolve'. And thus meditating, he wrings from the temporary sadness fresh conviction that the ebbing away, both in spirit and in appearance, of the brightest past, sad as it must ever be, is not so sad a thing as the weak yearning which, in departing, it often leaves stranded on the soul, to cling to the appearance when the spirit is irrecoverably lost. There is no other great poet who thus redeems new ground for spiritual meditation from beneath the very sweep of the tides of the most engrossing affections, and quietly maintains it in possession of the musing intellect. There is no other but Wordsworth who has led us 'to those sweet counsels *between head and heart*' which flash upon the absorbing emotions of the moment the steady light of a calm infinite world. None but Wordsworth has ever so completely transmuted by an imaginative spirit, unsatisfied yearnings into eternal truth. [Hutton goes on to elaborate and illustrate this point.]

. . . But it is by no means principally in treating these deeper themes that Wordsworth brings the most of this conscious, voluntary, imaginative force to bear upon his subjects. All his most characteristic poems bear vivid traces of the same mental process. In his poems on subjects of natural beauty it is perhaps even more remarkable than in his treatment of mental subjects where this contemplative withdrawal from the immediate tyranny of a present emotion, in order to gain a higher point of view, seems more natural.

. . . I may recall those daffodils transfigured before the 'inward eye, which is the bliss of solitude'; the cuckoo, which, though 'babbling only to the vale of sunshine and of flowers', he spiritualises into a 'wandering voice' that 'tellest unto me a tale of visionary hours'; the mountain echo, which sends her 'unsolicited reply' to the same babbling wanderer; the nut-laden hazel-branches, whose luxuriant feast first threw him into 'that sweet mood when pleasure loves to pay tribute to ease', and which then so 'patiently gave up their quiet being', that, haunted by remorse, he is compelled to exclaim, 'with gentle hand touch, for there is a spirit in the woods'; the daisy, that recalls him from 'stately passions' to 'the homely sympathy that heeds the common life our nature breeds'; and the mists, which 'magnify and spread the glories of the sun's bright head'. But there is no finer instance of Wordsworth's self-withdrawing mood in gazing at external things than that of the lines on the Boy of Windermere who mocked the owls. For real lovers of Wordsworth, these lines have effected more in helping them adequately to imagine the full depth of the human imagination, and to feel the inexhaustible wealth of Nature's symbols, than any magnificence of storm, or shipwreck, or Alpine solitude :

> There was a boy : ye knew him well, ye cliffs
> And islands of Winander ! many a time
> At evening, when the earliest stars began
> To move along the edges of the hills,
> Rising or setting, would he stand alone
> Beneath the trees or by the glimmering lake;
> And there, with fingers interwoven, both hands
> Pressed closely palm to palm, and to his mouth
> Uplifted, he, as through an instrument,
> Blew mimic hootings to the silent owls,
> That they might answer him; and they would shout
> Across the watery vale and shout again,
> Responsive to his call, with quivering peals,
> And long halloos and screams, and echoes loud
> Redoubled and redoubled; concourse wild
> Of mirth and jocund din : and when it chanced
> That pauses of deep silence mocked his skill,
> Then sometimes, in that silence while he hung
> Listening, a *gentle shock of mild surprise*
> *Has carried far into his heart the voice*
> *Of mountain torrents*; or the visible scene
> Would enter unawares into his mind,
> With all its solemn imagery, its rocks,
> Its woods, and that uncertain heaven, received
> Into the bosom of the steady lake.

No other poet but Wordsworth that the world ever produced could have written this; you feel in reading it that the lines 'a gentle shock of mild surprise has carried *far into his heart* the voice of mountain torrents', had for him an exactness as well as a fulness of meaning; – for he shows a curious power of carefully discriminating the degrees of depth in his poetic imaginations : some lie near the surface; others lie deeper, but still within the sphere of less meditative minds; others spring from a depth far beyond the reach of any human soundings. . . .

SOURCE: 'The Genius of Wordsworth', *Literary Essays* (1871) pp. 90–105 – extracts.

Walter Horatio Pater

An intimate consciousness of the expression of natural things, which weighs, listens, penetrates, where the earlier mind passed roughly by, is a large element in the complexion of modern poetry. It has been remarked as a fact in mental history again and again. It reveals itself in many forms; but is strongest and most attractive in what is strongest and most attractive in modern literature. It is exemplified, almost equally, by writers as unlike each other as Senancour and Théophile Gautier: as a singular chapter in the history of the human mind, its growth might be traced from Rousseau to Chateaubriand, from Chateaubriand to Victor Hugo: it has doubtless some latent connexion with those pantheistic theories which locate an intelligent soul in material things, and have largely exercised men's minds in some modern systems of philosophy: it is traceable even in the graver writings of historians: it makes as much difference between ancient and modern landscape art, as there is between the rough masks of an early mosaic and a portrait by Reynolds or Gainsborough. Of this new sense, the writings of Wordsworth are the central and elementary expression: he is more simply and entirely occupied with it than any other poet, though there are fine expressions of precisely the same thing in so different a poet as Shelley. There was in his own character a certain contentment, a sort of inborn religious placidity, seldom found united with a sensibility so mobile as his, which was favourable to the quiet, habitual observation of inanimate, or imperfectly animate, existence. His life of eighty years is divided by no very profoundly felt incidents: its changes are almost wholly inward, and it falls into broad, untroubled, perhaps somewhat monotonous spaces. What it most resembles is the life of one of those early Italian or Flemish painters, who, just because their minds were full of heavenly visions, passed, some of them, the better part of sixty years in quiet, systematic industry. This placid life matured a quite unusual sensibility, really innate in him, to the sights and sounds of the natural world – the flower and its shadow on the stone, the cuckoo and its echo. The poem of 'Resolution and Independence' is a storehouse of such records : for its fulness of imagery it may be compared to Keats's 'Saint Agnes' Eve'. To read one of his longer pastoral poems for the first time, is like a day spent in a new country : the memory is crowded for a while with its precise and vivid incidents –

> The pliant harebell swinging in the breeze
> On some grey rock ; –
>
> The single sheep and the one blasted tree
> And the bleak music from that old stone wall ; –
>
> In the meadows and the lower ground
> Was all the sweetness of a common dawn ; –
>
> And that green corn all day is rustling in thine ears.

Clear and delicate at once, as he is in the outlining of visible imagery, he is more clear and delicate still, and finely scrupulous, in the noting of sounds; so that he conceives of noble sound as even moulding the human countenance to nobler types, and as something actually 'profaned' by colour, by visible form, or image. He has a power likewise of realising, and conveying to the consciousness of the reader, abstract and elementary impressions – silence, darkness, absolute motionlessness : or, again, the whole complex sentiment of a particular place, the abstract expression of desolation in the long white road, of peacefulness in a particular folding of the hills. In the airy building of the brain, a special day or hour even, comes to have for him a sort of personal identity, a spirit or angel given to it, by which, for its exceptional insight, or the happy light upon it, it has a presence in one's history, and acts there, as a separate power or accomplishment; and he has celebrated in many of his poems the 'efficacious spirit', which, as he says, resides in these 'particular spots' of time.

. . . And so it came about that this sense of a life in natural objects, which in most poetry is but a rhetorical artifice, is with Wordsworth the assertion of what for him is almost literal fact. To him every natural object seemed to possess more or less of a moral or spiritual life, to be capable of a companionship with man, full of expression, of inexplicable affinities and delicacies of intercourse. An emanation, a particular spirit, belonged, not to the moving leaves or water only, but to the distant peak of the hills arising suddenly, by some change of perspective, above the nearer horizon, to the passing space of light across the plain, to the lichened Druidic stone even, for a certain weird fellowship in it with the moods of men. It was like a 'survival', in the peculiar intellectual temperament of a man of letters at the end of the eighteenth century, of that primitive condition, which some philosophers have traced in the general history of human culture, wherein all outward objects alike, including even the works of men's hands, were believed to be endowed with animation, and the world was 'full of souls' – that mood in which the old Greek gods were first begotten, and which had many strange aftergrowths.

In the early ages, this belief, delightful as its effects on poetry often are, was but the result of a crude intelligence. But, in Wordsworth, such power of seeing life, such perception of a soul, in inanimate things, came of an exceptional susceptibility to the impressions of eye and ear, and was, in its essence, a kind of sensuousness. At least, it is only in a temperament exceptionally susceptible on the sensuous side, that this sense of the expressiveness of outward things comes to be so large a part of life. That he awakened 'a sort of thought in sense', is Shelley's just estimate of this element in Wordsworth's poetry.

And it was through nature, thus ennobled by a semblance of passion and thought, that he approached the spectacle of human life. Human life, indeed, is for him, at first, only an additional, accidental grace on an expressive landscape. When he thought of man, it was of man as in the presence and under the influence of these effective natural objects, and linked to them by many associations. The close connexion of man with natural objects, the habitual association of his thoughts and feelings with a particular spot of earth, has sometimes seemed to degrade those who are subject to its influence, as if it did but reinforce that physical connexion of our nature with the actual lime and clay of the soil, which is always drawing us nearer to our end. But for Wordsworth, these influences tended to the dignity of human nature, because they tended to tranquillise it. By raising nature to the level of human thought he gives it power and expression : he subdues man to the level of nature, and gives him thereby a certain breadth and coolness and solemnity. The leech-gatherer on the moor, the woman 'stepping westward', are for him natural objects, almost in the same sense as the aged thorn, or the lichened rock on the heath. In this sense the leader of the 'Lake School', in spite of an earnest preoccupation with man, his thoughts, his destiny, is the poet of nature. And of nature, after all, in its modesty. The English lake country has, of course, its grandeurs. But the peculiar function of Wordsworth's genius, as carrying in it a power to open out the soul of apparently little or familiar things, would have found its true test had he become the poet of Surrey, say! and the prophet of its life. The glories of Italy and Switzerland, though he did write a little about them, had too potent a material life of their own to serve greatly his poetic purpose.[1]

. . . Sometimes as he dwelt upon those moments of profound, imaginative power, in which the outward object appears to take colour and expression, a new nature almost, from the prompting of the observant mind, the actual world would, as it were, dissolve and detach itself, flake by flake, and he himself seemed to be the creator, and when he would the destroyer, of the world in which he lived – that old isolating thought of many a brain-sick mystic of ancient and modern times.

At other times, again, in those periods of intense susceptibility, in which he appeared to himself as but the passive recipient of external influences, he was attracted by the thought of a spirit of life in outward things, a single, all-pervading mind in them, of which man, and even the poet's imaginative energy, are but moments – that old dream of the *anima mundi*, the mother of all things and their grave, in which some had desired to lose themselves, and others had become indifferent to the distinctions of good and evil. It would come, sometimes, like the sign of the *macrocosm* to Faust in his cell: the network of man and nature was seen to be pervaded by a common, universal life: a new, bold thought lifted him above the furrow, above the green turf of the Westmoreland churchyard, to a world altogether different in its vagueness and vastness, and the narrow glen was full of the brooding power of one universal spirit.

And so he has something, also, for those who feel the fascination of bold speculative ideas, who are really capable of rising upon them to conditions of poetical thought. He uses them, indeed, always with a very fine apprehension of the limits within which alone philosophical imaginings have any place in true poetry; and using them only for poetical purposes, is not too careful even to make them consistent with each other. To him, theories which for other men bring a world of technical diction, brought perfect form and expression, as in those two lofty books of *The Prelude*, which describe the decay and the restoration of Imagination and Taste. Skirting the borders of this world of bewildering heights and depths, he got but the first exciting influence of it, that joyful enthusiasm which great imaginative theories prompt, when the mind first comes to have an understanding of them; and it is not under the influence of these thoughts that his poetry becomes tedious or loses its blitheness. He keeps them, too, always within certain ethical bounds, so that no word of his could offend the simplest of those simple souls which are always the largest portion of mankind. But it is, nevertheless, the contact of these thoughts, the speculative boldness in them, which constitutes, at least for some minds, the secret attraction of much of his best poetry – the sudden passage from lowly thoughts and places to the majestic forms of philosophical imagination, the play of these forms over a world so different, enlarging so strangely the bounds of its humble churchyards, and breaking such a wild light on the graves of christened children.

And these moods always brought with them faultless expression. In regard to expression, as with feeling and thought, the duality of the higher and lower moods was absolute. It belonged to the higher, the imaginative mood, and was the pledge of its reality, to bring the appropriate language with it. In him, when the really poetical motive worked at all, it united, with absolute justice, the word and the idea; each, in the imaginative flame, becoming inseparably one with the other, by that fusion of matter and form, which is the characteristic of the highest poetical expression. His words are themselves thought and feeling; not eloquent, or musical words merely, but that sort of creative language which carries the reality of what it depicts, directly, to the consciousness.

The music of mere metre performs but a limited, yet a very peculiar and subtly ascertained function, in Wordsworth's poetry. With him, metre is but an additional grace, accessory to that deeper music of words and sounds, that moving power, which they exercise in the nobler prose no less than in formal poetry. It is a sedative to that excitement, an excitement some-times almost painful, under which the language, alike of poetry and prose, attains a rhythmical power, independent of metrical combination, and dependent rather on some subtle adjustment of the elementary sounds of words themselves to the image or feeling they convey. Yet some of his pieces, pieces prompted by a sort of half-playful mysticism, like the 'Daffodils' and 'The Two April Mornings', are distinguished by a certain quaint gaiety of metre, and rival by their perfect execution, in this respect, similar pieces among our own Elizabethan, or con-temporary French poetry. And those who take up these poems after an interval of months, or years perhaps, may be surprised at finding how well old favourites wear, how their strange, inventive turns of diction or thought still send through them the old feeling of surprise. Those who lived about Wordsworth were all great lovers of the older English literature, and often-times there came out in him a noticeable likeness to our earlier poets. He quotes unconsciously, but with new power of mean-ing, a clause from one of Shakespere's sonnets; and, as with some other men's most famous work, the 'Ode on the Recollec-tions of Childhood' had its anticipator. He drew something too from the unconscious mysticism of the old English language itself, drawing out the inward significance of its racy idiom, and the not wholly unconscious poetry of the language used by the simplest people under strong excitement – language, therefore, at its origin.

SOURCE: 'Wordsworth', *Appreciations* (1874) pp. 41–58 – extracts.

NOTE

1. A. C. Bradley quotes the Simplon Pass lines and asks whether they could have been written by ' "the poet of Surrey, say! and the prophet of its life" '.

Émile Legouis

Seldom had general uneasiness and moral disorder been so justifiable in England, rarely had the signs of their existence been so unequivocal, as during the winter of 1797–1798. By the peace of Campo-Formio, England was left in solitary opposition to the revolutionary government of France, which had compelled all its other enemies one by one to lay down their arms. Still in possession of her supremacy at sea, she had, nevertheless, as yet won no naval victory which so enhanced her prestige as to console her pride for defeats upon the Continent, none sufficiently decisive to convince her that she had an impregnable rampart in the waters which girdled her shores. So formidable had been the recent outbreaks of disaffection in her fleets, that scarcely even could she place reliance upon them. Ireland, shaking off her bondage, was meanwhile summoning the foreigner, and a scheme of invasion appeared to be ripening in France. There was not a point on the coasts of Britain but felt itself threatened. Worse still, those Englishmen, by far the more numerous party, who had at heart not only the success of their country's arms, but also the preservation of her time-honoured institutions, were asking one another with painful anxiety whether an invader, who landed on that British soil which had been so long free from desecration, would not find a thousand English hands outstretched in welcome, acclamation, and support. Well aware that the fascinations of revolution were strong enough to have destroyed the patriotism of an unknown number of their fellow-countrymen, they detected spies and traitors wherever they turned their restless glance. But a few months had elapsed since the death of Burke, and already they recognised the truth of those prophecies which, until his last hour, he had not ceased to repeat; already they perceived that he at any rate had accurately gauged the mighty strength of the subversive spirit against

which his eloquent voice had strenuously urged a new crusade.
No longer was it a question of crushing that spirit abroad;
fortunate indeed would they be, if they could prevent its
spread and victory at home.

Still more painful, at the same period, were the reflections
of those Englishmen who were well disposed towards France.
With unshaken fortitude they had supported the new Republic in the face of insult and suspicion, of enmity from their
friends and persecution from their rulers. They had forgiven
it the bloodiest days of the Terror, and the lingering fury of
that hurricane after which the most indulgent survey could
reveal nothing but wreckage without a single token of solid
reconstruction. Only yesterday they would have desired its
triumph over England, and some were prematurely enthusiastic at the thought of an invasion which, in their opinion, was
amply warranted by the attitude of their country. France
made no movement but in self-defence; in protecting herself
she protected the cause of human progress; she took up arms
in defence of future peace. She made war to put an end for
ever to all wars of ambition and self-interest. But now overwhelming intelligence reached them : the armies of the
Directory, during a time of European peace, had invaded
Switzerland – that country which, of all the nations of Europe,
should have been most sacred, on account of its weakness, and
from the fact that for centuries it had been throughout the
world the first refuge of liberty. The young Republic showed
itself no less the ruthless aggressor than the monarchs who had
formed a league for the spoliation of Poland. Nowhere in
Europe was there a corner left in which it was possible to pro-
long that dream of regeneration and of happiness on earth,
which for eight years had been so fearlessly pursued in face of
the most cruel disillusion. Those gloomy objections to their
theories which had already presented themselves again and
again to the minds of the most eager reformers, only to be
immediately thrust out of sight, now arose once more, vic-
torious and irresistible. Man, they concluded, is after all not
good by nature. It is not in his power to submit himself to the
guidance of reason. There is nothing in common between man

as he is and that being free alike from prejudice and from error, ready to be enlightened by the invincible logic of justice, whose glowing image philosophers have drawn with such delight. And reason, which has been so grossly deceived in its estimate of its own power, and has so completely misconceived the nature of the evil reality which it aspired to transform, is now seen to be condemned by the very experiment which it has been permitted to make.

Thus, between the two parties : — the Conservatives on the one hand, whose opinion from the outset has been that an imperfect state of society, woven out of good and evil, is all that man in his imperfection deserves; who have greeted with a smile of sarcastic incredulity the promise of another golden age and the regeneration of mankind; who, as the sky grows darker, and the hour of destruction seems near at hand, become more and more rooted in their distrust; — and, on the other hand, the reformers or revolutionists who persist in believing society as it is to be no longer tolerable, but who are losing hope of establishing in its place a better order of things — between these two parties we find a mutual and silent acquiescence in pessimism. Man is by nature perverse and unreasonable; life at best a poor possession; evil rooted in the very depths of human nature, and ineradicable save with that existence of which it forms a vital part; progress impossible, or so slow and inconsiderable that the contemplation of it brings no delight. The millennium of our dreams is the idlest of fancies.

. . . In the very heart of this crisis, on the 11th March 1798, a young Englishman, but a short time earlier one of the most fervent reformers, now living poor and unknown in a lonely nook in Somerset, was writing to a friend :

I have been tolerably industrious within the last few weeks. I have written 706 lines of a poem which I hope to make of considerably utility. Its title will be, The Recluse, or Views of Nature, Man, and Society.

The utility alluded to consists in restoring gladness to the heart of man. The poet's object is precisely that which every one seems ready to abandon as an idle dream : it is the recovery of happiness. He designs to increase the joys of life, and, though not denying the existence of its sorrows, to transform them into peace. He preaches no political or social reform. Whether the existing forms of society endure, or are destroyed, is for him at this time a matter of secondary importance. Nor does he speak in the name of any religion. He does not, as Chateaubriand already dreams of doing, offer to souls in search of pious emotion the solemn dogmas and the touching ceremonial of Christianity. He concerns himself with earthly happiness alone. From creeds and forms of worship, from national constitutions and legal codes, it may, according to circumstances, derive faint assistance, or meet with feeble opposition. But its deepest source is elsewhere; in the very centre of man's nature, in his senses and his heart. The one thing of true importance is the cultivation of the feelings, which, in the individual, may be, and ought to be, developed so as to be capable of the greatest possible amount of enjoyment. Already, in this world of pain, there are privileged beings whose eyes behold with quiet rapture the splendours of nature, whose ears detect her harmonies, whose hearts are thrilled spontaneously and with delight by all tender and lofty emotion.

> Why is this glorious creature to be found
> One only in ten thousand? What one is,
> Why may not millions be? What bars are thrown
> By Nature in the way of such a hope?
> Our animal appetites and daily wants,
> Are these obstructions insurmountable?
> If not, then others vanish into air. (*Prelude*, XIII 87–93)

When every man shall possess the poet's eye, the poet's ear, the poet's heart, that millennium, so fondly looked for in other paths of progress, will have been reached indeed. A distant end, no doubt, but one towards which every step is a delight, and for which men can strive, both individually and in unison, free from rivalry or wrath. In those very feelings which proud reason but lately despised and resolved to crush, lies the true worth of man; in those senses which that same reason regarded with suspicion or disgust, refusing to see in them anything beyond the evidence of his animal nature, lies man's true glory.

... Contempt for man as he is, contempt for the world of reality, such at bottom is the twofold source of the disease from which men are suffering. This contempt, born of pride and impotence, is the height of impiety, and those who indulge in it may be said to be justly punished by the despair in which it results. Nothing that this world contains is worthy of contempt; none who inhabits it has the right to despise.

> ... He who feels contempt
> For any living thing, hath faculties
> Which he has never used; ... thought with him
> Is in its infancy.
>> ('Lines left upon a seat in a yew-tree', 52-5)

Contempt means ignorance.

> 'Tis Nature's law
> That none, the meanest of created things,
> Of forms created the most vile and brute,
> The dullest or most noxious, should exist
> Divorced from good – a spirit and pulse of good,
> A life and soul, to every mode of being
> Inseparably linked. ('The Old Cumberland Beggar', 73-9)

If this is true of every created being, how much more of every human creature. Those lowly ones for whom hitherto the wise man has felt no sentiment but pity, of whom he has never thought without a sense of indignation at their degraded condition, to whom he has never spoken but to make them conscious by his very compassion of their insignificance and unworthiness – in order that such as these may be restored to their rights, it is useless to await the uncertain hour of the equal division of this world's false goods: wealth, shallow pleasures, adornments of the person, and intellectual gifts. We must recognise here and now their full value as they are. We must raise them in their own eyes and make them conscious of their usefulness, of the beauty and even of the brightness which may crown their simple life. Wretched and degraded as they are, they must be brought to feel that it is within their own power to shed a lustre round them in the cottage or the hovel in which they dwell.

And the proof that there is no occasion to despair of man's future will be all the more overwhelming, if we can determine the presence of the fundamental virtues and the moral perceptions in that class of men which is at once the most neglected and the most numerous. The proof that life is rich in pleasures will be the more impossible of refutation, if the joys of which the poet testifies are more accessible to all, more widely spread, less confined to particular seasons; if, unlike some rare plants, they require no journey to discover them, but blossom, like the daisy of the meadow, in familiar profusion beneath our feet. He, therefore, who would be the benefactor of his race, must be prepared both to point out those elements of the beautiful in man which are at once most essential and least understood, and to indicate those characteristics of the beautiful in nature, which are not only the most liable to be overlooked, but, at the same time, the most universal.

Such was the object of the great poem, designed to be of some 'utility' to a disheartened and sceptical generation, the composition of which was occupying Wordsworth's mind at twenty-eight years of age.

SOURCE : *The Early Life of William Wordsworth, 1770–1798* (1897) pp. 1–8 – extracts.

PART THREE

Modern Studies,
1926–1967

Helen Darbishire

WORDSWORTH'S *PRELUDE* (1926)

Between the years 1798 and 1805, the most fruitful years of
his poetic life, Wordsworth composed a long autobiographical
poem, known to his family and friends as 'the poem on his own
early life', or 'the poem on the growth of his mind', or 'the
poem addressed to Coleridge'. Of that work *The Prelude*, published after his death in 1850, is a much-revised version. The
original poem, preserved in two manuscript copies made by
Dorothy Wordsworth and Sara Hutchinson in the winter of
1805–06, has since remained in the hands of the Wordsworth
family. Mr Gordon Wordsworth recently entrusted these
manuscripts, together with others relevant to *The Prelude*, to
the careful hands of Professor de Selincourt, whose edition of
The Prelude, just published, gives us that early poem intact.
No event so important as this has happened in the literary
world for many years. The original *Prelude* is in a real sense a
different poem from *The Prelude* that we know. As we read it
we see into Wordsworth's mind at that very period when his
creative powers were at their height, and watch its first search-
ings after the true history of his inner life.

Wordsworth never intended to publish his autobiography
until his great philosophical poem *The Recluse* was completed.
But *The Recluse* was never completed, and he came to realise
that *The Prelude* must stand on its own merits and that he
must prepare it for posthumous publication. Thus began a process of periodic revision which ceased only with his life. The
first two finished manuscripts were made in the winter of
1805–06; the third was written probably between 1817 and
1819; the fourth round about 1828, corrected in 1832, and
completely overhauled in 1839; the fifth, which embodies
these corrections, was the copy from which the text of 1850

was printed. The first three manuscripts are closely in harmony; the fourth and fifth represent a thoroughly revised and altered poem. Professor de Selincourt's edition gives us in admirably critical form all the information that we need, and makes it possible for us to see the poem in all the stages of its growth. The text of 1850 is printed page by page opposite that of 1805–06, and the relevant readings from other manuscripts appear in the *apparatus criticus.*

The general trend of the alterations can be confidently foretold by anyone who knows Wordsworth's way of tinkering with his text. In style, bald simplicity will give place to a more decorative, more obviously literary form. In thought, a tendency to revolutionary politics will be checked, and moral and religious conceptions will be conformed to a more orthodox pattern. These familiar processes can be traced, surely enough, in the successive texts of *The Prelude.*

Another change, proper to that poem, springs from a change in his personal life. When he wrote and dedicated the poem to Coleridge the two were on terms of closest intimacy. In 1810 an unhappy estrangement divided them, and the old loving friendship was never regained. Many altered or omitted passages in *The Prelude* bear silent witness to the change. The tender address to Coleridge, 'most loving soul', is altered to 'capacious soul'; his 'gentle spirit' becomes a 'kindred influence'. The daring phrase in which Wordsworth claims their close intellectual kinship, 'though twins almost in genius and in mind', is struck out. And, most telling of all, the allusion to Dorothy, 'thy treasure also', is changed to the less poignant 'dear to thee also'. Further, the whole manner of the poem is altered. He had addressed himself to Coleridge heart to heart.

> I speak bare truth
> As if to thee alone in private talk,

he writes. In revising he changes the intimate and personal form, substituting general for particular expressions, replacing the pronoun 'I' by impersonal constructions. In short, with a touch here and a new patch there, he turns what was a glori-

fied private letter to Coleridge into a poetic confession, fit for
the medium of cold print.

But the most vital changes lie deeper still; they touch what
we should now call the psychology of the poem. The inspiration of Wordsworth's poetry had its vitalising source in the
power with which he realised a peculiar experience. The
experience begins in sensation and ends in thought. It begins
in such an adventure of the senses as that of his boyish birds-
nesting :

> Oh ! when I have hung
> Above the raven's nest, by knots of grass
> And half-inch fissures in the slippery rock
> But ill sustained, and almost (so it seemed)
> Suspended by the blast that blew amain,
> Shouldering the naked crag, oh, at that time
> While on the perilous ridge I hung alone,
> With what strange utterance did the loud dry wind
> Blow through my ear ! the sky seemed not a sky
> Of earth – and with what motion moved the clouds ! –

(a passage whose power and significance is inexplicable; for
what can we say of those last bare words except that they
'carry alive into the heart' something we have all heard with
our ears and seen with our eyes, yet never felt with so strange a
thrill ?).

It ends in such thought as that of the famous invocation :

> Wisdom and Spirit of the Universe !
> Thou Soul that art the eternity of thought,
> That givest to forms and images a breath
> And everlasting motion, not in vain
> By day or starlight thus from my first dawn
> Of childhood didst thou intertwine for me
> The passions that build up our human soul ;
> Not with the mean and vulgar works of man,
> But with high objects, with enduring things, –
> With life and nature –

The core of the experience was an intense consciousness of
Nature passing through his senses to his mind; and the growth

of that consciousness, its action and reaction upon his inner life, is the central theme of *The Prelude*. The experience was peculiar simply in its intensity. So pure and strong was the life his senses led that it passed, on a tide of feeling, into the life of his spirit. Here lies the mystery which he calls, in a significant phrase, 'the incumbent mystery of sense and soul'. What matters to us is not so much to understand the experience as to realise it, not so much to solve the mystery as to see where it lies. This is what the early *Prelude* helps us to do. In it Wordsworth told the inner workings of his mind as nakedly and truthfully as he could; and the changes most to be deplored in his later text are those which overlay or obscure that naïve immediate expression. They generally mar the poetry; they always disguise the truth.

The poet, Wordsworth has said elsewhere, is one

> Contented if he may enjoy
> The things which others understand.

That was written in 1800. The early *Prelude* insists again and again on the primacy and self-sufficiency of feeling. Of his Cambridge days we read :

> I lov'd and I enjoy'd, that was my chief
> And ruling business, happy in the strength
> And loveliness of imagery and thought.

In the final text these lines go out and a single line stands in their stead :

> Content to observe, to admire, and to enjoy.

Again, of his unsophisticated childhood he first wrote :

> I felt, and nothing else; I did not judge,

but rewrote :

> I felt, observed, and pondered, did not judge.

That bold trust in feeling meant a belief also in the value of sensation out of which such feeling springs. Seeking to tell how

in London, living amongst thousands of nameless human
beings, he was at times overpowered by the consciousness of
'the unity of man', he put it simply thus :

> When strongly breath'd upon
> By this sensation, whencesoe'er it comes
> Of union or communion doth the soul
> Rejoice as in her highest joy: for there,
> There chiefly, hath she feeling whence she is,
> And, passing through all Nature rests with God.

The conception came to him as a powerful sensation out of
which grew a profound feeling. The physical image 'strongly
breathed upon', and the naked language,

> There chiefly, hath she feeling whence she is,
> And, passing through all Nature rests with God,

seem to spring straight out of the experience itself. In revising
the lines he replaced the living fact by an intellectual statement
about it :

> The soul when smitten thus
> By a sublime *idea,* whencesoe'er
> Vouchsafed for union or communion, feeds
> On the pure bliss, and takes her rest with God.

The simple truth about his inner life which he set out to tell
in *The Prelude* was often strange and startling. Two sides of it
strike the common-sense mind as particularly strange. Physical
images have a power in the poet's inner life which the ordinary
man only knows in delirium. And Wordsworth is conscious of
two lives, or two levels of experience – the surface life to which
he belongs with the rest of the world, and another life beneath
this, in which, with a deep drop into himself, he seems to join
the inner life of the whole universe. His earlier text deals
boldly with these strange things. Poets, like lunatics and lovers
– and, we might add, like children – differ from the rest of us
in their power not only to see and hear images but to feel and
think them. Thus breath, air, or breeze is not for Wordsworth
merely a symbol for spiritual life – it actually becomes it. His

use of the image seems at first natural and innocent enough, as when he writes (in a cancelled passage) of the babe drinking in through its senses the tender passion of its mother :

> Such feelings pass into his torpid life
> Like an awakening breeze,

or of the 'gladsome air' (significantly altered later to 'absolute wealth') 'of my own private being'.

But under the image lay for Wordsworth a living fact. *The Prelude* opens with the blowing of a breeze 'from the green fields and from the sky' to greet him as he issues from the city. It does more than refresh him physically, for while it blows upon his body he feels within

> A corresponding mild creative breeze,
> A vital breeze which travelled gently on
> O'er things which it had made, and is become
> A tempest, a redundant energy
> Vexing its own creation.

That is, the air blowing from without passed within him and became a spiritual and creative energy. Other passages in the early *Prelude* tell in plain terms the same tale. Turning from his story of the Revolution, he invokes once more the powers of Nature :

> Ye motions of delight, that through the fields
> Stir gently, breezes and soft airs that breathe
> The breath of Paradise, and find your way
> To the recesses of the soul !

To place beside these lines the version of 1850 is to measure how much was lost in psychological truth when Wordsworth revised his poem :

> Ye motions of delight, that haunt the sides
> Of the green hills; ye breezes and soft airs,
> Whose subtle intercourse with breathing flowers,
> Feelingly watched, might teach man's haughty race
> How without injury to take, to give
> Without offence.

The bold fact of the first statement is omitted, the influence of the breeze tritely moralised.

'Motions of delight' is an arresting phrase, and Wordsworth's use of the word 'motion' is worth watching. Physical movement was to him, as it is perhaps to every imaginative mind, stimulating in a high degree. In Nature he was alive to the perpetual energy of motion. The Solitary of *The Excursion* longs to surrender his body to the elements,

> and reckless of the storm
> Be as a presence and a motion, – one
> Among the many : here.

Wordsworth seems to find in motion the very essence of life. God Himself, the divine principle in things, *is* motion :

> a motion and a spirit that impels
> All thinking things, all objects of all thought,
> And rolls through all things.

When he says :

> I felt a kind of sympathy with power,
> Motions raised up within me,

the word takes on a new meaning. If a breeze or a 'motion of delight' passes into the inner being, then a motion is a feeling as well as a physical movement. And so, indeed, he calls his first impulses of love towards man 'those motions of delight'; and again his early sensations of sympathy with Nature 'the first and earliest motions of my life'. These phrases occur in cancelled passages which now first see the light; but readers of Wordsworth are already familiar with 'those hallowed and pure motions of the sense' in the first book of *The Prelude*. The word in the sense of impulse or emotion was used by Shakespeare and by Milton, but was moribund in Dr Johnson's day.[1] Wordsworth's revival of it was necessary to his thought. It illustrates tellingly that fusion of physical with mental life, that direct, startling passage of image into thought or feeling, which he so freely expressed in his first draft of *The Prelude*. If the life of the spirit was motion and breeze, the suspension of that life was a deadly stillness. A cancelled passage, recalling his preoccupation with superficial interests at Cambridge, ends strangely thus :

> Hush'd, meanwhile,
> Was the under soul, lock'd up in such a calm,
> That not a leaf of the great nature stirr'd.

The soul lives a life of its own, shut away from our ordinary conscious life. Wordsworth even invents a new word for it, the under soul, a word of which the New English Dictionary gives no example before 1868. A still more surprising passage, which never found its way into a final draft of *The Prelude*, describes that state of mind, deeper than conscious thought, in which the individual is lost in the life of the whole universe :

> I seemed to learn
> That what we see of forms and images
> Which float along our minds, and what we feel
> Of action, and recognisable thought,
> Prospectiveness, or intellect, or will,
> Not only is not worthy to be deemed
> Our being, to be prized as what we are,
> But is the very littleness of life.
> Such consciousness I deem but accidents,
> Relapses from the one interior life
> That lives in all things, sacred from the touch
> Of that false secondary power by which
> In weakness we create distinctions, then
> Believe that all our puny boundaries are things
> Which we perceive and not which we have made, –
> In which all beings live with God, themselves
> Are God, existing in one mighty whole,
> As indistinguishable as the cloudless East
> At noon is from the cloudless West, when all
> The hemisphere is one cerulean blue.

There is no escape from the meaning of this – God is in the soul of man as He is in Nature. The only times when we truly

live are those in which, with no effort of will or intelligence, no
consciousness of forms or images, the soul merges into the life
of the universe and we *are God*. The great mind, Wordsworth
says, is one

> That is exalted by an underpresence,
> The sense of God, or whatsoe'er is dim
> Or vast in its own being.

Again, there is much significance in the word 'underpresence',
altered in another manuscript to 'underconsciousness', neither
word recorded in the New English Dictionary.

The experiences here described have a character which he
later shrank from allowing them. They were involuntary; they
had nothing to do with his conscious will or intelligence. Again
and again he tampered with his early record, cutting out words
that tell of involuntary action in the mind – things happening
of themselves – and substituting other words either nugatory
or expressly making the mind itself the agent. Thus his gift as a
poet, first described as an 'influx' vouchsafed to him, becomes
an 'insight'. 'Motions raised up within me' become 'motions
not treacherous or vain'. Of the vision on Snowdon in book
XIV he first wrote :

> A meditation rose in me that night
> Upon the lonely Mountain when the scene
> Had pass'd away, and it appear'd to me
> The perfect image of a mighty Mind,

but altered it significantly :

> When into air had partially dissolved
> That vision, given to spirits of the night
> And three chance human wanderers, *in calm thought
> Reflected,* it appeared to me the type
> Of a majestic intellect.

Perhaps the most interesting piece of psychology in the early
Prelude – no trace of it remains in 1850 – is found in the lines
leading up to his midnight encounter with the old soldier in

book IV. He is returning, tired from an evening's revelry, along a solitary mountain road.

> On I went
>   Tranquil, receiving in my own despite
>   Amusement, as I slowly pass'd along,
>   From such near objects as from time to time,
>   Perforce intruded on the listless sense
>   Quiescent, and dispos'd to sympathy,
>   With an exhausted mind, worn out by toil,
>   And all unworthy of the deeper joy
>   Which waits on distant prospect, cliff, or sea,
>   The dark blue vault, and universe of stars.
>   Thus did I steal along that silent road,
>   My body from the stillness drinking in
>   A restoration like the calm of sleep,
>   But sweeter far. Above, before, behind,
>   Around me, all was peace and solitude,
>   I look'd not round, nor did the solitude
>   Speak to my eye; but it was heard and felt.
>   O happy state! what beauteous pictures now
>   Rose in harmonious imagery – they rose
>   As from some distant region of my soul
>   And came along like dreams; yet such as left
>   Obscurely mingled with their passing forms
>   A consciousness of animal delight,
>   A self-possession felt in every pause
>   And every gentle movement of my frame.

Why did he strike the passage out? The mental exhaustion, the gradual restoration of the mind through the body, the involuntary images that rose as from some inner recess of his being, the consciousness of animal delight, make up a state which, reviewed in the cold light of reason, must have seemed to him confused, irrelevant to the purpose in hand. He was wrong. The passage is strictly relevant to his purpose. The sudden vision of the old soldier, still, uncouth, majestic, rising up as from another world, gets much of its sublime effect from its contrast with the mood that preludes it. This mood itself, described with an intimacy unparalleled elsewhere in Words-worth's writings, belongs to that undefined borderland between the physical and mental life which rational minds distrust. What makes the passage important to us is that it lets us see into his mind in a state not rapt and mystical, but shallow and calm – a mood that reveals, as distinctly as clear water shows pebbles in a brook, the simple elements of sensation that underlie thought and feeling. Who but Wordsworth would have dared to say that dreamlike visions rising from some distant region of the soul are bound up with, if they do not actually spring from, a 'consciousness of animal delight'? Who, at any rate, could have dared to say so in the year 1798? From such passages 'the incumbent mystery of sense and soul' receives illumination.

From the experiences which they record sprang his philosophy or faith. And of this again the first *Prelude* gives a firsthand statement. Wordsworth's creed may be said in three words : God, Man, Nature. These three were divine : it might almost be said that they were one divinity. God was necessarily greatest, Man came next, and Nature, who had taught him to know the divinity in man, was last yet first, the source of his inspiration and first step in all his vital knowledge. When he first confessed his faith in *The Prelude* he had only to use these words, simply and passionately, and all his meaning was conveyed. He had only to speak, in the lines already quoted, of the soul that 'passing through all Nature rests with God', and he had uttered the first article of his creed. The words were charged with power. What greater things can be said than God, Man, Nature? But the middle-aged Wordsworth who revised *The Prelude* had lost this vital sense. He was betrayed by the ineradicable weakness of civilised man; he had to explain, to rationalise, to moralise. Moreover, since he was not only a civilised man, but a devoutly religious Victorian Englishman, he had to translate his thought into the terms of an orthodox Christian creed. Thus the phrase 'to think with admiration and respect of man' becomes

> to think
> With a due reverence of earth's rightful lord
> Here placed to be the inheritor of heaven.

'God and Nature's single sovereignty' is amplified to

> presences of God's mysterious power
> Made manifest in Nature's sovereignty.

'Great God' gives place to 'Power supreme'! and in another context, ludicrously and lamentably, to 'How strange!' 'Living God', simplest sublime address to the Deity, becomes 'righteous Heaven'! At the time when he wrote *The Prelude* Wordsworth's faith, in one aspect a simple form of pantheism, in another a Hegelian belief in the power of the human mind, bore little, if any, trace of dogmatic Christianity. If he gave it afterwards a carefully Christian colouring, was this only, to use his own phrase of a famous expunction in *Peter Bell*, 'not to offend the pious'? Or did it portend some vital change of mind?

To answer that question we must examine some of the patched places in *The Prelude* text.

In the early version of book v, lines 11–14 ran:

> > > Hitherto
> In progress through this Verse, my mind hath look'd
> Upon the speaking face of earth and heaven
> As her prime Teacher, intercourse with man
> Establish'd by the sovereign Intellect
> Who through that bodily Image hath diffus'd
> A soul divine which we participate,
> A deathless spirit.

In revising this, he cut out the line which holds the essence of his meaning, 'A soul divine which we participate', and substituted an apologetic phrase to fill the gap, so that the triumphant passage now ends lamely thus:

> Who through that bodily image hath diffused,
> As might appear to the eye of fleeting time,
> A deathless spirit.

Again his apostrophe in book x:

> Great God !
> Who send'st thyself into this breathing world
> Through Nature and through every kind of life,
> And mak'st man what he is, Creature divine,

is reworded :

> O Power Supreme !
> Without Whose care this world would cease to breathe,
> Who from the fountain of Thy grace doth fill
> The veins that branch through every frame of life
> Making man what he is, creature divine.

The early versions here show a vital difference in thought, not only in expression. The great God who sends Himself into the world through Nature, who diffuses through her 'a soul divine which we participate', is the God of the pantheist. What Wordsworth has ejected in the process of revision is the naked fact of the soul of man meeting God in Nature.

One more passage will throw light. He altered the lines

> The feeling of life endless, the great thought
> By which we live, Infinity and God,

to

> Faith in life endless, the sustaining thought
> Of human Being, Eternity and God.

The verbal change is slight, but its import great. 'The feeling of life endless', his own personal intuition, comes to be called 'Faith in life endless', a faith which he shares with the Christian Church; the great thought by which we live, infinity and God, becomes the Christian thought of human immortality. Strange that the words 'infinity' and 'eternity' should mean the same thing with such a difference. The truth is that he both changed and did not change. That central experience, the merging of his soul with the divine soul in Nature, remained the core of his religion, 'the masterlight of all his seeing'; but it came to him more and more rarely : he distrusted its sufficiency, and he backed it up with the support of a traditional creed. Moreover, he had no intention of offending the pious, or of being himself misjudged. At no time of his life, except perhaps at the brief period of disillusion after his return from France in 1793, was Wordsworth a disbeliever in Christianity. 'There is no such thing as "natural piety",' said Blake, commenting on Wordsworth's phrase, 'because the natural man is at enmity with God.' But Wordsworth did not think so. For him natural piety was not inconsistent with Christian piety. The two creeds stood by him side by side : when one failed the other helped. But they never quite merged. In spite of all the tinkerings to which his text was submitted, many bold and challenging passages in *The Prelude* remain intact to vindicate the persistent strength of his early thought. The 'Prospectus' to *The Excursion* remains; the 'Lines composed above Tintern Abbey' remain. The passage which is the core of that poem,

> a sense sublime
> Of something far more deeply interfused,
> Whose dwelling is the light of setting suns,
> And the round ocean and the living air,
> And the blue sky, and in the mind of man :
> A motion and a spirit that impels
> All thinking things, all objects of all thought,
> And rolls through all things,

is quoted by Coleridge as an expression 'in language but not in sense or purpose' of a doctrine which he condemns with pain, the conception of God as the *anima mundi*. It was a poor compliment to Wordsworth to say that his language expressed what was not his sense and purpose. Whatever his other faults, Wordsworth always meant what he said.

Here, then, are two layers of thought, one superimposed upon but not displacing the other, a passionate intuition of God in the universe and a belief in the God of the Anglican Church : here, also, are two modes of expression, the one naïve and immediate, fitting the utterance of strong personal feeling, the other dignified and general, coloured by the language of a familiar creed.

In another direction his thought at once changed and did

not change. Everyone knows what Wordsworth thought of the human mind. Hegel could go no further in exalting it than Wordsworth went in his 'Prospectus' to *The Excursion* :

> For I must tread on shadowy ground, must sink
> Deep – and, aloft ascending, breathe in worlds
> To which the heaven of heavens is but a veil.
> All strength – all terror, single or in bands,
> That ever was put forth in personal form –
> Jehovah – with his thunder, and the choir
> Of shouting Angels, and the empyreal thrones –
> I pass them unalarmed. Not Chaos, not
> The darkest pit of lowest Erebus,
> Nor aught of blinder vacancy, scooped out
> By help of dreams – can breed such fear and awe
> As fall upon us often when we look
> Into our Minds, into the Mind of Man –
> My haunt, and the main region of my song.

Blake, speaking of this passage (to him so upsetting that it gave him a stomach complaint of which he nearly died), asked, 'Does Mr Wordsworth think his mind can surpass Jehovah?' This belief in the greatness of the human mind is at the very centre of Wordsworth's thought. As a young man he exulted almost to arrogance in the strength and power of his own mental life. In the early *Prelude* he uses such phrases as 'majestic thoughts', 'sovereignty within', 'religious dignity of mind', 'majesty of mind', 'majestic intellect'. In his revision these phrases are thrown out, or their fangs drawn. His 'majestic thoughts' become 'exalted thoughts'; 'sovereignty within' and 'religious dignity of mind' go out; 'majesty of mind' is displaced by 'a creed of reconcilement'; 'majestic intellect' becomes 'unfolding intellect'. A particular passage more closely scanned will show how his mind was working. It follows upon the account of his failure to fit into the students' life at Cambridge.

> But wherefore be cast down?
> Why should I grieve? I was a chosen Son.
> For hither I had come with holy powers
> And faculties, whether to work or feel :

> To apprehend all passions and moods
> Which time, and place, and season do impress
> Upon the visible universe, and work
> Like changes there by force of my own mind.
> I was a Freeman : in the purest sense
> Was free, and to majestic ends was strong.
> I do not speak of learning, moral truth
> Or understanding; 'twas enough for me
> To know that I was otherwise endow'd.

The meaning of these lines is unequivocal. The holy powers in which he exulted were the powers of his own mind freely communicating with Nature and drawing thence mysterious strength. They had nothing to do with intellectual training or moral worth, still less with religion in the orthodox sense, which he does not so much as refer to.

The passage appears in our known text shorn of all its daring, and decorously touched with Christian thought :

> But wherefore be cast down?
> For (not to speak of Reason and her pure
> Reflective acts to fix the moral law
> Deep in the conscience, nor of Christian Hope
> Bowing her head before her sister Faith
> As one far mightier), hither I had come,
> Bear witness, Truth, endowed with holy powers
> And faculties, whether to work or feel.

Hope bows before Faith : both are expressly Christian. Reason is tied to a moral function. Majesty, dignity, sovereignty, freedom, give place to a studious humility of mind. And here once more we touch a radical change in Wordsworth's thought. The pressure of the years and crushing personal sorrows had taught him the inherent weakness of human nature, a weakness from which neither mind nor spirit was exempt. And so the Christian doctrine of humility went home to his heart. When we find him after a magnificent eulogy of man, 'as of all visible natures crown', adding the words 'though born of dust and kindred to the worm', we are disgusted by what seems an irrelevant concession. But the words, out of key as they are with his earlier mood, were strictly relevant to his later position. They stand for something not only sincerely thought, but passionately felt. This will be acknowledged when we reflect upon some other lines in his final text, themselves magnificent and, as we thought, inevitable :

> Dust as we are, the immortal spirit grows
> Like harmony in music, –

which originally ran :

> The mind of man is fram'd even like the breath
> And harmony of music, –

with no reference to our dusty origin. The altered version vindicates itself. 'Dust as we are, the immortal spirit grows. . . .' Thought and feeling have been transmuted into pure poetry. The question 'Did Wordsworth mean what he says?' simply cannot be asked in the face of it.

In thought, then, the later *Prelude* records an inevitable change of mind. The increasing rarity of certain passionate experiences of his own lent force to his friends' warnings about the taint of pantheism; and he omits, or rewrites in a Christian sense, lines that record those passionate and possibly pantheistic experiences. Again, his exultant pride in the greatness of the human mind gives place at times to a truly Christian humility. At times only is that pride displaced. For here again, in certain passages, his earlier thought survives untouched. No terms could be stronger than these :

> Of genius, power
> Creation and divinity itself,
> I have been speaking, for my theme has been
> What passed within me.

Wordsworth could not help himself. When his religious thought flowed into the channel of Anglican doctrine he had to retouch his autobiography, and incidentally tamper with its poetry, in the spirit of that doctrine. But even in the interests of his creed he was wrong. If anyone has been converted to Christianity by *The Prelude*—and everyone who has really read it must have undergone conversion of some kind – it was not the Christianised passages that converted him, not the allusions to 'fountain of Thy grace', 'man inheritor of Heaven', 'Righteous Heaven', 'Power Supreme', but rather the poetry of a spiritual experience so intense, so pure, and so profound that it holds the essence of all religion. The text of the early *Prelude* gives us that elemental experience freed from the gloss of later interpretation. And it shows us, further, how its roots lay, where Wordsworth did not shrink from finding them, in the sensuous or animal life which is our common heritage. The poets of our own era have attempted to explore this region of the senses, with something, perhaps, of Wordsworth's daring. But he knew things which they do not know; and he kept himself severely aloof from knowledge that he did not need. He was innocent, where they are sophisticated. His extraordinary purity of mind and heart kept strong and pure to an almost supernatural degree those senses of his to which, as he is never tired of telling us, he owed everything that mattered.

SOURCE : *The Nineteenth Century,* XCIX (May 1926) 718–31.

NOTE

1. Cf. also his idea of 'truth' as

        'a motion or a shape
  Instinct with vital functions' (*Prel.* VIII 298).

J. R. MacGillivray

THE THREE FORMS OF *THE PRELUDE,* 1798–1805 (1964)

The Prelude was first published in 1850, shortly after Wordsworth's death. The composition of the poem, as distinct from its revision, had been completed forty-five years earlier, in 1805. It was revised on three occasions afterwards, the latest in 1839, and many minor changes were made, and a few larger ones. The fair copy of 1839 was the manuscript which was sent to the printer in 1850.

The next important date in the history of the poem was 1926, when Ernest de Selincourt published his edition 'from the manuscripts, with introduction, textual and critical notes'. The poem as it had been completed in 1805 was printed there for the first time, on verso pages opposite the corresponding lines of the well-known work of 1850. This convenient confrontation and the elaborate textual apparatus made it possible for the student to observe significant changes in thought and expression in Wordsworth's greatest poem over nearly the whole period of his literary life. However, neither de Selincourt's introductory account of the early history of *The Prelude*, nor Helen Darbishire's revision and correction of it in 1959, nor the textual apparatus, useful as it is, makes it clear that the poem of 1805 was not the first version of the autobiography, but rather the third. It had first been composed in 1798–1800 as a poem in two parts, less than one thousand lines in length. By the end of 1801, Wordsworth had decided to enlarge the poem and to give it a different emphasis. After working on it only rarely in the next two years and then continuously in February and March 1804, he had almost finished it, in five books, when he changed his plan once more, and

went on to write the much longer poem which he first completed the following year. Each of these three poems had its
particular biographical extent and literary organization. The
first poem was incorporated somewhat less than perfectly in the
second, and the second in the third. In this paper I intend to
trace the early history of the autobiographical writing which
became *The Prelude*, to distinguish the three forms which it
took, and to indicate how some puzzling features of the poem
of 1805 and later can be explained as unassimilated survivals
from the two earlier poems.

First a difficulty in designation should be mentioned. From
the beginning of its composition until shortly before its publication, more than half a century later, the poem in each of its
forms remained without a title. It was referred to in such
terms as 'a Poem . . . on my early life or the growth of my own
mind' or 'the poem to Coleridge'. It was Mrs Wordsworth,
after her husband's death, who gave the work its name : *The
Prelude, or Growth of a Poet's Mind; An Autobiographical
Poem*.[1]

It was intended both to *relate* and to *be* a prelude. It was to
relate the beginning of the poet's imaginative life, eventually
down to the year of the publication of *Lyrical Ballads*, when
he was twenty-eight years old. It was to be a prelude to a much
longer and more ambitious poem which he hoped would be
his greatest literary achievement, a work never completed –
hence the long delay in publication. We first hear of the plan
for the great poem and the beginning of its composition in
March 1798. 'I have been tolerably industrious within the last
few weeks. I have written 1300 lines of a poem which I hope to
make of considerable utility. Its title will be *The Recluse; or
views of Nature, Man, and Society*.'[2] A few days earlier he had
mentioned the poem without indicating the primary title : 'My
object is to give pictures of Nature, Man, and Society. Indeed
I know not any thing which will not come within the scope of
my plan.'[3]

Of the plan of *The Recluse* at this stage we learn no more
than that. It was both extensive and vague. It may have
originated in the mind of Coleridge, so productive of large

schemes. Certainly for many years he was to continue to show an almost proprietary interest in the project. Since the previous summer (1797), the two poets had been living near each other in Somerset. An established friendship had been followed by mutual dependence for intellectual and literary stimulation. They had wandered over the neighbouring Quantock Hills together or down to the shore of the Bristol Channel – where a government spy with a Bardolph nose, sent to find out what those suspected radicals were discussing so frequently, was incensed to learn that they were talking about him. He was sure he heard them, several times, refer to Spy Nozy.[4] In November, accompanied by Dorothy Wordsworth, they had walked as far as Lynmouth, on the border of Devon, and during the first evening as they tramped along they had planned and begun to compose as a joint effort 'The Ancient Mariner'. Day after day they retraced the well-worn path between Coleridge's humble cottage on the edge of Nether Stowey and the handsome country mansion of Alfoxden, three miles to the west, where the Wordsworths had obtained a year's tenancy at a nominal rent which even they could afford. And always they discussed poetry and literary plans. In the three weeks that began with the first reference to *The Recluse*, as Dorothy Wordsworth's journal shows, there were not more than three days in all when Wordsworth and Coleridge did not see each other.

At this time, in March 1798, both poets were thinking of publishing, but neither had yet considered the joint volume of poems which was to appear in only a few months, the famous *Lyrical Ballads*. Coleridge was negotiating with Cottle of Bristol for a third and much revised edition of his poems, but he also proposed a volume to be made up of his unpublished tragedy *Osorio* and Wordsworth's *The Borderers*. In addition to his tragedy, Wordsworth's only sizable literary commodities were two fairly long narrative poems of social comment, 'Salisbury Plain' and 'The Ruined Cottage'. The latter poem, recently revised and enlarged, was probably now thought of as eventually to form part of *The Recluse*.

'The Ruined Cottage' had been finished, Wordsworth then

believed, in the previous summer. It was the pathetic story, in
blank verse, of the misfortunes of one family in a time of un-
employment, scarcity, and war. The central character was a
woman whose husband was driven in the desperation of
penury to take the King's shilling, leaving her and their children in the cottage which, as it gradually falls into ruin, becomes
the suggestive counterpart of a ruined family. The sympathetic
observer and narrator was a pedlar of philosophic cast of mind,
whose occasional returns to the neighbourhood accounted for
the observed stages in the decline of Margaret's fortune. The
pedlar was little more than a narrative convenience when the
poem was first finished, merely the poet's source of information and a quite secondary figure in the story. But by the beginning of 1798 Wordsworth had become dissatisfied with the
poem. The pedlar was, in a way, the poet's surrogate, and he
probably found it necessary to explain how so unlikely a person
had become a sensitive and imaginative observer of life. So he
began to enlarge the poem with a history of the boyhood of
the pedlar, in Cumberland, the region of the poet's birth, and
particularly with a history of the growth of his imagination.
The composition went on rapidly, in January and February.
The sombre story of Margaret and her ruined cottage was
joined to another story, related with subtlety and passion,
about a youth's feelings for the world of nature. By 5 March,
Dorothy Wordsworth reported that the poem had grown to
900 lines and 'The Pedlar's character now makes a very, certainly the *most*, considerable part of the Poem'.[5] Wordsworth
could have had no idea where the new theme would lead him.
However, we can recognize in about 250 lines of MS. B of
'The Ruined Cottage' the first clear statement of some dominant ideas and the anticipation of some parts and episodes in
The Prelude.[6]

I shall make only summary reference to a few points of
similarity. Here, as in *The Prelude*, Wordsworth distinguishes
stages in the development of an imaginative mind, and records
a boy's passionate joy in the world of nature and in the very
experience of being alive. In all nature the youth came to
recognize life and the presence of mind, even in the very rocks :

> Even in their fixed and steady lineaments
> He traced an ebbing and a flowing mind,
> Expression ever varying. (106–8)

At last,

> From Nature and her overflowing soul
> He had received so much, that all his thoughts
> Were steeped in feeling. He was only then
> Contented, when, with bliss ineffable
> He felt the sentiment of being, spread
> O'er all that moves, and all that seemeth still. . . .
>   Wonder not
> If such his transports were; for in all things
> He saw one life, and felt that it was joy. (238–52)

This final passage in the story of the pedlar's youth was afterwards transferred to the second book of *The Prelude*. The only change was the substitution of *I* and *my* for *he* and *his*. The youth described in 'The Ruined Cottage' was really the poet himself.

The most memorable literary accomplishment of 1798 for both Coleridge and Wordsworth was the publication of *Lyrical Ballads*. Wordsworth's share in the joint project was to demonstrate what could be done to make events from humble and rustic life described in a deliberately, even defiantly, plain language into poetry of permanent interest and appeal. The experiment was hardly a success, and it was tacitly abandoned or the conditions much altered thereafter, though the reasoned and stubborn apologia first published with the second edition in 1800 gave the literary public for a long time, perhaps down to our own day, the ineradicable belief that the most typical poetry of Wordsworth is to be found in *Lyrical Ballads*, 1798, and all his critical ideas in the preface of 1800. Yet the best poem by Wordsworth in the volume was not in the least of the sort in question. The 'Lines Composed a few miles above Tintern Abbey' was written when *Lyrical Ballads* was already in the hands of the printer, and it was added as an afterthought. The Wordsworths were in Bristol to see the poems through the press and in mid-July went for a few days up the

Wye Valley into South Wales, a region which the poet had visited once before. The literary result was the composition, in one day, of an autobiographical poem of reminiscence and speculation, a poem in which he traces the stages in the development of his mind and feelings, and expresses a sense of a living universe of man and nature pervaded by the power of the unknown Being,

> A motion and a spirit, that impels
> All thinking things, all objects of all thought,
> And rolls through all things –

motion and spirit, the ultimate mysteries of the physical and the biological realms, and beyond them a 'something', for the name of God does not occur in the poem.

The themes which Wordsworth had first used in MS. B of 'The Ruined Cottage' and to which he had given the first formal poetic expression in 'Tintern Abbey' could not be ignored for long. In the autumn, Coleridge, his disciple Chester, and the Wordsworths went to Germany to spend the winter. Financial circumstances and temperamental preferences sent the first pair to the social gaieties of a North German town and the Wordsworths to a thrifty solitude in Goslar, near the Harz Mountains. In a foreign land, shut out from society by poverty and a merely elementary knowledge of German, with few books to read, Wordsworth was compelled to draw on his inner resources of memory and thought. One day, probably late in October, he opened one of the pocket-notebooks he had with him (the one in which he had already written a report of Coleridge's and his interview with Klopstock in Hamburg and in which Dorothy had entered her journal of the trip from Hamburg to Goslar) and on the last recto page of the notebook he began to write :

> Was it for this
> That one, the fairest of all rivers loved
> To blend his murmurs with my nurse's song
> And from his alder shades and rocky falls
> And from his fords and shallows sent a voice
> To intertwine my dreams. . . .

He was writing the beginning of *The Prelude*. The 'this' of his question, the end toward which nature and fortunate circumstance had conspired, was that the child whose earliest memories were of the garden-terrace back of the house, washed by the Derwent 'fairest of all rivers', should mature in mind and imagination to become the poet Wordsworth hoped to be.[7] He continued composing, using pages and parts of pages in an order often confusing to the student who would follow him, but in general setting down passages of reminiscence alternated with others of interpretation or of generalization about the early development of a poet's imagination. Several of the most memorable passages of the first book of *The Prelude* are there in their earliest form, in the notebook now designated JJ.[8]

When the travellers returned to England the next summer (1799), Wordsworth should have gone on with *The Recluse*, the poem which he and Coleridge had decided was to be his most ambitious work. But he felt unprepared, perhaps inadequate for the task. The quite indefinite extent and unpredictable content of a work called 'Views of Nature, Man, and Society' might well have given him pause. In a lost letter to Coleridge, to which we have part of the reply, he must have announced that he was first going to expand and complete the poem begun in Germany about the growth of his imagination, that it was to be a poem addressed to Coleridge as a personal record between friends and fellow poets, and that although it would be a composition complete in itself and could be so published, he expected to publish it only when *The Recluse* was finished and as an appendix to that poem. Coleridge was less than enthusiastic, though he did not directly oppose the scheme : 'O let it be the tail-piece of "The Recluse"! for of nothing but "The Recluse" can I hear patiently.'[9] So in the autumn and winter of 1799–1800, the first winter at Grasmere, Wordsworth added greatly to the work begun in Germany, completing a poem in two parts, of about 960 lines, addressed to Coleridge, and describing the early development of a poet's mind. This poem survives in two manuscripts, one complete (MS. U), the other lacking only the first 54 lines of

the second part (MS. V). It has never been published, though
many of its readings are given in the de Selincourt–Darbishire
variorum edition, and most of the poem, revised, rearranged,
and in some parts broken up, appears somewhere in *The
Prelude* as published, mostly in books I and II, but also in
books V, VIII, and XI.

In this proto-*Prelude* of 1798–1800 one observes a much
more unified theme and a much stronger sense of formal structure than in the poem completed first in 1805 and published
in 1850. The time covered is restricted to childhood and school
days only. The single theme is the awakening of the imagination. Each of the two parts has its own limit in time : the first
being of childhood and to the age of about ten, the second until
the end of school days when the narrator was seventeen. The
whole poem, and each separate part, shows an unusual number, for Wordsworth at least, of devices of formal structure,
used, I think, with considerable success. In the First Part, for
example, of which the first two hundred lines had been largely
written, or at least drafted, in Germany, we find, as I have
mentioned earlier, alternating passages of reminiscence and of
comment, or reflection, or psychological generalization. The
reminiscences are varied to represent, not only the particular
activities of the child, usually at play, but activities of each of
the four seasons, of day and night, morning and evening,
within doors and without, in society and in solitude. We begin
with 'the five years' Child' who 'made one long bathing of a
summer's day' and go on next to the boy who aspired to be 'a
fell destroyer', snaring woodcocks in the moonlight when

> The frost and breath of frosty wind had snapp'd
> The last autumnal crocus ... (I 312–13)

or later to the same boy, with his friends or alone, skating on
a winter evening :

>   while the stars,
> Eastward, were sparkling clear, and in the west
> The orange sky of evening died away. (I 471–3)

Always, in every remembered episode there is the primary
matter-of-fact event usually described vividly and with a sense
of joy, but there is also the secondary event that really
mattered, in the boy's mind and imagination, the awareness of
beauty or mystery or of purposeful power and life in all the
world of nature about him. These moments of imaginative
intensity, Wordsworth would say, of insight, come rarely, and
sometimes on unlikely occasions. Here, for example (1 339–
50), the poet remembers the boy-mountaineer risking his life
on a rock-face for no better purpose than to rob a raven's nest:

> Though mean
> My object, and inglorious, yet the end
> Was not ignoble. Oh ! when I have hung
> Above the raven's nest, by knots of grass
> And half-inch fissures in the slippery rock
> But ill sustain'd, and almost, as it seem'd,
> Suspended by the blast which blew amain,
> Shouldering the naked crag; Oh ! at that time,
> While on the perilous ridge I hung alone,
> With what strange utterance did the loud dry wind
> Blow through my ears ! the sky seem'd not a sky
> Of earth, and with what motion mov'd the clouds !

Toward the end of this First Part of the poem of 1798–
1800, three memories are recorded of a quite different character, of the boy's first glimpses of the dark side of life, his first
awareness of death. These are the memories of watching the
recovery of the body of a drowned man (an episode now in
book v of *The Prelude*) and the two illustrative 'spots of
time' (later transferred to book xi of the poem), of the child's
fears when left alone, near the Border Beacon of Penrith, at
the place where a murderer had been hanged at the scene of
his crime, and the particularly poignant memory for Wordsworth from his school days of his impatient wait in the wind
and the rain near Hawkshead, at the beginning of the Christmas holidays, for the horses which his father was to send to
carry him and his brothers home to the anticipated gaieties of
the season, unaware that before the holidays would be over his
father would be taken ill suddenly and die.

The Second Part of the poem of 1798–1800 generally corresponds to the second book of *The Prelude*. Here too we observe the use of contrast as a formal feature. In four episodes the noisy athletic activities of the 'boisterous race' of schoolboys at play are associated and contrasted with the occasional experience of 'calmer pleasures' by at least one of their number. To mention only the last of these four – after a noisy afternoon of bowling on the green at the fashionable 'White Lion' at Bowness, by Windermere, with indecorous juvenile shouts that 'Made all the mountains ring', darkness fell on the lake and stillness broken only by the music of a flute played from across the water by one of their number :

> Oh ! then the calm
> And dead still water lay upon my mind
> Even with a weight of pleasure, and the sky
> Never before so beautiful, sank down
> Into my heart, and held me like a dream. (ii 176–80)

Wordsworth tries also in this part to trace systematically the stages in the development of his mind, more fully than he had attempted for the Pedlar in 'The Ruined Cottage' and for himself in 'Tintern Abbey', and to distinguish between the contributions of reason and imagination. But he soon gave up the attempt, remembering that he was writing for Coleridge who was far more practised than he was in these speculations :

> Thou, my Friend ! art one
> More deeply read in thy own thoughts. . . . (ii 215–16)

A good many things are included in *The Prelude*, and others omitted for the same reason, that the poem was addressed to Coleridge. This early version reaches its climax when the youth of seventeen can be described in words originally written of the Pedlar, and quoted above, that 'all his thoughts were steeped in feeling'. He was ready in mind to try to learn the art of poetry.

This poem was finished and put aside. It was complete in itself, but it was not to be published except with *The Recluse*.

We hear no more of it for two years, until in December 1801 Dorothy Wordsworth made a brief reference in her diary to the composition 'of the third part' of the poem to Coleridge. Evidently the two-part poem of 1798–1800 was to be enlarged. Over a year later, in January 1803, there is another even slighter reference. Then another year passes. In mid-January 1804, after a visit of several weeks with the Wordsworths, Coleridge set out for London and eventually to the Mediterranean region where he was to spend more than two years, mostly at Malta, for the recovery of his health. About two weeks after Coleridge left Grasmere, Wordsworth wrote to Francis Wrangham: 'At present I am engaged in a Poem on my own earlier life, which will take five parts or books to complete, three of which are nearly finished.'[10] On 6 March, in a letter to De Quincey, he reported: 'I am now writing a poem on my own earlier life; and have just finished that part in which I speak of my residence at the University. . . .'[11] Writing to Coleridge the same day to report progress he said: 'When this next book is done, which I shall begin in two or three days' time, I shall consider the work as finished.'[12]

This second poem which had evidently been planned as to length and form, and to a large extent composed, was never finished – or rather before it could be finished Wordsworth changed and enlarged the scheme once more and went on to write the much longer work in thirteen books completed in 1805. We have no manuscript of the second poem to correspond to U and V, the fair copies of the first. We have a few references in letters, the most helpful of which I have quoted in part. We have also one notebook, W, containing perhaps 700 lines of autobiographic verse in about a dozen discontinuous passages plus minor drafts and jottings written over a period of two years and a half; but in what order the passages were composed is not always discernible, and only a few of them can be dated with moderate certainty.

Several points, however, about the second form of the poem seem quite clear. Wordsworth became dissatisfied with the original two-part poem because it related nothing about the influence of books and formal education upon his imagination in childhood and youth. In notebook W he composed a considerable amount on this subject, much of it now in book v of *The Prelude*. He wrote in ridicule of the educational theorists who would give the child only factual and improving books. He was ponderously ironic about the model child in moral and didactic tales (like Thomas Day's famous *Sandford and Merton*) – a diminutive man, obedient, unselfish, industrious, and prodigiously learned.

> Briefly, the moral part
> Is perfect, and in learning and in books
> He is a prodigy. . . .
> With propositions are the younker's brains
> Filled to the brim, the path in which he reads
> Is chok'd with grammars. . . . (v 318–20; 323–5, W)

His master, the educational theorist, is ever on the watch to restrain him within limits as if he were a stray domestic animal in the village pound :

> Some busy helper still is on the watch
> To drive him back and pound him like a Stray
> Within the pinfold of his own conceit; . . . (v 360–2)

A few years ago, David Erdman discovered and published a letter, written in 1797 to William Godwin by Thomas Wedgwood, afterwards the friend and patron of Coleridge, suggesting the establishment with Wedgwood money of a sort of Centre for Child Study and Controlled Education where a truly efficient formal education could be given by shutting the child away entirely from the confusing complexities of nature ('the child must never go out of doors or leave his own apartment'), where he could learn only what the educational theorists in charge chose to teach him, when they thought he was properly conditioned to learn.[13] The most incredible feature of this remarkable letter was that Wedgwood confided to Godwin that he was thinking of offering the wardenship of his projected institution to a bright young man whom he had not actually met – his name William Wordsworth ! All this, of course, came to nothing, except perhaps book v of *The Prelude*. It may be significant that in January 1803 when we know that Wordsworth was engaged, briefly, on the second form of the poem, Thomas Wedgwood had come north with Coleridge to spend a month in the Lake District. He could be a reminder of the preposterous among theories of education.

The original two-part poem to Coleridge, then, was enlarged to be about the development of the imagination under the dual influence of nature and books. There are at least two passages in notebook W (passages now in the fifth book of *The Prelude*) where the key words appear linked together and capitalized, Nature and Books. Wordsworth's remarks afterwards about his first year at Cambridge (now book III) were to carry his formal education far enough to allow for all he had to say on that subject, and the poem was to be completed in one book more which was to include two striking passages, one now in the fourth book, the other at the beginning of the final one. They both appear in an early stage in notebook W. The first passage is the description of scene and feeling as he crossed Hawkshead Moor returning home from a party in a glorious summer dawn during his first Long Vacation from Cambridge and recognized that he was called and dedicated to poetry.

> Ah ! need I say, dear Friend, that to the brim
> My heart was full; I made no vows, but vows
> Were then made for me; bond unknown to me
> Was given, that I should be, else sinning greatly,
> A dedicated Spirit. On I walk'd
> In blessedness, which even yet remains. (IV 340–5)

The other memory first recorded in notebook W is of climbing Snowdon in the darkness until he found himself suddenly in the light above the clouds, which the poet interpreted as an allegory of the imagination. As this passage is preceded by the heading '5th Book', it seems clear that even at this time Wordsworth had decided that this episode should introduce the conclusion of his poem. So we may surmise that the second poem to Coleridge was to be about a poet's education, by nature and by books, down to the end of his formal education when he was twenty. It was to reach its climax and conclusion in the allegorical experience by night on Snowdon and the recognition of a poet's dedication in the splendour of dawn and sunrise. Again, the poem was to be of comparatively limited extent and of a clearly discernible formal structure.

Only a few days after 6 March 1804, when Wordsworth told both Coleridge and De Quincey that his poem was almost finished, he must have decided to enlarge it further. Some weeks earlier, Coleridge had asked the women of the Grasmere household to make him a fair copy of all Wordsworth's unpublished poetry to take with him to the Mediterranean. In February and March they were engaged on this very demanding task. The packets of manuscript which they prepared survive, MS. M. The last section transcribed is of books I–V of *The Prelude*, and *they are in the order and otherwise substantially the same as in the 1805 text*. This fair copy of five books on the new and final plan must have been completed by about 20 March. Incidentally, this is the first manuscript in which one finds the first 270 lines of book I of the poem.

By the time Coleridge had received the fair copy of five books, Wordsworth was well on with the sixth. After a long rest in the summer he took up the task again and finished it the following May.

Of the theme and structure of the published poem, much has been written, and I would only make a few comparative generalizations. Although no one could question Wordsworth's assertion in the last book that the theme of the imagination 'hath been the moving soul of our long labour', this central interest in *The Prelude* is often obscured by somewhat peripheral matters of political, social, and intellectual history. There is a good deal of external autobiography, of particular places, people, and public events. It may be that the particularities in the first of the books about life at Cambridge (March 1804) indicated the new direction. More than once the poet showed that he was aware of writing a chronology of external events when he should have tried to concentrate on the inner

events which had been of the greatest importance in the first
two plans of the poem.

Several features of the published poem, including oddities
and anomalies, can be understood better when we are aware
of the history of the writing. From book I 270 to the end of
book II still makes a poetic unity which the general reader
may recognize without knowing that here we have still a large
proportion of the earliest poem. It is odd, however, that the
farewell to Coleridge which was its formal conclusion still
remains at the end of book II. Many readers have wondered
why the poet after writing of his life at Cambridge should in
book V, on 'Books', say so much about tales for children and
nothing about books read at the university and after. The
inadequate explanation, of course, is that this section was
written to pair with the education of the child by nature, in
the second plan of the poem, and was, incidentally, composed
before he wrote anything about Cambridge. Also, anyone
reading books IV, V and VI can see that VI appears to follow
right after IV and that V is an interruption in every way.
Again, the explanation is that the scheme of the second poem
has not been sufficiently suppressed in the third. Books IV and
VI were written in that order, and most of V had been composed earlier than either for another poem. Some readers may
also have observed that book III, about the poet's first year at
Cambridge, includes a great variety of description and comment, but book VI, entitled 'Cambridge and the Alps', tells
hardly anything about the last two-and-a-half years of his
academic career. The explanation is that book III was written
for the second plan of the poem and was intended to be complete in itself. It left little to be related afterwards when the
poet found it necessary to provide more chronological autobiography.

In the Preface to *The Excursion* (1814), Wordsworth
wrote of *The Prelude*, then still unnamed and unpublished,
and of *The Recluse* that 'the two Works have the same relation
to each other, if I may so express myself, as the ante-chapel
has to the body of a gothic church'. An architectural comparison is appropriate, but *The Prelude* seems to me to be rather

more like a work of domestic than of ecclesiastical architecture. The first building was a well-proportioned structure of moderate size, varied yet congruous in its parts. But the owner, as often happens, came to think that it lacked some essential features for his satisfaction and decided to extend the edifice, changing its design and more than doubling its size. However, before this had been completed, no doubt encouraged in his extravagance by his wife and by his sister who had a great interest in these matters, he changed the plan again and, extending the building in several directions, he finally made it very much larger than he had ever envisaged. Visitors nowadays to this massive and complex structure may sometimes lose their way in its connecting passages or stumble at some abrupt change of level in different parts, but the amateur student of this kind of architecture can enjoy a harmless pleasure in discovering how the whole edifice was put together. As often happens in building, some of the material used quite evidently antedates the earliest part of the triple structure. Some of it derived from a ruined cottage; some may be traced back to Tintern Abbey.

SOURCE: *Essays in English Literature from the Renaissance to the Victorian Age, Presented to A. S. P. Woodhouse* (1964) pp. 229–44. In an earlier form, this paper was read at a meeting of Section II of the Royal Society of Canada at McMaster University on 4 June 1962.

NOTES

Notes 4 and 8 (7 in the original) are here printed in an abbreviated form.

1. Christopher Wordsworth, *Memoirs of William Wordsworth* (London, 1851) I 313.

2. *The Early Letters of William and Dorothy Wordsworth,* ed. E. de Selincourt (Oxford, 1935) p. 190.

3. Ibid., p. 188.

4. *Biographia Literaria,* ed. J. Shawcross (Oxford, 1907) I 126–7. The government spy was once thought to have been a

comic invention of Coleridge, but there actually was such a person. His name was G. Walsh, his instructions and reports are in the Public Record Office (H.O. 42/41), and he was sent to keep under surveillance the Wordsworths who had just settled at Alfoxden. . . . Though there is no question about Spy Nozy, there is one about Spinoza. Were Coleridge and Wordsworth actually discussing him frequently in the summer of 1797 when the spy was shadowing them? . . .

5. *Early Letters,* p. 176.

6. MS. B. of 'The Ruined Cottage' is printed at length among the notes to *P.W.*, v 379–404.

7. This appears to be an oversight. The JJ lines from which MacGillivray is quoting have no context. In context, however, Wordsworth's question is ironical, and the 'this' is Wordsworth's equivocation and 'listlessness from vain perplexity' (1 266). [Ed.]

8. Miss Darbishire's transcript of the drafts of *The Prelude* in MS. JJ are given in the second edition, pp. 633–42. My quotations from the poem are from the text of 1805 unless otherwise indicated. . . .

9. *Collected Letters of Samuel Taylor Coleridge,* ed. E. L. Griggs (Oxford, 1956) 1 538.

10. *Early Letters,* p. 355.

11. Ibid., p. 370.

12. Ibid., p. 368.

13. David V. Erdman, 'Coleridge, Wordsworth, and the Wedgwood Fund', *Bulletin of the New York Public Library,* LX (Sep–Oct 1956) 425–43, 487–507.

Ellen Douglass Leyburn

RECURRENT WORDS IN *THE PRELUDE* (1949)

From the time of Coleridge critics have delighted to show the discrepancy between Wordsworth's theory of poetic diction and his practice. Coleridge's comments are familiar:

I reflect with delight, how little a mere theory, though of his own workmanship, interferes with the processes of genuine imagination in a man of true poetic genius, who possesses, as Mr. Wordsworth, if ever man did, most assuredly does possess, 'The Vision and the Faculty Divine'.

. . . feeling a justifiable preference for the language of nature and good sense, even in its humblest and least ornamented forms, he suffered himself to express, in terms at once too large and too exclusive, his predilection for a style the most remote possible from the false and showy splendour which he wished to explode.[1]

On such authority we feel easy about enjoying Wordsworth's poetry while setting aside the theory as a mere case of overstatement. Josephine Miles has gone further than Coleridge in her book, *Wordsworth and the Vocabulary of Emotion*,[2] to show that Wordsworth is linked to the eighteenth century exactly by his taste for stated emotion in contrast to our twentieth-century preference for poetry that conveys emotion by indirection. There is indeed beyond the vocabulary of emotion treated by Josephine Miles a wealth of sheer abstraction in *The Prelude* which might seem another link with eighteenth-century poetry.

As we contemplate such a weight of evidence, we wonder what becomes of Wordsworth's feeling that he was making a revolution in poetic diction by using the real language of men, a conviction from which he never departed, though he somewhat modified his statement of what he meant by 'the real language of men'. Yet somehow there persists in us as in Wordsworth himself the feeling that he did bring about a revolution in poetic diction. The language of *The Prelude* is not the language of *The Essay on Man*, though both are philosophic poems and both abound in abstractions. We sense a difference between Pope's abstractions and Wordsworth's, or indeed between Wordsworth's own abstractions in his early poems and those in *The Prelude*. The difference is so pronounced that when we come upon old fashioned personified abstractions in *The Prelude*, we are startled if not dismayed. Wordsworth seems to have lost his own tone of voice and to speak with a sort of ventriloquism in the lines :

> And here was Labour, his own Bond-slave, Hope
> That never set the pains against the prize,
> Idleness, halting with his weary clog,
> And poor misguided Shame, and witless Fear,
> And simple Pleasure, foraging for Death,
> Honour misplaced, and Dignity astray; (III 630-5)[3]

Likewise when he uses conventional descriptive epithets : 'spreading Pine', 'froward Brook', 'roaring wind', 'clamorous rain', 'vernal heat' (IV 36, 40, 76, 77, 94) we feel as if he has lapsed into an earlier idiom and is not writing in the way we have come to think of as 'peculiarly unborrowed and his own'.

The explanation of our feeling that Wordsworth does have his own idiom, even though his poetry abounds in abstractions and stated emotions, lies, I think, in his philosophy. Professor Pottle provides the clue for an analysis of Wordsworth's diction in *The Idiom of Poetry* : 'The moment he had it [the religion of Nature] everything was clear. He had his subject matter and he had his idiom.'[4] The 'religion of Nature' to which Wordsworth attained rested upon the idea of the earth

as the visible language of God.[5] Since this is a warmly anim-
ated view of nature and demands more than intellectual assent
if it is to be believed at all, we should expect the poet holding
it to be in a state of vivid sensation and to convey his response
in the words of his poetry. Just so Wordsworth does communicate in his diction the vitality of his belief.

A glance at a sample of Pope's diction in *The Essay on Man*
will help to explain how achieving his particular philosophy
sharpened and enriched Wordsworth's use of words. It might
almost be said that the difference between Pope's diction and
Wordsworth's is demanded by the difference in their philo-
sophies. The word which dominates the first book of the *Essay
on Man* is *System*. It is the Chain of Being as set forth by King
and Bolingbroke which Pope is celebrating. He communicates
his admiration for the beauty and order of a universe where
'system into system runs' (1 25). But he is not recording – still
less advocating – any personal response of the individual to the
system, unless mere acceptance be considered a response. The
conception remains remote because 'a system' cannot be
immediately apprehended. The word suits the philosophic
structure about which Pope is speaking; but it would be impossible to express Wordsworth's view of nature with its
emphasis on the percipient mind of man without a warmer
diction.

An analysis of certain recurrent words in *The Prelude*
demonstrates this warmth and shows why Wordsworth clung
to the idea that he was reforming the language of poetry,
though he dropped his insistence on using the 'language of
conversation'. It is perhaps not amiss to quote once more the
crucial sentences in which he propounds his own view of his
diction because he worked out the theory during the period
when he was writing the first books of *The Prelude* :

Advertisement to *Lyrical Ballads* (1798)

They were written chiefly with a view to ascertain how far the
language of conversation in the middle and lower classes of
society is adapted to the purposes of poetic pleasure.

Preface to *Lyrical Ballads* (1800)

It was published, as an experiment, which, I hoped, might be of some use to ascertain, how far, by fitting to metrical arrangement a selection of the real language of men in a state of vivid sensation, that sort of pleasure and that quantity of pleasure may be imparted, which a Poet may rationally endeavour to impart. . . . The principal object, then, proposed in these Poems was to choose incidents and situations from common life, and to relate or describe them, throughout, as far as was possible in a selection of language really used by men, and, at the same time, to throw over them a certain colouring of imagination, whereby ordinary things should be presented to the mind in an unusual aspect; . . . There will also be found in these volumes little of what is usually called poetic diction; as much pains has been taken to avoid it as is ordinarily taken to produce it; this has been done for the reason already alleged, to bring my language near to the language of men; . . . I have at all times endeavoured to look steadily at my subject.

Appendix to *Lyrical Ballads* (1802)

The earliest poets of all nations generally wrote from passion excited by real events; they wrote naturally, and as men : . . . It is indeed true, that the language of the earliest Poets was felt to differ materially from ordinary language, because it was the language of extraordinary occasions, but it was really spoken by men, language which the Poet himself had uttered when he had been affected by the events which he described, or which he had heard uttered by those around him.[6]

These passages are a comment on what Wordsworth was actually doing. We have to agree with him that in *The Prelude* as much as in the humblest of the Lyrical Ballads he is using the real language of men exactly because the language conveys to us his state of vivid sensation. The diction itself confronts us with the conviction about nature which is Wordsworth's reality.

He is indeed looking steadily at his subject. He is not simply taking a familiar philosophy and 'poetizing it'. He is doing just what he declares he is doing, taking a 'review of his own mind'

and showing how it has developed through the beneficent
influence of nature. His new perception of the speaking face of
nature gave him the means of interpreting his own experience.
It also gave him his own language. Just as the richness of texture which we feel in his terms comes into the poetry exactly
concurrently with a fresh richness of thought and feeling, so it
might also be suggested that the enriching of Wordsworth's
diction is almost in proportion to the enriching of his understanding of his relation to nature during his sojourn at
Alfoxden.

Wordsworth's new perception of the universe is perhaps
most clearly incorporated in his use of the word *earth*.

> the earth
> And common face of Nature spake to me
> Rememberable things; (1614-16)

is a peculiarly Wordsworthian statement. The richness of effect
is achieved partly by what Wordsworth does with the word
earth itself. He keeps us conscious of the plainest meaning,
ground, dirt, and even emphasizes this meaning by going on
to the *common* face of Nature. Yet the larger meaning of the
whole world that surrounds us, 'the earth on which [Man]
dwells' (xii 447-8) is the one to which our attention is called
by the comment on what the earth does: it not only speaks,
but it speaks rememberable things. This seeing our ordinary
surroundings as the speaking voice of God is the heart of the
Wordsworthian philosophy. As Wordsworth communicates his
thought, he enlarges his diction by the very process of communication. *Earth,* as Wordsworth uses it, takes on the whole
feeling of the conception of the earth in the philosophy; but
the philosophic conception is given ballast by the retaining in
the word of the plain everyday meaning of ground. Thus
Wordsworth's philosophy is literally rooted in the earth. It is
hardly necessary to multiply examples such as 'the speaking
face of earth' (v 12) which incorporate the spiritualized view
and at the same time give it substance by retaining the plain
meaning of the word. We know Wordsworth's regard for substance from his use of *substantial* as a word of praise in such

phrases as 'substantial lineaments' (I 628) and 'substantial things' (XII 234). With world, which is a more imposing word than earth in ordinary usage, Wordsworth is likely to put in an extra term, 'visible world' (II 293) or 'circumambient world' (VIII 47) which specifically calls to mind that he is speaking of something to be sensuously perceived. The doubleness of Wordsworth's intention in the use of *earth* (or world when it is a synonym) is explained in a pair of lines where the word does not occur :

> To the end and written spirit of God's works,
> Whether held forth in Nature or in Man. (IV 358–9)

In the passage near the beginning of book v, where Wordsworth summarizes the substance of the earlier books, he shows the relation of the divine mind through the language of nature to the mind of man :

> Hitherto,
> In progress through this Verse, my mind hath look'd
> Upon the speaking face of earth and heaven
> As her prime Teacher, intercourse with man
> Establish'd by the sovereign Intellect,
> Who through that bodily Image hath diffus'd
> A soul divine which we participate,
> A deathless spirit. (v 10–17)

He has already insisted on the essential part of the perceiver in this active universe :

> Emphatically such a Being lives,
> An inmate of this *active* universe;
> From nature largely he receives; nor so
> Is satisfied, but largely gives again,
> For feeling has to him imparted strength,
> And powerful in all sentiments of grief,
> Of exultation, fear, and joy, his mind,
> Even as an agent of the one great mind,
> Creates, creator and receiver both,
> Working but in alliance with the works
> Which it beholds. (II 265–75)

The position given to the percipient mind by Wordsworth is revealed to us in his use of the word *being*, and at the same time the philosophy enriches the word. When Wordsworth feels 'the sentiment of Being' (II 420) or speaks of 'the immortal being' (v 22), he is clearly aware of something beyond himself. But just as clearly it is something in himself. So when the word refers directly to man's being, the idea of divinity is still in it, as is vividly revealed in such phrases as 'Great birthright of our Being' (II 286) or

> spreads abroad
> His being with a strength that cannot fail. (IV 160–1)

It is there even when he uses the word in the sense of 'a being', 'the progress of our Being' (II 239), 'A favor'd Being' (I 364). This is the sort of being who can perceive the objects in the earth as part of the balance 'Both of the object seen and eye that sees' (XII 379). Such a being reads in the hills 'The changeful language of their countenances' (VII 727). The relation of man to being itself is given in the lines:

> There came a time of greater dignity
> Which had been gradually prepar'd, and now
> Rush'd in as if on wings, the time in which
> The pulse of Being everywhere was felt,
> When all the several frames of things, like stars
> Through every magnitude distinguishable,
> Were half confounded in each other's blaze,
> One galaxy of life and joy. Then rose
> Man, inwardly contemplated, and present
> In my own being, to a loftier height;
> As of all visible natures crown; and first
> In capability of feeling what
> Was to be felt; in being rapt away
> By the divine effect of power and love,
> As, more than anything we know instinct
> With Godhead, and by reason and by will
> Acknowledging dependency sublime. (VIII 624–40)

Object as it is used in *The Prelude* is clearly a complex word,

if we may adopt the Empsonian terminology.[7] Of the meanings given in the N. E. D., those which seem to me to fall within
Wordsworth's feeling of the scope of the word are '3. Something placed before the eyes . . . a material thing . . . b. Something which on being seen excites a particular emotion, as
admiration, horror, disdain, commiseration, amusement . . .
4. That to which action, thought, or feeling is directed.'
3b apparently links the meanings 3 and 4 in the Wordsworthian phrases: 'an object in my mind of passionate intuition' (x 587–8), 'the object of its fervour' (x 819), and
'objects of its love' (iii 369). This emotional quality seems to
inhere in the word as Wordsworth uses it and to be retained
with emphasis just on the emotional richness in the uses:
'affinities in objects' (ii 403–4), 'objects that were great or
fair' (viii 450), 'Nature and her objects' (viii 522), 'all
objects being themselves capacious' (viii 756–7), 'Imagination . . . tried her strength among new objects' (viii 796–8),
'objects which subdu'd and temper'd them' (ii 71–2),
'objects, even as they are great' (x 142). Yet the ostensible
meaning is only the simple one of 'something placed before
the eyes'. So strong is the feeling that outward objects are
objects of emotion, and of beneficent emotion, that when
Wordsworth wants to use the word without this suggestion, he
has to give it an opposite derogatory emotion: 'I was betray'd
by present objects' (x 883–4). He has so charged the word
itself with feeling that he has almost lost it in the meaning
merely of something placed before the eyes, though that meaning is almost always part of his richer use of the word. When
he wants to convey this meaning uncolored by the connotations
he has given *objects*, he sometimes resorts to the phrase 'outward things' (vii 623). But he also uses this phrase for more
than objects in the sense of bodies:

> Not of outward things
> Done visibly for other minds. (iii 174–5)

When he wants the two meanings of *object* distinct in the same
passage, he clarifies the senses by modifiers:

> Holds up before the mind, intoxicate
> With present objects and the busy dance
> Of things that pass away, a temperate shew
> Of objects that endure. (XII 33–6)

His lines:

> ... I thus convoked
> From every object pleasant circumstance
> To suit my ends; (X 737–9)

might be taken as a comment on what he does to the word itself.

One of the most interesting words in the Wordsworthian language is *forms*. Sometimes it is specifically limited, as in the phrases, 'outward forms' (VI 668), 'exterior forms' (III 159), and 'vulgar forms of present things' (XII 361). Frequently it seems to be used in the quite simple sense of 'shape, arrangement of parts', and it is often accompanied by the word *colour* as if to emphasize the externality of the meaning: e.g. 'the quick dance of colours, lights and forms' (VII 156–7), 'an impassion'd sight of colours and of forms' (VI 608–9), 'Their hues and forms' (I 639), or with a more extended list of physical properties in the lines:

> 'Tis true that Earth with all her appanage
> Of elements and organs, storm and sunshine,
> With its pure forms and colours, pomp of clouds
> Rivers and mountains, ... (XI 108–11)

Yet even into these comparatively simple uses of the term we carry the enlargement which Wordsworth has given it in such phrases as 'her awful forms and viewless agencies' (VIII 484–5), where forms seem almost as much 'powers' as the viewless agencies themselves. Here too, the simple meaning is present; but the feeling with which the word is used in this rhapsody to nature calls into play its whole philosophical content: 'the essential creative quality' or 'the formative principle which holds together the several elements of a thing'; it per-

haps even suggests Plato's ideas. Wordsworth seems somewhat
to explain the process by which the very word is heightened
when he says:

> Even forms and substances are circumfus'd
> By that transparent veil with light divine; . . .
>   (v 625–6)

Clearly it is the formative power of nature about which he is
talking when he says:

> such virtue have the forms
> Perennial of the ancient hills; . . . (vii 725–6)

Yet in his highest reaches of the word he never loses the plain
idea of shapes. Indeed in this very passage he has just spoken
of 'The mountain's outline and its steady form'. In one of the
passages omitted from the edition of 1850 there is a curious
double use where both the simple and the rich meanings of
the word seem emphasized:

> his mind spreads,
> Tenacious of the forms which it receives. (ii 253–4)

Perhaps it was this very doubleness that seemed to Wordsworth confusing as he revised the poem and made him omit
the passage. But in most of his uses the layers of meaning in the
word, far from making for confusion, clarify one of his essential conceptions of nature as conveying impressions to man
through a visible language. He seems to be giving an explica-
tion of his use of *forms* in the familiar passage where he speaks
of the manifestations of nature after he has crossed the Alps as
'types and symbols of Eternity' (vi 571). Accordingly, when
he speaks of 'lovely forms' (iii 366), 'beauteous forms' (ii
51), and 'mighty forms' (vi 347), there is a richness of connotation which suggests far more than outward beauty and
grandeur. This feeling incorporated in the word *forms* that
the outward forms of the visible world are types and symbols of

an invisible presence is enforced by the frequent juxtaposition of 'images' and 'forms'. The two words are generally used almost synonymously in the simple meaning of forms, i.e. shapes, which I take to be the explicit meaning in the lines:

> Nor am I naked in external things,
> Forms, images; (I 165–6)

>   by form
> Or image unprofaned; (II 325–6)

> And earth did change her images and forms
> Before us, fast as clouds are chang'd in Heaven.
>   (VI 429–30)

Thus when Wordsworth expresses gratitude for 'forms distinct to steady me', he goes on to explain:

>   I still
> At all times had a real solid world
> Of images about me. (VIII 603–5)

Images seem likewise identified with forms in the heightened passage:

> Wisdom and Spirit of the universe!
> Thou Soul that art the Eternity of Thought!
> That giv'st to forms and images a breath
> And everlasting motion! (I 428–31)

But here clearly both are made the types and symbols of eternity. The juxtaposition enforces the feeling that the forms are images, so strongly suggested when the word *forms* is used alone.

There is a parallel doubleness of effect in the word *image* used alone. Indeed the effect is more than double, for in his use of this term Wordsworth seems regularly to call into play at least three of the meanings given in the N.E.D.: 'An artificial imitation or representation of the external form of any object', 'A mental representation of something (esp. a visible object), not by direct perception, but by memory or imagination; a mental picture or impression; an idea, conception', and 'A thing in which the aspect, form, or character of another is reproduced; a counterpart, a copy . . . A thing that represents or is taken to represent something else; a symbol, emblem, representation'. There may be even a fourth dictionary meaning : 'A representation of something to the mind by speech or writing' in the use :

> For images, and sentiments, and words,
> And everything with which we had to do
> In that delicious world of poesy,
> Kept holiday; (v 603–6)

> The notions and the images of books. (viii 516)

The sense 'artificial imitation' is dominant in the use 'waxen Image which yourselves have made' (viii 434). But this feeling of artificiality is usually remote rather than prominent in Wordsworth's use of *image*. It may be in a measure present in the many uses where the word seems to mean : 'A mental representation . . . not by direct perception, but by memory or imagination; a mental picture' as in the phrases, 'a mind beset with images' (vi 179–80), 'leave behind a dance of images' (viii 164), 'The gladsome image in my memory' (x 995), 'Some fair enchanting image in my mind' (iv 104). Certainly, however, in these examples the feeling of artifice is very faint. What is emphasized is the vividness of the picture in the mind. Indeed the strength of Wordsworth's power of visual representation, his 'disposition to be affected more than other men by absent things as if they were present',[8] was so strong that the images seem to have been presented to him as actual forms. This power of visualization helps, I think, to explain the use of the word *images* so frequently in conjunction with *forms* in a way that suggests simple reduplication, or at most intensification, of the plainest meaning of *form* itself : i.e. shape.

But the word *image* goes through the same sort of heightening that Wordsworth gives to *forms*. The meaning 'counterpart, copy' is in such uses as 'images of danger and distress' (VIII 211) and 'no composition of the thought, abstraction, shadow, image' (XII 84–5). From this meaning of copy, we move to the meaning 'symbol, emblem, representation'. The phrase 'the perfect image of a mighty Mind' (XIII 69) used of a mountain night scene seems to have a purely figurative or symbolic intent. And this is true when Wordsworth speaks of the 'image of right reason' (XII 26), and

> An image not unworthy of the one
> Surpassing Life. (VI 154–5)

It is, of course, impossible to make an image, an actual copy, of a mind or spirit. But here again, even in the most highly spiritualized use of the word, we are conscious of the actual images, the shapes, in nature on which the symbolic use is based. The symbol and the essence symbolized are both present in the word. The same combination is brought home to us in the use of the word *imagery* :

> or the visible scene
> Would enter unawares into his mind
> With all its solemn imagery, its rocks,
> Its woods, and that uncertain Heaven, receiv'd
> Into the bosom of the steady Lake. (V 409–13)

The double intent of the diction again reveals Wordsworth's view of God and nature : nature as actually and in her sensuous forms the means of communication between God and man. The spirit speaks through nature.

Wordsworth's frequent term for this spirit in nature is *Presence* or *Presences*. His very choice of a word emphasizes the vitality of his conception of 'living Nature' (VI 119). The immediacy with which he can apprehend the forms as symbols is made possible by the actual presence of what is symbolized. The simple meaning of 'being present' is a basic one for Wordsworth and, I think, determines his choice of this particular word to stand for spirit. But the emphasized meaning is 'Something present, a present being, a divine, spiritual, or incorporeal being or influence felt or conceived as present'. This is so much Wordsworth's sense that there is an example from him to explain this meaning in the N.E.D. All the power of divinity is in the Presences in the lines :

> Yet would the living Presence still subsist
> Victorious; (v 33–4)

> Add unto this, subservience from the first
> To God and Nature's single sovereignty,
> Familiar presences of awful Power. (ix 236–8)

But part of this very force comes from our feeling of the actuality of the sheer being present. Such an exclamation as :

> Ye Presences of Nature, in the sky
> And on the earth ! (i 490–1)

within the expression itself intensifies the meaning 'present being' by the meaning 'being present'; but I think the double effect is always felt in Wordsworth's usage, whether he calls attention to it or not. Indeed we can hardly think of Wordsworth's objects, forms, and images without thinking of the presences in them.

A word that acquires a special force, though perhaps no complexity of meaning, through Wordsworth's view of nature is *intercourse*. He uses it almost regularly to describe his communion through nature itself with the spirit in nature :

> I held unconscious intercourse
> With the eternal Beauty. (i 589–90)

> Nor was this fellowship vouchsaf'd to me
> With stinted kindness . . .
> In solitude, such intercourse was mine. (i 442–3, 449)

The means of apprehending the Presences in nature, of holding such intercourse, is imagination, which Wordsworth calls a 'Power' (vi 527, vii 498). His use of the word *power* has a curious complexity, for he not only shifts among definitions of it as a quality, but goes over into the meaning: 'A celestial or spiritual being having control or influence; a deity, a divinity.' The reverence with which he viewed the imagination perhaps enabled him to make the transition from 'holy powers and faculties' (III 83–4), imagination, awful Power, to 'a plastic power' (II 381), 'visionary power' (II 330),

> that universal power
> And fitness in the latent qualities
> And essences of things, by which the mind
> Is mov'd by feelings of delight. (II 343–6)

Indeed, he links two meanings in the sequence: 'Of Genius, Power, Creation and Divinity itself' (III 171–2), and he enforces the connection in the lines:

> I felt a kind of sympathy with power,
> Motions rais'd up within me, nevertheless,
> Which had relationship to highest things. (x 417–19)

Consequently we have rather the feeling that the divine and human power are all one in such passages as: 'the hiding-places of my power' (XI 336),

> What there is best in individual Man,
> Of wise in passion, and sublime in power, (x 667–8)

'incommunicable powers' (III 188),

> 'Tis a power
> That does not come unrecogniz'd. (I 47–8)

There are other earthly gifts besides man's imagination that partake of this sublime quality: 'names . . . were Powers' (IX 180), 'words in tuneful order . . . a passion and a power' (v 579–80).

> speak of them [books] as Powers
> For ever to be hallowed; only less,
> For what we may become, and what we need,
> Than Nature's self, which is the breath of God.
>
> (v 219–22)

The idea of goodness is associated with *power* as with *object*. Again Wordsworth has to reduce the word by derogatory modifiers such as 'false, secondary power' (II 221), or 'vulgar power' (v 595), if he wants the meaning simply of ability. In the lines:

> such object hath had power
> O'er my imagination since the dawn
> Of childhood, (XII 146–8)

while the word seems to mean simply force, the juxtaposition with *object* and *imagination* gives it some of the favourable connotation of these words; and its own aura of divine power still comes with it.

Indeed the interrelation of all these terms, and especially the fact that they come together in the passages where the poetry is most impassioned, is exactly what makes them seem peculiarly Wordsworthian. Their occurring in clusters in the most characteristic lines is precisely the basis for picking these particular words to analyze. Their very frequency makes it impossible to quote the passages in proof; but there is at least one in almost every book of the poem.[9] It is perhaps these linked uses of the words that seem to belong peculiarly to him which most justify Wordsworth's feeling that he was adding a new vitality to the language of his poetry, that it is indeed the language of man in a state of vivid sensation that he is speaking. It is worth noting that most of the words which belong to him in a special way are not 'learned words'; but what is significant for Wordsworth, at least by 1800, is their conveying his reality. The richness of his diction goes with the richness of his thought. It is the poet of Wordsworth's definition, 'a man speaking to men',[10] whom we hear in the lines:

> In one beloved Presence ... there exists
> A virtue which irradiates and exalts
> All objects through all intercourse of sense.
> No outcast he, bewilder'd and depress'd;
> Along his infant veins are interfus'd
> The gravitation and the filial bond
> Of nature, that connect him with the world.

Emphatically such a Being lives,
An inmate of this *active* universe;
From nature largely he receives; nor so
Is satisfied, but largely gives again,
For feeling has to him imparted strength,
And powerful in all sentiments of grief,
Of exultation, fear, and joy, his mind,
Even as an agent of the one great mind,
Creates, creator and receiver both,
Working but in alliance with the works
Which it beholds. (II 255–75)

SOURCE: *English Literary History,* XVI (1949) 284–98.

NOTES

1. *Biographia Literaria,* II 45 and 70.
2. Univ. of California Press, Berkeley and Los Angeles, 1942.
3. The 1805 text is cited throughout.
4. F. A. Pottle, *The Idiom of Poetry* (Cornell U.P., 1946) p. 133.
5. This view I think he owed partly to a discovery of Berkeley's philosophy during the period of his first intimacy with Coleridge. The chief elements in the Berkeleian system : the conconception of the universe as the visible language of God and the emphasis on the percipient mind in relation to the physical world with the consequent relation between man and man and between God and man, all are present in Wordsworth's poetry after 1797. See my 'Berkeleian Elements in Wordsworth's Thought', *Journal of English and Germanic Philology,* XLVII (1948) 14–28.
6. *Wordsworth's Literary Criticism,* ed. Nowell C. Smith (London, 1905) pp. 1, 11, 13–14, 18, 41, 42.
7. William Empson, 'The Structure of Complex Words', *Sewanee Review* LVI (1948) 230–50. Empson's categories of equations seem to me to be arbitrary; but it is possible to profit by the enrichment of our reading which his attention to hidden meanings in diction has brought about without taking over the paraphernalia of his system of equations. The word *sense,* though clearly part of the set of terms under consideration, is omitted from the present study because of the careful attention Empson

gives to it. But his analysis, brilliant as it is, is apparently based
on what I think a false assumption that *The Prelude* is a piece of
casuistry in Wordsworth's self-defence.

8. *Wordsworth's Literary Criticism*, p. 23.

9. I 427–41; II 250–80; III 121–38, 359–71; V 615–29; VI
661–7; VII 716–40; VIII 593–605; XI 105–223; XII 278–379
XIII 66–119.

10. *Wordsworth's Literary Criticism*, p. 23.

Jonathan Bishop

WORDSWORTH AND THE 'SPOTS OF TIME' (1959)

The Prelude is at the center of our experience of Wordsworth; at the center of our experience of *The Prelude* are those 'spots of time' where Wordsworth is endeavoring to express key moments in the history of his imagination. Basil Willey[1] has suggested that we might isolate the genuine element in Wordsworth by collating these passages; this essay is an attempt in that direction.

Narrowly speaking, the 'spots of time' are the two incidents introduced by Wordsworth's own use of the phrase: 'There are in our existence spots of time,/That with distinct pre-eminence retain/A renovating virtue',[2] that is, the little boy's encounter with the gibbet and his wait for his father's horses. Yet the poet's language implies that there were in fact many such 'spots' from which his mind could draw new strength, and every reader of *The Prelude* will at once associate with these two those other 'passages of life' which collectively establish the greatness of the poem. Using the phrase in a looser sense, the 'spots of time' must include the descriptions of Wordsworth's boyhood exploits as a snarer of woodcocks, a plunderer of birds' nests, a skater, a rider of horses, and such single events as the famous Stolen Boat episode, the Dedication to poetry, the Discharged Soldier, the Dream of the Arab-Quixote, the memory of the Winander Boy, the Drowned Man, Entering London, the Father and Child and the Blind Beggar, Simplon Pass, The Night in Paris, Robespierre's Death, and Snowdon. Some would wish to include the memories of childhood play at Cockermouth, and the moment under the rock when Wordsworth heard 'The ghostly language of the ancient earth' (II 309), or such border-line cases as the

Druid Reverie. But a list incorporating every moment of excitement in *The Prelude* would be unwieldy and tendentious. The passages I have named everyone can agree upon; they must form the major items in any argument which seeks, in whatever terms, to express a sense of the poem.

I will assume for the purposes of this article that my reader has in fact appreciated the power of these 'spots' and that I need not devote space to quotation and exegeses intended to establish their poetical existence. Let us agree that the job of introducing Wordsworth's excellences has been done, perhaps more often than is strictly necessary. I should like to raise here a question that emerges after we have made ourselves acquainted with the general limitations and strengths of *The Prelude*, and recognized the peculiar interest of the 'spots'. How do we get into them? What sense do these crucial experiences make as we go over them in our minds? What do they appear to be *about*?

The first thing that strikes us is the degree to which they tend to share common themes. Consider the way they commence: 'Oh, many a time have I, a five years' child' (I 288); 'Not less when spring had warmed' (I 326); 'And in the frosty season' (I 425); 'many a time/At evening' (v 365–6); 'When summer came,/Our pastime was' (II 54–5); the opening lines set the date and the season of adventures many times experienced by the boy Wordsworth. This note of repetition recurs as each memory develops. Wordsworth is always conscious of movements; the river Derwent 'blends' and 'flows' and 'winds' and the young boy 'plunges', 'scours', and 'leaps'; and movement tends to become a rhythm of repeated actions: 'Basked in the sun, and plunged and basked again' (I 291), or 'Scudding away from snare to snare, I plied' and 'sounds/Of indistinguishable motion, steps' (I 313; 323–4). Motion often means climbing, the ascent of a road or crag or mountain, and when the protagonist himself does not rise, another participant in the experience may. Repeated action seems to be linked with the presence of animals; the boy Wordsworth ranges heights 'where woodcocks run' (I 311); his skiff heaves 'through the water like a swan' (I 376); the skating boys are a 'pack' and 'hare' (I 437); even the ascent of Snowdon is diversified by the antics of a dog. Horses are especially prominent; they appear more or less importantly in Entering London, Robespierre's Death, The Dream (in the form of a dromedary), and the Gibbet and Waiting for Horses. Perhaps we are closest to the meaning horses have for Wordsworth in his recollection of mounted expeditions to the seashore, when 'Lighted by gleams of moonlight from the sea/We beat with thundering hoofs the level sand' (II 136–7).

The presence of powerfully repeated action seems linked with another common element, the emergence of a solitary figure from a crowd. While skating the boy Wordsworth detaches himself from the games of his playmates to 'cut across the reflex of a star' (I 450) as he says in a wonderful image, and the Dedication and his encounter with the Discharged Soldier each follow upon dancing parties from which Wordsworth is returning alone. There is a crowd to witness the Drowned Man's rise from the lake, and to listen as the solitary flautist 'blew his flute/Alone upon the rock' (II 169–70). Is there perhaps an analogy between the separation of an individual from a crowd and the theme of repeated action? Just as, at the climax of a 'spot', the protagonist detaches himself from his companions, so the rhythm of motion, rising to a height, often receives a check, a breaking in of new experience. The skating memory illustrates this clearly: 'and oftentimes,/When we had given our bodies to the wind/And all the shadowy banks on either side/Came sweeping through the darkness, spinning still/The rapid line of motion, then at once/Have I, reclining back upon my heels,/Stopped short' (I 452–8); transferring the skater's motion to the cliffs around him, which wheel by him giddily. Similarly, the climax of the nest-plundering memory comes at the moment when, his own movement checked, the boy hangs on the face of the rock while wind and clouds move for him. More developed is the experience of the Winander boy, calling repeatedly across a lake; at moments as he 'hung/Listening', he felt 'a gentle shock of mild surprise' which 'carried far into his heart the voice/Of mountain torrents' exchanging for his proud shouts a heartfelt impression of the 'visible scene' (v 381–4). Wordsworth was conscious of the importance of this formula in his mental life and twice instanced the Winander 'spot' as evidence that 'an act of steady observation, or . . . expectation', suddenly relaxed, might carry to the heart whatever at that moment impressed the senses.[3] The most vivid example of reciprocation is the famous Stolen Boat memory. The boy rows his skiff out into the lake, his eyes fixed on a peak behind as a mark, 'lustily' enjoying his rhythmical motion through the water. Suddenly his own actions bring about another, vaster motion and a farther peak rises up behind his mark : 'I struck and struck again,/And growing still in stature the grim shape/Towered up between me and the stars, and still,/For so it seemed, with purpose of its own/And measured motion like a living thing,/Strode after me' (1 380–5). Reciprocation has become retaliatory. His action is guilty; he has stolen the boat, and nature's reaction is correspondingly punitive. We may recall the 'low breathings' the boy heard following him when he stole birds from others' snares, and remember that there is often a degree of guilt attached even to innocent actions; running out into the fields is 'wantonness' and climbing after eggs 'plundering'. At the climax of the Stolen Boat episode the language seems to put us in touch with a more severe crime than theft; we read that, astonished, he 'struck and struck again' with his oars, as if an act more violent than rowing alone were meant.

The 'low breathings' just noticed may also remind us of the role moving air plays in the 'spots'. Wind is literally present as the boy scales the heights; it blows 'amain,/Shouldering the naked crag' (1 334–5) where the birds' nests are found, and sweeps the skaters over the ice. Raised to its human equivalent the wind blows 'strange utterance', or, as personified Nature, 'breathes'. The recurrence of occasions on which sounds are heard over a watery surface seems linked with this half-human air. The Winander boy shouts across the lake, and church bells, voices, and echoes combine in an 'alien sound/Of melancholy' (1 443–4) that resounds over the icy surface of the lake in the skating memory. In an interestingly linked series, the music of bird song from an island is echoed by 'that single wren/Which one day sang so sweetly' over ground wet from 'recent showers' (II 118–20) and the climactic image of a boy sitting on an island blowing his flute over 'dead still water' (II 171). In the memories of youth and adulthood we encounter, in place of natural sounds, a voice speaking words, inarticulate or cryptic, threatening or relieving. This sound or voice seems most often to occur at the extreme moment of the repeated action, to enunciate, as it were, the check or reversal which climaxes the experience; though in the case of the Winander boy, the voice is itself the repeated action. Perhaps the presence of something written, like the initial carved in the turf in the Gibbet episode, or the pamphlet in the Paris Night memory, or the 'books' carried by the Arab-Quixote, are derivations from the commoner and more vivid image of an articulate cry.

Surfaces hide depths. The boy shouts over water, rows upon it, gallops beside it; he also bathes in it, and we are soon made aware of water as a powerful image of the apprehensive mind. The 'uncertain heaven, received/Into the bosom of the steady lake' (V 387–8) is a famous and explicit image for the impression made upon the boy's heart, and the sound of his companion's flute makes him feel that the 'calm/And dead still water lay upon my mind/Even with a weight of pleasure, and the sky,/Never before so beautiful, sank down/Into my heart, and held me like a dream' (II 170–5). These words place the boy first under the water, then identify him with it; imaginatively, he dissolves into the element that drowns him. We recall Wordsworth's comparison of his effort to remember to 'one who hangs down-bending from the side/Of a slow-moving boat, upon the breast/Of a still water' (IV 256–8), seeking to distinguish objects on the bottom.

This metaphor is dramatized in the Drowned Man 'spot'. Walking alone around a silent lake as a schoolboy Wordsworth had seen a heap of garments on the opposite shore, and the next day he watched as the body, grappled to the surface, 'bolt upright/Rose, with his ghastly face, a spectre shape/Of terror' (V 449–51). A very similar figure, described in virtually the same terms, appears in the encounter with the Discharged Soldier. Wordsworth leaves a party, and starts home 'up a long ascent,/Where the road's watery surface, to the top/ Of that sharp rising glittered. . . .' His reverie is suddenly interrupted by 'an uncouth shape. . . . Stiff, lank, and upright; a more meagre man/Was never seen before by night or day./ Long were his arms, pallid his hands; his mouth/Looked ghastly in the moonlight' (IV 379–96). Can we connect these spectral figures with the ghostly retaliator who lurked in nature, whose 'low breathings' and 'steps' he heard behind him, the 'grim shape' whose 'head' 'upreared' behind the mountain horizon, and see him again in the 'blind Beggar, who, with upright face,/Stood, propped against a wall' (VII 639–40) in one of the London memories? It seems relevant that the sight of this beggar made Wordsworth's mind turn 'round/As with the might of waters' and that he gazed 'as if admonished from another world' (VII 643–9). In these experiences the other world is literally beyond the limits of this; the grim shape emerges from behind the horizon, from under the surface of the water, at the crest of a road. To pass a boundary is to evoke the unknown. In Entering London he is riding on a vehicle surrounded by crowds when he suddenly becomes aware that 'The threshold now is overpast' (VIII 549), as if these words were spoken to his inner ear; whereupon 'A weight of ages did at once descend/Upon my heart; no thought embodied, no/Distinct remembrances, but weight and power, – /Power growing under weight' (VIII 552–5). *Power growing under weight*; the image expresses a paradoxical release of inner force complementing the very pressures which inhibit it, as if suffering authorized strength. Does not such language, echoed in so many of the 'spots', suggest that the moment of illumination is irresistibly followed by a punitive crushing, a death by a weight like that of water and all that water obscurely symbolizes? To be sure, Wordsworth tells us as often as not that such experiences are matter for self-congratulation, and perhaps ultimately they are, yet we should not allow his often rather sanctimonious afterthoughts to blur for us the clear drift of his language. The immediate experience is terror.

As we go over the 'spots', and recall the associated areas of

Wordsworth's other poetry, we come upon other evidences of a shared vocabulary. We notice how often key experiences take place in darkness, especially darkness qualified, perhaps at the moment of inner illumination, by the sudden presence of light; the role of the moon is worth following for its own sake through the whole body of Wordsworth's work. Trees, too, have a special meaning for him, though their place in the 'spots' seems less prominent than one might expect. Buildings, especially ruined buildings, do appear : Cockermouth Castle, 'a shattered monument' (1 284), stood beside the river in which the 'five years' child' bathed; in the memories of book II a bird sings in a ruined shrine; a chapel on an island is part of the scenery in Robespierre's Death; cottages, huts, and tenements appear in other 'spots'. But moonlight, trees and even buildings seem relatively isolated images; to pursue them is to leave behind the context in which, if anywhere, they acquire a meaning. Our job as readers is less to establish the presence of individual items than to articulate the latent argument these recurrences suggest. What we seem to have are fragments of a drama, moments in a single action which has retired behind the reach of direct expression, leaving in our hands fragments of imagery. In what sentences will this vocabulary combine?

Perhaps a recapitulation will clarify. We seem to have in the 'spots' a repeated action, something a crowd does, or the protagonist does over and over, an action with guilty overtones, expressive of power and pride, rising as it proceeds to a boundary, there to be checked and retaliated upon from without, by counter-motion, or by a voice or the appearance of a grim shape, whose arrival precipitates an oppressive catastrophe. Is this rehearsal too abstract? Objections will arise, for many a 'spot' mixes or omits elements of this story : the relation between the protagonist and the grim shape, for example, is very changeable, in some memories reducing to identity. And many of the early memories never rise to a distinct crisis; we hear of customary actions, repeated experiences which stay, as it were, in the back of Wordsworth's mind, pleasant but indistinct. When something does happen, though, the event follows at a greater or lesser distance this curious pattern.

Wordsworth himself is not certain what to name these moments. They demonstrate the workings of 'unknown modes of being' (I 393) as dreams do and we recall that the hills swirling about the skater calm down 'Till all was tranquil as a dreamless sleep' (I 464), and that the music of the flute sinks into his heart to hold him 'like a dream' (II 176). One of the major 'spots' of adult life is literally a dream; others are nearer hallucination (Paris Night) or vision (Snowdon). Wordsworth offers interpretations when he feels he can put the event satisfactorily into philosophic terms. The Snowdon experience appears to him 'The type/Of a majestic intellect' (XIV 66–7), a symbol of the mind, a view which clearly embodies a real insight, yet the language in which the insight is elaborated, most readers will agree, is invincibly prosaic. The 'philosophic mind' can interpret, but only in abstract terms; the feelings embodied in the original mysterious event remain attached to the structure of the event itself.

Let us turn, with this caveat in mind, to a related group of 'spots' experienced in young manhood, and see how far the pattern we have been able to find may help us to disengage a meaning. Book x begins with Wordsworth returning to Paris in October, 1792. He is on his way home, leaving Annette pregnant behind him. It is a moment of public tension. The king is in prison, and the massacres of September just past. Entering the city, Wordsworth crosses the empty square where men had died a few weeks before, looking on the sights 'as doth a man/Upon a volume whose contents he knows/Are memorable' (x 58–60) but which he cannot read. He ascends to his bed in a 'large mansion', and with 'unextinguished taper' begins to read. The elements necessary to significant experience begin to combine, as he climbs out of the populous city to his lonely nocturnal eminence, lit by a single light, and broodingly works upon himself, recalling reasons why the massacres of the previous month must be followed by new terrors:

> The fear gone by
> Pressed on me almost like a fear to come.
> I thought of those September massacres,

> Divided from me by one little month,
> Saw them and touched : the rest was conjured up
> From tragic fictions or true history,
> Remembrances and dim admonishments.
> The horse is taught his manage, and no star
> Of wildest course but treads back his own steps ;
> For the spent hurricane the air provides
> As fierce a successor ; the tide retreats
> But to return out of its hiding-place
> In the great deep; all things have second birth;
> The earthquake is not satisfied at once ;
> And in this way (x 71–85)

He works upon himself, piling images of retaliation one upon another, including as he goes references to horses, wind and sea, drugging himself to the point where a hallucinatory voice breaks in, crying 'To the whole city, "Sleep no more".' It is the cry of Macbeth after killing his king.

The next morning Wordsworth walks out to find a pamphlet being sold in the streets. This pamphlet reprints a speech made by a brave Girondist named Louvet, who, provoked by Robespierre's challenge, had while 'no one stirred,/In silence of all present, from his seat/. . . walked single through the avenue,/And took his station in the Tribune, saying,/"I, Robespierre, accuse thee !" ' (x 109–13). This story accidentally repeats the formula of the previous night; again we have a solitary man, separating himself from a crowd, walking to an eminence, and again a voice challenges the bloody deeds of a murderer. The ambiguity of the grammar allows us to make the necessary connections : Wordsworth feels himself both as the utterer of the cry and the murderer to whom it is directed.

The depths of Wordsworth's imaginative involvement in the political events that followed that night is easy to read in his own actions. He returned to England in December, 1792; in January Louis XVI was executed. Typically, the poem does *not* mention this; we hear instead of the 'shock' Wordsworth's moral nature felt when England joined the allies against France. In the middle of January he wrote his unmailed letter to the Bishop of Llandaff, accusing this fellow north countryman, liberal, and Cambridge man of apostasy from the revolutionary creed, and taking pains to defend the execution of the king. As the Terror commenced and gathered strength, Wordsworth found himself nightly engaged with dreams of imprisonment and 'long orations, which I strove to plead/Before unjust tribunals' (x 411–12) like Louvet, with a terrifying sense of impotence and desertion. His explanation for the atrocities is interesting; he believed them the result of a 'terrific reservoir of guilt' which could no longer hold its 'loathsome charge' and 'burst and spread in deluge through the land' (x 477–80).

These events and preoccupations serve as a chain of associations to bind the Paris Night 'spot' to the next crucial experience. One August day in 1794 he was walking on the sands of the Leven estuary. As he admired the cloud effects he meditated upon memories of his old teacher, whose grave he had that morning visited. He recalled this worthy man's last remark to him, ' "My head will soon lie low" ' (x 538); and wept a little, for Taylor had put him on the way to be a poet.

> As I advanced, all that I saw or felt
> Was gentleness and peace. Upon a small
> And rocky island near, a fragment stood
> (Itself like a sea rock) the low remains
> (With shells encrusted, dark with briny weeds)
> Of a dilapidated structure, once
> A Romish chapel, where the vested priest
> Said matins at the hour that suited those
> Who crossed the sands with ebb of morning tide.
> Not far from that still ruin all the plain
> Lay spotted with a variegated crowd
> Of vehicles and travellers, horse and foot,
> Wading beneath the conduct of their guide
> In loose procession through the shallow stream
> Of inland waters; the great sea meanwhile
> Heaved at safe distance, far retired. (x 553–68)

The elements of significant experience begin to combine. Here is the wide surface, associated with the presence of water;

here is a crowd, including horses, a multiplicity of movement; here is an island and on it a ruined building. The sea is benign; it 'heaves', but at a distance. At this moment Wordsworth is accosted by a stranger, who without prologue cries out ' "Robespierre is dead" ' (x 573).

We may speculate that the shock of this news is compounded for Wordsworth by the theme of his meditations, for he had just been complacently enjoying a diminished version of an analogous experience. Taylor, his amiable foster father, had predicted a death, and the prediction unexpectedly comes true for a man with whom Wordsworth has for many years felt a profound connection, a villain who acted out fantasies of murderous rebellion in which Wordsworth, it is not too much to say, half-consciously participated.

He is free to respond with joy; Robespierre has suffered the punishment of a regicide and Wordsworth may therefore allow himself some liberty from the apprehensions his conscience has burdened him with. 'Sleep no more' is no longer addressed to *him*. The image of the deluge is evoked again as he dissociates himself from the wicked who have been 'swept away' by the 'river of blood' (x 584, 586) they had affected to direct. His mind takes him back to a more innocent moment on this very shore, when the implications of action were uncontaminated, and the deluges of metaphor were a real ocean, as 'Along the margin of the moonlight sea – /We beat with thundering hoofs the level sand' (x 602–3).

Such a paraphrase of the political 'spots' and the biographical material with which they are associated may bring out the additions these particular 'spots' make to the pattern. We notice that the grim shape of the earlier memories has become a definite human figure, who speaks articulate words, and that the criminal activity hinted at in some of the earlier memories has acquired, in the new context provided by political awareness, a definite outline. The violent death of a king and of his executioner is at the center of Wordsworth's political preoccupations.

If with the clues suggested by these revolutionary memories we turn back to the private experiences with which Wordsworth explicitly linked his general remarks about the 'spots', we find this theme of violent death re-translated into terms which, we may feel, come closer to the emotional sources of Wordsworth's disquiet. Consider the Gibbet episode. As a very young child Wordsworth finds himself lost among barren hills, leading a horse. He stumbles upon a ruined gibbet: 'The gibbet-mast had mouldered down, the bones/And iron case were gone; but on the turf,/Hard by, soon after that fell deed was wrought,/Some unknown hand had carved the murderer's name' (XII 237–40). Terrified, he runs away up a hill, 'Faltering and faint, and ignorant of the road:/Then, reascending the bare common, saw/A naked pool that lay beneath the hills,/A beacon on the summit, and, more near,/A girl, who bore a pitcher on her head,/And seemed with difficult steps to force her way/Against the blowing wind' (XII 247–53). The event preserves several of the images we have noticed, including wind, water, something written, a horse, a ruin, and an ascent toward a limit. The theme of murder is explicit. Yet the order in which the images appear is broken. We may identify the initials on the turf with the voice whose cry climaxes so many 'spots', but here it appears at the beginning, rather than the end. And in place of a grim and ghostly masculine shape we have a living girl. Can we read the extraordinary concentration upon the separate images of pool, beacon, and girl as a displacement of feeling from the evidences of crime and punishment to accidental concomitants of an experience too overwhelming to be faced directly? The three static impressions have become symbols which bear all the weight of a meaning not directly their own. Some portion of that meaning presumably resides in the gibbet from which the boy flees; we may gather hints of the rest when we recall that this experience takes place at Penrith, that it is to be dated at a time close to his mother's death, and that his later associations with the scene were those of young love.

The Gibbet memory is immediately followed by the memory of climbing a crag with his brothers to wait for the horses that would take them all home from school for the Christmas holidays:

> There rose a crag,
> That, from the meeting-place of two highways
> Ascending, overlooked them both, far stretched;
> Thither, uncertain on which road to fix
> My expectation, thither I repaired,
> Scout-like, and gained the summit; 'twas a day
> Tempestuous, dark, and wild, and on the grass
> I sate half-sheltered by a naked wall;
> Upon my right hand couched a single sheep,
> Upon my left a blasted hawthorn stood;
> With these companions at my side, I watched,
> Straining my eyes intensely, as the mist
> Gave intermitting prospect of the copse
> And plain beneath. (XII 292–305)

The expectation depicted in these lines is not consummated then and there; Wordsworth breaks off, as he so often does in an important memory; it was, he says, days later that his anticipation was reciprocated unexpectedly by his father's death. The feelings roused by this event revert upon the experience of waiting, fastening upon the 'single sheep, and the one blasted tree,/And the bleak music from that old stone wall' (XII 319–20), making of these symbols to which, as he writes, he can repair to 'drink,/As at a fountain' (XII 325–6). Is it an accident that these two 'spots' should be linked together, and that the first should appear to deal with the child's fantasies about his mother, the other about the death of a father? Does the presence of a gibbet in the first memory suggest that, in fantasy though not in fact, the later event preceded the earlier? It is interesting that the 'spots' which Wordsworth chooses to illustrate his general theory of the restorative value of childhood memories should be the ones which most directly concern family feelings, and that in both the weight of emotion shifts from the human occasion to associated images. Such memories bring us some distance from the public world of the political 'spots': 'The hiding-places of man's power/ Open; I would approach them' (XII 279–80), but the threshold cannot be passed either by Wordsworth himself or by his readers.

This does not of course prevent us from essaying acts of interpretation: my own is implied in the manner in which I have paraphrased the 'spots' we have just been considering. The prevailing tendency among critics of Wordsworth has been to see the experiences the 'spots' record in quasi-mystical terms, to find their subject the relation of mind to nature and reality. Havens' massive study is perhaps the best representative of what can be done in this line. Yet there are obvious objections to linking Wordsworth with the mystics. The experiences recorded in the 'spots' are not impersonal, but private; in them Wordsworth, far from finding himself rapt from the world, discovers a special importance in the details of common life. He does not feel, as the mystic traditionally does, an unqualified joy, nor are claims made of insight into a supernatural reality; the claims that are made are imaginative and emotional. Indeed Wordsworth's *religious* life tends to be quite distinct from the 'spots', and to mean, psychologically, a state of affairs in opposition to the part of life they embody. The mystic rejects words; the 'spots', as we have seen, are embodied in a special vocabulary. We have besides the negative evidence that Coleridge, who would have known, never thought of them as mystical.[4] If we stress the mystical dimension in these experiences we are forced to rule out certain 'spots' in favor of others,[5] yet if any one is important, they all are; if they vary, it is in poetical fullness and imaginative authority, not mystical purity. Is there perhaps a certain unconscious devaluation of the imagination on the part of readers who wish to make Wordsworth over into a thinker or mystic?

An analogous short-circuiting may be behind the desire to associate the 'spots' with a single period in Wordsworth's creative life. The boyhood memories of books I and II were written at Goslar in 1798–99; the existence of MS. V proves this. But the speculation that the equally significant Snowdon 'spot' was written at the same time can be called no more than probable.[6] The same is true of the Gibbet. The Discharged Soldier is definitely early,[7] but Paris Night and Robespierre's Death were as far as anyone knows written in late 1804. The Simplon Pass experience, I shall argue in a moment, takes place in the act of composition, i.e. sometime in March or April 1804. The temptation to translate one's awareness of the literary and psychological equality of the 'spots' into bibliographical terms must, it seems to me, be resisted. Wordsworth's creativity was not limited to the Goslar period.[8]

My re-telling of the political and personal 'spots' makes plain the direction it seems to me most rewarding for the modern reader to go. We have a group of memories; these share a vocabulary of imagery, a vocabulary which seems to combine into a story, a story which, so far as it is interpretable, tells of the fears, curiosities, and guilt of childhood. The memories we have seem to acquire their special meaning from other and more remote sources; the repetition of language and situation becomes, once it is noticed, a clue to something farther back.

A recent article in the *Psychoanalytic Quarterly* 'On Earliest Memories' is suggestive.[9] Its authors, in summing up professional work on this subject, point out how similar one's earliest memories are to dreams, how they are chosen, as it were, to represent one's life style. They 'reveal, probably more clearly than any other single psychological datum, the central core of each person's psychodynamics, his chief motivations, form of neurosis, and emotional problem'. Selected and distorted to express their possessor's 'nuclear emotional constellation',[10] they persist through life, less influenced by superficial experience than dreams. They are added to only through some major shift in the interior balance of power. Do we not have, in the 'spots', experiences to which these generalizations will apply? To be sure, there are obvious differences between the fragmentary recollections recorded in the autobiographical portion of Christopher Wordsworth's *Memoirs*, memories we can literally call 'earliest', and the much more developed and expressed experiences, occurring at intervals well into adult life, which the 'spots' articulate. Yet we have seen that they share common themes. Can we suppose that we have, in Wordsworth, a mind with an extraordinary capacity to re-create, or have recreated for it, moments which embody the significance of its own life, as the ordinary mind can no longer do, once it has emerged from early childhood, except in the very much weaker and more ambiguous forms of dreams? Given a chance conjunction in Wordsworth's environment of certain elements which have an *a priori* significance for him, together with a state of mind under a sufficient condition of tension, waking experiences as vivid, symbolic, and mysterious as a dream could overwhelm him, with all the advantages of his waking mind at hand to help him articulate the event. Legouis quotes a saying of Landor that Wordsworth gives us the protoplasm of poetry, rather than poetry itself.[11] Perhaps, in Wordsworth's case, the distinction is not worth drawing. For it is precisely the most poetic moments which come closest to their creator's central concerns. We may even claim that *The Prelude* constitutes the record, half-concealed in a commonplace autobiographical structure, of a process which, in these days, we would call a self-analysis; the precipitate of an interior battle, a sequence of maneuvers against the incomprehensible, fought out in the public domain of verse. To be sure, every artist, so far as he achieves an imaginatively convincing structure, embodies in that structure a dramatic self-illumination from which he may, merely as a man, profit : it is Wordsworth's special genius that he should have devoted himself so massively to the imagination taken in this sense as to be, virtually, the first and last of his line. With all this held in mind I should like to forestall some of the criticisms my argument may have evoked in my reader by returning to the poetry, and address myself to two 'spots' in which the imagination as such explicitly figures.

At one point during his first visit to France Wordsworth and his friend Jones found themselves climbing among mountains up a dubious path in pursuit of their guide. As they climb they meet a peasant, from whom they ask direction. He tells them they have crossed the Alps. Obscurely depressed by the news, they hurry downwards through a gloomy chasm, whose rocks, torrents, and tumult seem 'like workings of one mind, . . . symbols of Eternity' (vi 636, 639).

As it stands this is no more than a minor experience, though the descent into the chasm is vividly expressed and reminds the

re-reader of *The Prelude* of the chasm in the Snowdon 'spot'
from which the roar of water ascended. What makes this section of the poem extraordinary is an interruption in the
description of this past event. As Wordsworth writes the words,
'we had crossed the Alps', the articulation of this old experience of passing a limit takes effect in the present; Wordsworth
breaks off, filled with an immediate emotion. And here we see
the heroic quality of the poet's mind; instead of allowing his
feelings simply to be, his pen put down until the spasm passes,
he sets out to express what he feels: 'Imagination – here the
Power so called/Through sad incompetence of human speech,/
That awful Power rose from the mind's abyss/Like an unfathered vapour' (vi 593–5). The peasant's words were, he
has just said, 'translated by our feelings'; a symbol was interpreted. As he reviews this event it suddenly acquires a double
sense. Just as he and Jones had interpreted the peasant's
remark once, so now, as he writes, Wordsworth finds himself
'interpreting' the meaning of the whole experience. The tone
shifts and he speaks directly to a new companion: 'Imagination –' The imagination itself becomes as it were a solitary, a
grim shape of greater dignity than the literal peasant from
which by association it derives; an 'awful power', ghostlike, it
rises, self-born; the dead father of the other 'spots' lurks here
as an adjective.

'. . . unfathered vapour that enwraps,/At once, some lonely
traveller. I was lost;/Halted without an effort to break
through' (vi 595–7). His forward movement as a writer is
checked by a half-comprehended shock of recognition. He sees
obscurely, why *not* checking his climb over the mountain
range was so moving. When is he 'halted'? Presumably right
after he tried to start, that is, right after writing the key word,
'Imagination'. May we speculate that he was preparing to say
something prosy *about* the imagination, something analogous
to the lecture he does read us in the last books of the poem,
when it came over him that the word was also a cry, a call to
a person? Whereupon there rose within him the reality of
which, in its abstract form, he was about to speak. The interior
power holds him, enwraps him, halts him; he is checked by the

very power which, if he could break through, would endow him with some scarcely imaginable flow of strength. He is caught at the moment of psychic paradox; his true self is his enemy.

A moment of silence follows the semi-colon; then, 'But. . . .' There are several possibilities. 'I will make an effort? I *have* made an effort and I give up? In any case?' The tense shifts to the present: this is what he finds he can say: 'But to my conscious soul I now can say' (vi 598). We should not mistake the 18th-century meaning of 'conscious' for the sense the word has now; but there has been a shift of address, a movement, perhaps accompanied by a loss, from the all-inclusive name 'Imagination' to the limited, traditional, 'conscious soul'. Is there also some dwindling of the original impact in the distance implied by *what* he says? ' "I recognize thy glory" ' is spoken from a place apart. The imagination, now the conscious soul, is 'recognized' as a legitimate ruler; yet the emotion in all its ambiguity is still alive, for it is the 'usurpation' accomplished by the imagination with its primitive strength that he goes on boldly to praise, following the fruitful inconsistency of the political metaphor with a more explicit paradox, a 'light' that goes out in a 'flash': ' "I recognize thy glory": in such strength/Of usurpation, when the light of sense/Goes out, but with a flash that has revealed/The invisible world, doth greatness make abode,/There harbours; . . .' From here on the development is firm, unqualified; the voice honors the reality hc has experienced magnificently:

> whether we be young or old,
> Our destiny, our being's heart and home,
> Is with infinitude, and only there;
> With hope it is, hope that can never die,
> Effort, and expectation, and desire,
> And something evermore about to be.
> Under such banners militant, the soul
> Seeks for no trophies, struggles for no spoils
> That may attest her prowess, blest in thoughts
> That are their own perfection and reward,
> Strong in herself and in beatitude

That hides her, like the mighty flood of Nile
Poured from his fount of Abyssinian clouds
To fertilise the whole Egyptian plain. (vi 603–16)

To feel intuitively and directly some portion of the meaning of the memory he is describing, to apprehend as a present experience what is symbolized by the breaking of a barrier is to release the associated stores of emotion as an overwhelming power, a power which Wordsworth with wonderful courage and, we can be sure, exact insight, immediately names the source of poetry itself, the efficient cause of the splendid lines on the page before us. The psychic reserves locked in the key experiences of his life are at rare moments available to a mind strong enough to face them, to address a lifetime to their articulation. At such times the mind may joyfully congratulate its own nature, and the flood of unconscious energies are, like those of the Nile, benign.

Floods, however, are not always fertilizing. Consider the other 'spot' which deals explicitly with the imagination, the famous dream of the Stone and the Shell. I don't want to spend time on the details of the dream as such; anyone who has come so far with me and recalls the story will understand the degree to which the adventure of the dream incorporates the vocabulary of the other 'spots', with its wide waste of sand, its movement, its grim shape in the form of a strange Arab, who rides a dromedary instead of a horse. This figure carries a stone, representing geometry and a shell, standing for poetry. He presents the shell to the dreamer, who puts it to his ear, 'And heard that instant in an unknown tongue,/Which yet I understood, articulate sounds' (v 93–4), prophesying destruction by deluge to the inhabitants of the world. Explaining that he intends to bury the two objects, which he calls 'books', the Arab races away, with the dreamer in chase. As he rides the Arab looks back; following his glance, the dreamer sees 'over half the wilderness diffused,/A bed of glittering light' (v 128–9). He is looking at ' "The waters of the deep/Gathering upon us" ' (v 130–1). Pursued by the 'fleet waters of a drowning world' (v 137), the dreamer wakes in terror.

Let us look first at the shell. The Arab tells the dreamer in so many words that it represents poetry, and though the allegory is a little stiff, we need not hesitate to accept this interpretation as broadly correct. There are two facts about shells which make this interpretation exciting. First, they come from the sea. If the shell is a book of poetry, the sea from which it has its being must be the creative mind. We have seen how the experience of the imagination eventuated, in the Simplon 'spot', in an image of a fertilizing river : here, the destructive aspect of this image predominates, pursuing life to destroy it. Once again, the act of understanding an image is dangerous; as one handles the symbol one evokes the reality for which it stands; and this is as likely to mean destruction as renewed creativity. Comprehension too often means catastrophe. The real source from which catastrophe comes we learn when we consider the other fact about shells. When you hold one to your ear, the roar you hear is the tide of your own blood. The deluge, in other words, wells up from within.

We may now paraphrase the dream as follows : 'If you choose poetry as a way of life, as you have done and are bound to do, you run the severe risk of being overwhelmed by the unconscious forces from which your poetry must derive its vital inspiration and the significant portion of its subject matter; if you lose your nerve, you will find yourself "burying" your talent to escape the emotional turmoil it brings upon you.'

As Wordsworth himself understood when he contemplated his hopes for his poem, 'This is, in truth, heroic argument,/. . . which I wished to touch/With hand however weak, but in the main/It lies far hidden from the reach of words./Points have we all of us within our souls/Where all stand single; this I feel, and make/Breathings for incommunicable powers' (iii 184–90).

Source : *English Literary History,* xxvi (1959) 45–65.

NOTES

Twelve footnotes in the original text are here deleted.

1. Basil Willey, *The Eighteenth Century Background* (London : Chatto & Windus, 1940) p. 274.

2. XII 208–10 ff. 1850 version cited throughout.

3. The relevant autobiographical passages are most easily available in de Selincourt (1926 edition) p. 531, and R. D. Havens, *The Mind of a Poet* (Baltimore, 1941) II 392.

4. Havens admits this himself (1 167).

5. Havens, 1 168.

6. See de Selincourt, p. xxxv, and Havens, p. 638. [In fact it belongs to MS. W in 1804 – Ed.]

7. De Selincourt, p. xxxiii.

8. Nor was everything written at Goslar good. A VII 721–9 is entirely dull stuff, and A VII 21–37 merely cute.

9. Leon S. Saul, Thoburn R. Snyder, Jr, and Edith Sheppard, 'On Earliest Memories', *Psychoanalytic Quarterly*, XXV (1956) 228–37.

10. Ibid., pp. 229–30.

11. Legouis, *The Early Life of William Wordsworth,* p. 317.

Colin Clarke

FROM *ROMANTIC PARADOX**
(1962)

. . . In the years 1797–8 Wordsworth discovered his main theme : the place of mind in nature. And at the same time we find him using the words 'image', 'form' and 'shape' with a greatly increased range of suggestion. The relevant pieces for study here are the tale of the discharged soldier, which was later incorporated in *The Prelude*; the tale of 'The Pedlar', as contained in the first extant MS. of 'The Ruined Cottage'; and some fragments of blank verse to be found in the Alfoxden Note Book.

Here is the account of his meeting with the soldier :

> On I went
> Tranquil, receiving in my own despite
> Amusement, as I slowly pass'd along,
> From such near objects as from time to time,
> Perforce, intruded on the listless sense
> Quiescent, and dispos'd to sympathy,
> With an exhausted mind, worn out by toil,
> And all unworthy of the deeper joy
> Which waits on distant prospect, cliff, or sea,
> The dark blue vault, and universe of stars.
> Thus did I steal along that silent road,
> My body from the stillness drinking in
> A restoration like the calm of sleep,
> But sweeter far. Above, before, behind,

* These extracts from Colin Clarke's book have been chosen with care, but for the full argument with all its complex over-tones and applications the reader should turn to the original context. [Ed.]

> Around me, all was peace and solitude,
> I look'd not round, nor did the solitude
> Speak to my eye; but it was heard and felt.
> O happy state ! what beauteous pictures now
> Rose in harmonious imagery – they rose
> As from some distant region of my soul
> And came along like dreams; yet such as left
> Obscurely mingled with their passing forms
> A consciousness of animal delight
> A self-possession felt in every pause
> And every gentle movement of my frame.
>   While thus I wander'd, step by step led on,
> It chanc'd a sudden turning of the road
> Presented to my view an uncouth shape
> So near, that, slipping back into the shade
> Of a thick hawthorn, I could mark him well,
> Myself unseen. (1805 : IV 375–405)

The passing forms in the mind behave so like the near objects that *intrude* on the listless sense as though they were within the mind as well as outside it that rigid distinctions between outer and inner become irrelevant. (The observer steals *along* the silent road, and the pictures come *along* like dreams; both the prospect and the region of the soul are *distant*; the outward solitude is heard and *felt*, the self-possession is *felt* in every pause; etc.) The uncouth shape that confronts the young man unawares is located, firmly enough, in the world of the senses; and yet there is a hint that it belongs also to that world of 'intervenient imagery' (to borrow an apt expression from the third book of *The Prelude*) that lies mid-way between the substantial waking world and the world of sleep; or rather embraces them both. In other words the context tends to assimilate the 'shape' to the passing forms in the mind, although the surface narrative makes it clear that it is a three-dimensional shape known to sight.

> He was of stature tall,
> A foot above man's common measure tall,
> Stiff in his form, and upright, lank and lean;
> A man more meagre, as it seem'd to me,

> Was never seen abroad by night or day.
> His arms were long, and bare his hands; his mouth
> Shew'd ghastly in the moonlight : from behind
> A milestone propp'd him, and his figure seem'd
> Half-sitting, and half-standing. I could mark
> That he was clad in military garb,
> Though faded, yet entire. He was alone,
> Had no attendant, neither Dog, nor Staff,
> Nor knapsack; in his very dress appear'd
> A desolation, a simplicity
> That seem'd akin to solitude. Long time
> Did I peruse him with a mingled sense
> Of fear and sorrow. From his lips, meanwhile,
> There issued murmuring sounds, as if of pain
> Or of uneasy thought; yet still his form
> Kept the same steadiness; and at his feet
> His shadow lay, and mov'd not.

The repetition of 'form' and its association with 'lean', 'meagre' and 'shadow' just keeps alive the possibility that the form of the soldier somehow belongs with the passing forms or harmonious imagery in the mind. Although the word 'image' is not in fact applied to the uncouth shape in this original version, it might well have been. In the later version we get :

> How gracious, how benign, is Solitude;
> How potent a mere image of her sway;
> Most potent when impressed upon the mind
> With an appropriate human centre.

The paragraph from which these lines are taken irritates the reader not only because, in de Selincourt's words, 'it was unnecessary, and [because] the rather elaborate style in which it is written contrasts awkwardly with the bare, telling simplicity of the narration that follows' (*Notes*, p. 525), but because it precedes that narration, so that the significance of 'image', the crucial word in this context, seems to be imposed upon the narrative instead of emerging from it unobtrusively. The

uncouth shape of the original is an image in the primary sense
that it is an object of perception and yet seems to rise out of
the perceiver's own consciousness; and beyond this, it is an
image or emblem of the potent sway of Solitude. The 'image'
of the later version however, which is also – potentially – an
image in a double sense (both 'sensation "impressed upon the
mind"' and 'type'), is merely abstract, an emblem that is
virtually devoid of content and emblematic of nothing.

The next passage I shall consider is to be found early in 'The
Ruined Cottage':

> So the foundations of his mind were laid
> In such communion, not from terror free.
> While yet a child, and long before his time
> He had perceived the presence and the power
> Of greatness, and deep feelings had impressed
> Great objects on his mind, with portraiture
> And colour so distinct (that on his mind)
> They lay like substances, and almost seemed
> To haunt the bodily sense. He had received
> A precious gift, for as he grew in years
> With these impressions would he still compare
> All his ideal stores, his shapes and forms,
> And being still unsatisfied with aught
> Of dimmer character, he thence attained
> An *active* power to fasten images
> Upon his brain, and on their pictured lines
> Intensely brooded, even till they acquired
> The liveliness of dreams. Nor did he fail,
> While yet a child, with a child's eagerness,
> Incessantly to turn his ear and eye
> On all things which the rolling seasons brought
> To feed such appetite. Nor this alone
> Appeased his yearning; in the after day
> Of boyhood, many an hour in caves forlorn
> And in the hollow depth of naked crags
> He sate, and even in their fixed lineaments,
> Or from the power of a peculiar eye,
> Or by creative feeling overborne,

> Or by predominance of thought oppressed,
> Even in their fixed and steady lineaments
> He traced an ebbing and a flowing mind,
> Expression ever varying.

In order to convince himself of the solidity and externality of the visible world, the child Wordsworth 'grasped at a wall or tree' (just as Dr Johnson, with the intention of refuting Berkeley, vigorously kicked a stone). And Bonamy Price had this tale to tell of the poet in old age (it is quoted by de Selincourt in his notes to 'Ode. Intimations Of Immortality'):

The venerable old man raised his aged form erect; he was walking in the middle, and passed across me to a five-barred gate in the wall which bounded the road on the side of the lake. He clenched the top bar firmly with his right hand, pushed strongly against it, and then uttered these ever-memorable words : 'There was a time in my life when I had to push against something that resisted, to be sure that there was anything outside me. I was sure of my own mind; everything else fell away, and vanished into thought.'

Though a phenomenalist may assure us that the tactile and kinaesthetic senses provide no better proof of the 'otherness' of objects than the sense of sight, the layman instinctively touches things and tests their resistance in order to convince himself that they have substance. (In his book *Looking At Pictures* Sir Kenneth Clark, discussing Vermeer's 'eye', writes : 'For the first, and almost for the last, time in European painting, it is an eye which felt no need to confirm its sensations by touch. The belief that what we touch is more real than what we see is the basis of drawing. A firm outline denotes a tangible concept.') So we shall not be surprised to find that Wordsworth, who bears such wavering testimony to the solidity of the natural world, should assure us in one and the same context that images are 'pictured lines' and that they 'lie upon the mind' like things that have weight.

In the 1814 edition of *The Excursion* the lines immediately following 'and deep feelings had impressed' were altered to read :

>   and deep feelings had impressed
> So vividly great objects that they lay
> Upon his mind like substances, whose presence
> Perplexed the bodily sense.

In a copy of his own Poetical Works (1836–7) which he used for correction and redrafting of his text Wordsworth altered the lines again so as to read :

>   and deep feelings had impressed
> Upon his mind great objects so distinct
> In portraiture (lineament), in colouring so vivid
> That on his mind they lay like substances
> And almost indistinguishably mixed
> With things of bodily sense.

And finally in the 1845 edition this is altered once more and becomes :

>   and deep feelings had impressed
> Great objects on his mind, with portraiture
> And colour so distinct, that on his mind
> They lay like substances, and almost seemed
> To haunt the bodily sense.

The weakest of these versions is the one published in 1814. The others make it clear that the great objects are not only substances but pictures; and it is the paradoxical relationship between imagery as picture and imagery as substance that the ensuing paragraph is, above all, concerned with. The word 'vividly' in the 1814 edition is insufficiently precise : it leaves us guessing at what seems to have been the intended meaning – namely, that a colourful and sharply defined *picture* lay upon the mind. In the first and the last two versions however we are left face to face with the full paradox of sense-perception : the images lie heavily, like substances, and yet are to be thought of

as a kind of portraiture. (Compare *The Prelude*, II 176 ff.
1805.) So when shortly afterwards we come upon the expression 'fixed lineaments', the impression of stability and solidity
that the phrase seems so surely to evoke is insensibly qualified,
for 'lineaments' recalls 'pictured lines' and so points inwards,
if only dimly, as well as outwards. As a result, when the word
is used a second time, we are fully prepared to accept the
implication that the 'fixed and steady lineaments' are not
merely the line of the crags but are lines depicted on a mind.
And beyond that, we are ready to respond to the suggestion
that this mind is eternal, and that it finds expression in the line
of the crags much as the human mind finds expression in the
lineaments of the face.

Further on in the *addendum* to 'The Ruined Cottage'
(*P.W.*, v 402) we find the following :

> Or was it ever meant
> That this majestic imagery, the clouds
> The ocean and the firmament of heaven
> Should lie a barren picture on the mind ?

What the syntax demonstrably asserts here is that imagery and
clouds (and ocean, and firmament) are identical : images are
things and things are images. Moreover the imagery has
weight and substance, for it *lies* on the mind. But this is only
half the story. For the imagery is a mental picture (though a
hypothetically barren one) and must therefore be insubstan-
tial. And this picture in turn is also both tenuous and solid, for
it lies on the mind just as certainly as the imagery does.

This brings me to one of the most remarkable uses of the
word 'image' in the whole of Wordsworth :

> Yet still towards the cottage did I turn
> Fondly, and trace with nearer interest
> That secret spirit of humanity
> Which, 'mid the calm oblivious tendencies
> Of Nature, 'mid her plants, her weeds and flowers,
> And silent overgrowings, still survived.

The old man, seeing this, resumed, and said
My Friend, enough to sorrow have you given,
The purposes of Wisdom ask no more,
Be wise and cheerful, and no longer read
The forms of things with an unworthy eye.
She sleeps in the calm earth and peace is here.
I well remember that those very plumes,
Those weeds and the high spear-grass on that wall,
By mist and silent rain-drops silvered o'er,
As once I passed, did to my mind convey
So still an image of tranquillity,
So calm and still, and looked so beautiful,
Amid the uneasy thoughts which filled my mind,
That what we feel of sorrow and despair
From ruin and from change, and all the grief
The passing shews of being leave behind
Appeared an idle dream that could not live
Where meditation was. I turned away
And walked along my road in happiness.

The lines make even more impact in *The Excursion* than they do here in the original version, because the long reflective argument from the *addendum* – much of which was worked into *The Excursion*, book IV – is deleted. The decision to abridge this discourse was a wise one; for the Wanderer's prolonged reflections had had the effect of partially severing the moral from the narrative. In the published version we cannot fail to recognize that the cottage overgrown with plants is not merely the *occasion* of moral reflections but a pictorial embodiment of their meaning: the narrative, the moral commentary, and the picture or setting are inseparable. The contradiction between the extreme ordinariness of this picture – composed as it is of common plumes and weeds and spear-grass – and the quantity of moral meaning it is called upon to express gives to the conclusion of the Wanderer's tale an appearance almost of paradox. The depth of his feelings as he contemplates the spear-grass on the wall might well seem – judged by common-sense standards – out of proportion to the cause assigned. Yet the incident does not strike us as improbable. And the reason is that the poetry leaves no room for doubt that the scene contemplated exists inwardly as well as outwardly; we can believe that the plants and weeds are the cause of profound effects in the life of the mind because they are, demonstrably, of the same stuff as the mind. Wordsworth's success here is partly due to his play on the word 'image'. Qua 'picture', the 'image of tranquillity' is as unremarkable as it could well be; qua 'emblem', it records a spiritual experience that is both remarkable and valuable. (Compare the plural meaning of the word in line 69, book XIII of *The Prelude*, 1805.) The image is 'calm and still', first because it is a faithful picture of the plumes, weeds and spear-grass – and these are still; secondly because it virtually *is* these objects, since it is indistinguishable from them; and finally because it is a copy not only of tranquil external things but of tranquillity itself. (The heart is so calm that its tranquillity might be considered the very emblem of tranquillity.) The syntax strongly implies that it was not merely the weeds etc. but also their image that 'looked so beautiful', as though image and thing were equally distant from the mind contemplating them – and therefore equally objective. In other words the image tends to become, or dissolve into, the thing itself, the object imaged. And the curious but very characteristic use of the word 'Amid', which manages to connote spatial as well as temporal location, also serves to put thing and image on the same footing, by seeming to locate them both amid uneasy thoughts. (There is a similar use of 'amid' a few lines above : '. . . 'mid the calm oblivious tendencies Of Nature, 'mid her plants . . .'.) So it comes about that the poetry acts out the stated meaning; for the lesson the Wanderer has to teach is that 'the forms of things' – of commonplace things – can carry a great weight of moral meaning, and this is precisely what, to the eye of the reader as well as of the Wanderer himself, the form (or image) of the weeds and so on appears to do.

Before he achieved these austerely beautiful lines about the image Wordsworth made 'three different attempts at a reconciling passage for the close of the poem' (de Selincourt, p. 400). Two of them are of interest for the way they spell out the paradox which in the final version has become implicit. It will be enough to look at the first of these.

> The old man ceased : he saw that I was moved.
> From that low bench rising instinctively
> I turned away in weakness, and my heart
> Went back into the tale which he had told,
> And when at last returning from my mind
> I looked around, the cottage and the elms,
> The road, and pathway, and the garden wall
> Which old and loose and mossy o'er the road
> Hung bellying, all appeared, I know not how
> But to some eye within me all appeared
> Colours and forms of a strange discipline.
> The trouble which they sent into my thoughts
> Was sweet, I looked and looked again, and to myself
> I seemed a better and a wiser man.

Wordsworth explicates the paradox with some deliberation : the colours and forms of cottage, elms and so on impress themselves at one and the same time on an outer and an inner eye, so that the forms can only be forms in a double sense.

The Alfoxden Note Book contains a number of fragments that bear upon my theme (they are printed by de Selincourt in an appendix to vol. v); but I shall choose only one for comment – and select the following because of the way it looks forward to 'Tintern Abbey' :

> Why is it we feel
> So little for each other, but for this,
> That we with nature have no sympathy,
> Or with such things as have no power to hold
> Articulate language?
> And never for each other shall we feel
> As we may feel, till we have sympathy
> With nature in her forms inanimate,
> With objects such as have no power to hold
> Articulate language. In all forms of things
> There is a mind.

These lines were written at a period when the word 'forms' was coming to have for Wordsworth a persistently ambiguous connotation. But here the ambiguity is not realized; and as a result he is reduced to merely *asserting* his faith that there is a mind 'in all forms of things'. On numerous occasions, and particularly in 'Tintern Abbey', Wordsworth was to demonstrate this faith poetically, the demonstration depending very much on his persuading us that the forms of things are shapes in a human mind as well as the shapes of a landscape. But the 'forms inanimate' of the lines under review show no signs of being of the same stuff as the mind of the observer and remain purely external. So we have to take the 'doctrine' or 'belief' on trust. Still, the fragment is an interesting pointer to 'Tintern Abbey' (or rather to a dominant theme of that poem) because mind is declared to be universally present not, simply, in things but in the forms of things.

II

. . . In the following section I shall endeavour to consolidate my argument. I shall range over the poems freely to show that the conclusion that Wordsworth uses the words 'form', 'shape' and 'image' equivocally has not been arrived at on the evidence of half a dozen cannily selected instances, and that almost anywhere we turn and dip (in the poetry of the great decade, that is) we discover the same feeling for the ambiguity of perception.

The first passage is taken from the 1805 version of *The Prelude*:

> Yet in the midst
> Of these vagaries, with an eye so rich
> As mine was, through the chance, on me not wasted,
> Of having been brought up in such a grand
> And lovely region, I had forms distinct
> To steady me; these thoughts did oft revolve

> About some centre palpable, which at once
> Incited them to motion, and control'd,
> And whatsoever shape the fit might take,
> And whensoever it might come, I still
> At all times had a real solid world
> Of images about me; ...

The primary meaning of 'images' here seems to be 'Nature's image-work' : the young poet is surrounded by pictures, but real solid pictures. However, given the context, a comparison-and-contrast with *mental* images seems also to be implied : 'the images were pictures, as all images are, including images in the mind; yet they were *not* images in the mind, for they were solid'. As so often in poetry the effect of this denial of a meaning is that the meaning denied begins to assert itself as a positive value, thus : 'The images were solid *and yet* were optical appearances'. Moreover we have learnt a few lines earlier that the 'forms distinct' steadied the mind and the thoughts revolved 'About some centre palpable' as though both thoughts and forms were operating in a space at once mental and physical. When therefore the metaphor of the circle ('*About* some centre . . .') is covertly repeated ('. . . a real solid world Of images *about* me') the reader tends to assume that the relationship between the images and the self, like that between the forms and the thoughts, is not purely external : in other words 'about me' is not interpreted simply as 'outside and independent of me' but also as 'centred upon me' and even perhaps, in some sense, 'dependent upon me'.

Here, from *The Prelude*, is a further example of ingenious double-talk :

> No familiar shapes
> Remained, no pleasant images of trees,
> Of sea or sky, no colours of green fields;
> But huge and mighty forms, that do not live
> Like living men, moved slowly through the mind
> By day, and were a trouble to my dreams.

> Wisdom and Spirit of the universe !
> Thou Soul that art the eternity of thought,
> That givest to forms and images a breath
> And everlasting motion, not in vain
> By day or star-light thus from my first dawn
> Of childhood didst thou intertwine for me
> The passions that build up our human soul . . .
>
> (1850; 1 395–407)

Shapes, images, forms – our three key terms do a great deal of work here. Moreover 'shape' has been used shortly before, in reference to the 'huge peak' :

> I struck and struck again,
> And growing still in stature the grim shape
> Towered up between me and the stars . . .

The solidity of the peak is a distinctly qualified solidity, for 'shape', we know, can mean spectre or phantom. (Compare *Paradise Lost*, II 649, 666 ff., and 681. For 'grim' see *P.L.*, II 804; and also 'Fragment of a Gothic Tale' – de Selincourt's edition, *P.W.*, I 291.) When we come upon the next usage we shall not have forgotten the mobility and ambiguous status of the huge, black peak – the grim shape – and this will predispose us to find in the familiar shapes or pleasant images a like mobility, a capacity to be at once there and here, to exist both outwardly and inwardly. (It was precisely this mobility that Hobbes denied to the image : '. . . and yet the introducing of *Species visible* and *intelligible* [which is necessary for the maintenance of that Opinion] passing to and fro from the *Object*, is *worse* than any Paradox as being a plain *impossibility*.') 'To remain' can mean both 'to continue in the same state' and 'to be left over – as a residue or trace'. The shapes are, first and foremost, impressions left on the mind. But 'familiar', taken in conjunction with the alternative meaning of 'Remained', suggests that they are also objects in the natural world – well-known objects that endure : no familiar shapes remained either inwardly or outwardly. In short the sinister power of the language can largely be traced to an unstated meaning: viz. that the darkness hangs over both the boy's thoughts and the whole visible world. (The 'huge and mighty forms . . . moved slowly through the mind' not only at night but also 'by day'.) The inner chaos has spread outwards and engulfed the entire imagery of nature.

In his invocation to the 'Wisdom and Spirit of the universe' Wordsworth is elaborating and modifying some earlier lines which are to be found in Manuscript V. (De Selincourt publishes them as a footnote.)

> Oh not in vain, ye Beings of the hills,
> And ye that walk the woods and open heaths
> By moon or starlight, thus from my first dawn
> Of childhood, did ye love to intertwine . . .

The rural and pagan charm of these lines gives way to splendour and sublimity in the published version. And it is largely because of the substitution of those 'forms and images' for the 'hills . . . (and) woods and open heaths' of the original that Wordsworth's sudden ascent to the sublime is so easy and convincing. For the 'forms and images' are both configurations in the mind and configurations in the external world; so their presence justifies the appeal to a Spirit diffused widely through time and place and residing, indifferently, in nature or the mind of man. Moreover, because of the preceding lines about the pleasant images and huge and mighty forms, the *mobility* of the natural world is already suggested by the equivocal 'forms and images' before we reach the words 'breath' and 'motion'; and indeed without this equivocation the reality of the Spirit would have been largely a matter of assertion.

Wordsworth's 'imagination' – in the sense of inner vision or 'inward eye' – seems to have been most active when the outward vision was also engaged (despite what the poem 'I wandered lonely . . .' might suggest).

> At length, the dead Man, 'mid that beauteous scene
> Of trees, and hills and water, bolt upright
> Rose with his ghastly face; a spectre shape
> Of terror even! and yet no vulgar fear,

> Young as I was, a Child not nine years old,
> Possess'd me; for my inner eye had seen
> Such sights before, among the shining streams
> Of Fairy land, the Forests of Romance :
> Hence came a spirit hallowing what I saw
> With decoration and ideal grace;
> A dignity, a smoothness, like the works
> Of Grecian Art, and purest Poesy.

This 1805 version is a clear improvement on the lines to be found in MS. V :

> Rose with his ghastly face. I might advert
> To numerous accidents in flood or field
> Quarry or moor, or mid the winter snows
> Distresses and disasters, tragic facts
> Of rural history that impressed my mind
> With images to which in following years
> Far other feelings were attached, with forms
> That yet exist with independent life
> And like their archetypes know no decay.

There is a sharp disjunction here of outer and inner – i.e. of tragic facts and impressions on the mind, inward forms and their outward archetypes – and the lines are colourless and flat. In the 1805 version all this gives way to characteristic equivocation : the scene is now both actual and ideal. The word 'scene' itself, in MS. V, already implies that the eye is contemplating a picture or image, and this suggests however faintly that the existence of the trees and hills and water is not *merely* objective – a meaning (or intimation of a meaning) that is confirmed in the 1805 version by the introduction of the word 'shape'. Because the child's mind is not confronted by a reality entirely alien to itself – that is, because the anxiety-experience occurs within a scenic context, a realm of shapes as much as things – we easily accept the statement about the transforming power of the 'inner eye' and the assurance that the soul was not debased by terror. (In MS. V the record of this incident is followed by the lines that became xi 258 ff. of

The Prelude – i.e. the famous passage about the 'spots of time', those moments of high significance when we feel deeply

> that the mind
> Is lord and master, and that outward sense
> Is but the obedient servant of her will.)

The inward streams and forests, and the dead man and beauteous scene, are alike 'sights' – or intervenient images. Incidentally, the comparison of the spectre shape with an artefact is in accordance with Wordsworth's inclination to merge art and nature – his partial equation of natural (or sense) images, ideal (or inward) images, and poetic images :

> On Man, on Nature, and on Human Life,
> Musing in solitude, I oft perceive
> Fair trains of imagery before me rise . . .

or :

> Some lovely Image in the song rose up
> Full-formed, like Venus rising from the sea . . .

In the Fenwick note to 'Resolution and Independence' he makes the quaint remark : 'The image of the hare I then observed on the ridge of the Fell.'

III

. . . Wordsworth's poetry often implies, and occasionally claims explicitly, that the feeling attendant upon an act of sense-perception is quite as objective as the things that are sensed. Indeed no poet does more justice to the fact that, as Bosanquet remarked, 'feelings get into objects'. In *The Recluse* he writes :

> Joy spreads, and sorrow spreads; and this whole Vale,
> Home of untutored Shepherds as it is,
> Swarms with sensation, as with gleams of sunshine,
> Shadows or breezes, scents or sounds. Nor deem

> These feelings, though subservient more than ours
> To every day's demand for daily bread,
> And borrowing more their spirit, and their shape
> From self-respecting interests, deem them not
> Unworthy therefore, and unhallowed ...

The manifest meaning of 'sensation' here is 'feelings' or 'emotions'; but a further, latent meaning is 'sense-perceptions'. We accept the assurance that sensations *qua* feelings exist out there in the Vale along with the gleams of sunshine, the shadows, breezes, scents and sounds, partly because we recognize that where sensations *qua* sense-perceptions are concerned, object so easily becomes subject and subject object. In 'The Ruined Cottage' (*P.W.,* v 388) we see how this tendency to objectify emotion is associated with the disposition to see nature as a world of forms or shapes as much as a world of things :

> To every natural form, rock, fruit and flower
> Even the loose stones that cover the highway
> He gave a moral life, he saw them feel
> Or linked them to some feeling. In all shapes
> He found a secret and mysterious soul,
> A fragrance and a spirit of strange meaning.

Is it not because Wordsworth is concerned here with natural forms and shapes more than things that he has the confidence to assert that he saw the stones and so on feel? In other words, is it not implied that the forms can feel and the shapes have a soul because they are images, and therefore not alien to the mind? Here is a clearer instance, involving a characteristic use of the verb 'to be' :

> the tall rock,
> The mountain, and the deep and gloomy wood,
> Their colours and their forms, were then to me
> An appetite; a feeling and a love ...

Rock, mountain and wood were not merely the occasion and object of feeling; also — and more mysteriously — they *were* that feeling. At first these natural objects are offered to contemplation as being, unquestionably, solid and material : 'The

tall rock, The mountain . . .'. But then the phrase 'their colours
and their forms' quietly shifts the reader's attention from
things themselves to images of things (we are suddenly aware
of the landscape as a scene, with a pattern) and this prepares
the way for the subsequent fusion, or partial fusion, of inner
and outer, feeling and sensation. If Wordsworth had made
the bald, startling assertion that rock, mountain and wood
were to him an appetite – that is, if the phrase 'their colours
and their forms' had not been inserted where in fact it was
inserted – the resultant cancelling of the distinction between
inner and outer would have struck the reader as so violent as
to be absurd.

It is true that in order to explain the apparent existence of
feelings out there in nature Wordsworth often resorts to the
common-sense associationist theory which he inherited from
the eighteenth century; and in the lines quoted above from
'The Ruined Cottage' the words 'he saw them feel' are
balanced by 'Or linked them to some feeling'. But he was as
ready to believe that feelings are *found* in nature as to believe
that they are transferred to nature :

> For me, when my affections first were led
> From kindred, friends, and playmates, to partake
> Love for the human creature's absolute self,
> That noticeable kindliness of heart
> Sprang out of fountains . . . (*The Prelude,* VIII; 1850)

Clearly, his belief in the pervasiveness of feeling is not only
arrived at by contemplating the *appearances* of nature (the
kindly power that wells up with mysterious impartiality in
fountains and the human heart is not known by sense-
perception). Nevertheless this faith in the ubiquity of life and
spirit is also dependent on knowledge provided by the senses,
and is related to Wordsworth's perplexity concerning images
or forms. Again and again the poetry demonstrates that joy
spreads, and sorrow spreads, because sensations have dimensions that are at once mental and spatial.

IV

... To appreciate the function of the image in Wordsworth's poetry is to understand better why he could so frequently extract pleasure from experience – or the recollection of experiences – that were painful. It is the image of tranquillity conveyed by the plumes and weeds and spear-grass that gives the poet strength to face the anguish of Margaret's history ('I turned And walked along my road in happiness'); and the image of the leech-gatherer (an intervenient image – a kind of dream-image as well as sensation) so fortifies him that the sense of solitude and anxiety by which he had previously been haunted ceases to dismay. In his loneliness and grotesqueness and spectral dignity the old man at once embodies and allays the poet's anxieties. And this is what we learn to expect of the Wordsworthian image, which is apt to be both disturbing and reassuring. A spectre of the mind – a 'spectre shape Of terror' – suddenly confronts the observer as an object in the given world; and the experience exalts while it disturbs, or terrifies. Usually the exaltation comes in the process of recollection. It is in later life that the blank misgivings of a creature moving about in worlds not realized cause the poet to raise 'The song of thanks and praise'. In the same way the child's vision of 'unknown modes of being' is alarming at the time but later exhilarating and consoling. The account of the anxiety-experience here leads directly into an ecstatic apostrophising of the Wisdom and Spirit of the Universe. For such experiences prove that our rigid, everyday distinctions between mind and nature are in part illusory. (Or there are these lines from the Preface to *The Excursion*, where the fear is somewhat distanced, and the note of triumph – due in some measure at any rate to uncertainty as to what is inward and what outward – is justified for the most part indirectly, through insistence on the *spaciousness* of the human mind :

> Not Chaos, not
> The darkest pit of lowest Erebus,
> Nor aught of blinder vacancy, scooped out

By help of dreams – can breed such fear and awe
As fall upon us often when we look
Into our Minds, into the Mind of Man—
My haunt, and the main region of my song.)

Joy, then, is the normal accompaniment in Wordsworth's poetry of 'fear and awe', though no doubt it was rarely blended with these emotions in the original experience. The Wisdom and Spirit of the Universe, that gives to forms and images a breath and everlasting motion, sanctifies

Both pain and fear, until we recognize
A grandeur in the beatings of the heart.

So images not only provide the poet with the courage to face his spectres; they enable him actually to rejoice in those spectres. Images are a frequent source of anxiety, but also an ultimate source of consolation.

SOURCE: *Romantic Paradox* (1962) pp. 26–38, 53–9, 62–5, 85–7.

Geoffrey H. Hartman

A POET'S PROGRESS: WORDSWORTH AND THE *VIA NATURALITER NEGATIVA* (1962)

The exact role that Nature played in Wordsworth's experience
has not been defined beyond controversy. A number of readers
have felt that his poetry honors and even worships Nature; and
in this they have the support of Blake, a man so sensitive to
any trace of 'Natural Religion' that he blamed some verses of
Wordsworth's for a bowel complaint which almost killed him.[1]
Scholarship, luckily, tempers the affections, and the majority
of scholarly readers have emphasized the poet's progression
from Nature Worship or even Pantheism to a highly qualified
form of natural religion, with increasing awareness of the
'ennobling interchange' between mind and Nature and a late
yielding of primacy to the activity of the mind or the idealizing
power of Imagination. A very small group, finally – represented by occasional insights rather than by a sustained position – has pointed to the deeply paradoxical or problematic
character of Wordsworth's dealings with Nature and suggested that what he calls Imagination may be *intrinsically*
opposed to images culled or developed from Nature. This last
and rarest position seems to me quite close to the truth, yet I
do not feel it conflicts totally with the more traditional readings, which stress the poet's adherence to Nature. My purpose
is to show, via three important episodes of *The Prelude*, that
Wordsworth came to realize that Nature itself led him beyond
Nature; and how and when the realization was achieved. The
poet's sense of a reality in Nature is kept alive by the very fact
that Nature itself weans his mind, and especially his poetic
mind, from its early dependence on immediate sensuous

stimuli. And since this movement of transcendence, or what mystics have often called the negative way, is shown by Wordsworth as inherent in life, and as achieved without violent or ascetic discipline, I have thought to name it a *via naturaliter negativa*.

I

The Prelude opens with a success immediately followed by a failure. Released from the 'vast city' and anticipating a new freedom, the poet pours out a rush of fifty lines: 'poetic numbers came/Spontaneously to clothe in priestly robe/A renovated spirit' (1 51–3).[2] Here is the consecration, the promise of poetry as a sacrament, a gift efficacious beyond the moment. Why should a chance inspiration assume such significance? The reason is that Wordsworth was not used to make 'A present joy the matter of a song'; yet here, apparently, is evidence that he may soon become self-creative, or need no more than a 'gentle breeze' (the untraditional muse of the epic's opening) to produce a tempest of poetry. 'Matins and vespers of harmonious verse!' is the hope held out to him, and having punctually performed Matins the poet is content to slacken, to be gradually calmed by the clear autumn afternoon.

He meditates beneath a tree on a great poetic work soon to be begun. The sun sets, and city smoke is 'ruralized' by distance. He starts to continue his journey, but now it is clearly time for vespers:

> It was a splendid evening, and my soul
> Once more made trial of her strength, nor lacked
> Aeolian visitations (94–6)

An outside splendor challenges the creative mind. Is the poet strong enough to answer it spontaneously, as if he needed only a suggestion, the first chord?

> but the harp
> Was soon defrauded, and the banded host
> Of harmony dispersed in straggling sounds,

And lastly utter silence ! 'Be it so;
Why think of anything but present good?' (96–100)

Wordsworth once again sees present good, like present joy, strangely opposed to the quickening of verse. The poetic outburst which he had considered a religious thing ('punctual service high . . . holy services') is now disdained as profane and *servile* :

So, like a home-bound labourer I pursued
My way beneath the mellowing sun, that shed
Mild influence ; nor left in me one wish
Again to bend the Sabbath of that time
To a servile yoke. (101–5)

His reversal of mood is surprisingly complete. One who, at the impassioned outset of his reflections, had been so sure of the freely creative, autonomous nature of his poetic soul that famous passages on the emancipated spirit – from *Paradise Lost* and *Exodus*[3] – swell the current of his verse, while he thinks to possess total freedom of choice,

now free,
Free as a bird to settle where I will

that same person now writes of himself, with a slight echo of Gray's *Elegy* :

So, like a home-bound labourer I pursued
My way. . . .

The meaning of the reversal is not immediately clear. It does not deject the poet; it endows him, on the contrary, with a Chaucerian kind of cheer and leisure :

What need of many words?
A pleasant loitering journey, through three days
Continued, brought me to my hermitage.

I spare to tell of what ensued, the life
In common things – the endless store of things

(105–9)

The form of the reversal is that of a return to Nature, at least
to its rhythm. For the moment no haste remains, no tempest,
no impatience of spirit. It is the mood of the hawthorn shade,
of a portion of Wordsworth's Cambridge days, when he
laughed with Chaucer and heard him, while birds sang, tell
tales of love (III 278–81).

In the exultant first lines of *The Prelude* Wordsworth had
foreseen the spirit's power to become self-creative. Though
fostered by Nature it eventually outgrows its dependence, sings
and storms at will (33–8). The poet's anticipation of autonomy is probably less a matter of pride than of necessity : he
will steal the initiative from Nature, so as to freely serve or sustain the natural world, should its hold on the affections
slacken. His poetic power, though admittedly in Nature's gift,
must perpetuate, like consecration, vital if transitory feelings.
Without poetry the supreme moment is nothing.

Dear Liberty ! Yet what would it avail
But for a gift that consecrates the joy? (31–2)

The reversal teaches that this desire for immediate consecra-
tions is a wrong form of worship. The world demands a
devotion less external and wilful, a wise passiveness which the
creative will may profane. The tempest 'vexing its own
creation' is replaced by a 'mellowing sun, that shed/Mild influence'. Nature keeps the initiative. The mind at its most free
is still part of a deep mood of weathers.

Wordsworth's failure to consecrate, through verse, the
splendid evening is only the last event in this reversal. It begins
with the poet placing (so to say) the cart before the horse,
Poetry before Nature : 'To the open fields I told/A prophecy :
poetic numbers came . . .' (50 ff.). He never, of course, forgets
the double agency of inward and outward which informs
every act of poetry. So his heart's frost is said to be broken by

both outer and inner winds (38 ff.). Such reciprocity is at the
heart of all his poems. Yet he continually anticipates a movement of transcendence : Nature proposes but the Poet disposes.
Just as the breeze engendered in the mind a self-quickening
tempest, so poetry, the voice from that tempest, re-echoing in
the mind whence it came, seems to increase there its perfection
(55 ff.). The origin of the whole moves farther and farther
from its starting point in the external world. A *personal* agent
replaces that of Nature : 'I paced on . . . down I sate . . .
slackening my thoughts by choice' (60 ff.). There is a world
of difference between this subtle bravado and the ascendancy
of *impersonal* constructions in the final episode : 'Be it so;
Why think of anything but . . . What need of many words? . . .
I pursued My way . . . A pleasant loitering journey . . . brought
me to my hermitage.'

This change, admittedly, is almost too fine for common
language. Syntax becomes a major device but not a consistent
one. In the 1850 text, while the poet muses in the green, shady
place, certain neoclassical patterns, such as the noble passive
combined with synecdoche, create an atmosphere in which
personal and impersonal, active and passive, blend strongly :

> Many were the thoughts
> Encouraged and dismissed, till choice was made
> Of a known Vale, whither my feet should turn (70–2)

Devices still more subtle come into play. In the passage immediately preceding, Wordsworth describes the quiet autumn
afternoon :

> a day
> With silver clouds, and sunshine on the grass,
> And in the sheltered and the sheltering grove
> A perfect stillness. (67–70)

'Sheltered and sheltering' – typical Wordsworthian verbosity?
The redundance, however, does suggest that whatever is happening here happens in more than one place; compare 'silver

clouds and sunshine on the grass'. The locus doubles, re-
doubles : that two-fold agency which seems to center on the
poet is active all around to the same incremental effect. The
grove, sheltered, shelters in turn, and makes 'A perfect stillness'. The poet, in a sense, is only a single focus to something
universally active. He muses on this intensifying stillness, and
within him rises a picture, gazing on which with *growing* love
'a higher power than Fancy' enters to affirm his musings. The
reciprocal and incremental movement, mentioned explicitly in
lines 31 ff., occurs this time quite unself-consciously, clearly
within the setting and through the general influence of Nature.

No wonder, then, that the city, which the poet still strove to
shake off in the first lines, appears now not only distant but
also 'ruralized', taking on the colors of Nature, as inclosed by
it as the poet's own thought. The reversal is finalized by the
episode of the splendid sunset. Wordsworth not only cannot,
he *need* not steal the initiative from Nature. Her locus is universal, not individual; she acts by expedients deeper than will
or thought. Wordsworth's failure intensifies his sense of a principle of generosity in Nature. That initial cry of faith, 'I cannot
miss my way' (18), becomes true, but not because of his own
power. The song loses its way.

Wordsworth's first experience is symptomatic of his creative
difficulties. One impulse vexes the creative spirit into self-
dependence, the other exhibits Nature as that spirit's highest
guardian object. The poet is driven at the same time from and
toward the external world by dynamic dissatisfaction. No
sooner has he begun to enjoy his Chaucerian leisure than
restiveness breaks in. The 'pilgrim', despite 'the life in common
things – the endless store of things', cannot rest content with
his hermitage's sabbath. Higher hopes, 'airy phantasies',
clamor for life (114 ff.). The poet's account of his creative
difficulties (146–269) documents in full his vacillation between a natural and a more-than-natural theme, between a
Romantic tale and one of 'natural heroes', or 'a tale from my
own heart' and 'some philosophic song' – but he adds, immediately swinging back to the humble, 'Of Truth that cherishes
our daily life'. Is this indeterminacy the end at which Nature

aims, this curious and never fully clarified restlessness the ultimate confession of his poetry?

It would be hard, in that case, to think of *The Prelude* as describing the 'growth of a poet's mind'; for what the first part of book 1 records is, primarily, Wordsworth's failure to be an epic poet, a poet in the tradition of Spenser and Milton. 'Was it for this', he asks, that Nature spent all her care (269 ff.)? The first six books of *The Prelude* trace every moment of that care. There is little doubt in Wordsworth that Nature intended him for a poet. Why else that continual prediction and fostering of the spirit's autonomy from childhood on? And yet, the very moment the spirit tries to seize autonomy, to quicken like Ezekiel's self-moved chariot, Nature humbles it by an evidence of subtle supremacy, or Wordsworth humbles himself by shrinking from visionary subjects.

Wordsworth never achieves his philosophic song. *Prelude* and *Excursion* are no more than 'ante-chapels' to the 'gothic church' of his unfinished work. An unresolved antagonism between Poetry and Nature prevents him from being a sustained visionary poet in the manner of Spenser and Milton. It is a paradox, though not an unfruitful one, that Wordsworth should so scrupulously record Nature's workmanship, which prepares the soul for its independence from sense experience, yet refrain to use that independence out of respect to Nature. His greatest verse *takes its origin* in the memory of given experiences to which he is often pedantically faithful. He adheres, apparently against Nature, to natural fact. That is his secret, and our problem.

II

It might seem that the failure of poetic nerve recorded in *Prelude* 1 is simply a sign of Nature's triumph over the poet. He recognizes poetry is not prophecy or a sacramental gift. Though Wordsworth suffers a reversal, and the splendid evening shows his soul's weakness, such a conclusion is premature. Nature, for Wordsworth, is never an enemy but always a guide

or guardian whose most adverse-seeming effects are still peda-
gogy. *Prelude* I is filled with examples of Nature's unpredictable, often fearful methods. Even if we do not appeal to
further knowledge of his work, the poem's opening drama
shows only that Wordsworth cannot write poetry about Nature
as an immediate external object. That may appear to contradict what readers have valued most, his power to represent
the natural world with childhood intensity, to give it back its
soul, to awaken the mind (as Coleridge remarked) to the
lethargy-shrouded loveliness of common things. There is, however, a distinction to be made between the immediacy of
Nature and the immediacy of a poem dealing with Nature,
though they are often so close that Matthew Arnold sees
Nature herself guiding the pen in Wordsworth's hand.

Wordsworth's poetry places itself at a significant remove
from the founding experience. This is not a naïve or purely
personal fact. *The Prelude* never represents Nature simply as
an immediate or ultimate object, even where the poet's recall
is most vivid. Every incident involving Nature is propaedeutic
and relates to that 'dark Inscrutable workmanship' mentioned
by *Prelude* I 340 ff. I have suggested elsewhere how the fine
skating scene of the first book (425–63), though painted for
its own sake, to capture the animal spirits of children spurred
by a clear and frosty night, moves from vivid images of immediate life to an absolute calm which foreshadows a deeper yet
also more hidden or mediate source of life.[4] This apparent
action of Nature on itself, to convert the immediate or external
into the quietly mediate, which then unfolds a new, less
exhaustible source of life, is analogous to the action of the mind
on itself which characterizes the poet in the 1800 Preface to
Lyrical Ballads. Poetry, says Wordsworth, is the spontaneous
overflow of powerful feelings, but qualifies at once: 'It takes
its origin from emotion recollected in tranquillity: the emotion is contemplated till, by a species of reaction the tranquillity gradually disappears, and an emotion, kindred to that
which was before the subject of contemplation, is gradually
produced, and does itself actually exist in the mind.'

One process potentially results in poetry, the other in the

mind making that poetry. The two have a similar, perhaps continuous structure. Both show the passing of immediacy into something more mediate or meditative, but also its revival as a new kind of immediacy. Now this, surely, is like the basic movement of the *Prelude*'s first episode. It begins with an outburst, a 'passion' of words rising immediately from the poet like animal spirits from children, having no full external cause. Then as the moment of fervor spreads, the landscape reveals its secret pressures, blends with and overshadows the thoughts of the poet. A splendid image, finally, outspeaks the poet, just as Nature in 1 458 ff. foretells her ever calmer presence to the reflective child. Thus Nature is not an 'object' but a presence and a power; a motion and a spirit; not something to be worshiped or consumed, an immediate or ultimate principle of life, but – and here it becomes most hard to find terms that preserve the poet in the thinker – something whose immediacy, like that of a poem, is not separable from the work of perfect mediation. Wordsworth fails to celebrate his sunset because poetry is not an act of consecration and Nature not an immediate external object to be consecrated. When the external stimulus is too clearly present, the poet falls mute and corroborates Blake's strongest objection : 'Natural Objects always did and now do weaken, deaden and obliterate Imagination in Me.'[5]

A second, though chronologically earlier failure vis-à-vis the external world is related in *Prelude* VI. It occurs just before Wordsworth feels love for man begin to emerge out of his love for Nature. The poet, having finished his third year of studies at Cambridge (he is twenty years old), goes on a walking tour of France and Switzerland. It is the summer of 1790, the French Revolution has achieved its greatest success and acts as a subtle, though in the following books increasingly human, background to his concern with Nature. Setting out to cross the Alps by way of the Simplon Pass, Wordsworth and his friend are separated from their companions and try the ascent by themselves. After climbing some time and not overtaking anyone, they meet a peasant who tells them they must return to their starting point, and follow a stream down instead of further ascending, i.e., they had already crossed the Alps. Disappointed, 'For still we had hopes that pointed to the clouds', they start downward beset by a 'melancholy slackening', which, however, is soon dislodged (557–91, 617 ff.).

This simple episode stands, however, within a larger, interdependent series of events. An unexpected revelation comes almost immediately (624–40), while the whole is preceded by a parallel instance of disappointment with the natural world followed by a compensatory vision (523 ff.). In addition to this temporal structure of blankness and revelation, of the soulless image and the sudden renewed immediacy, we find an amazing instance of a past event's transtemporal thrust. The poet, after telling the story of his disappointment, is suddenly, in the very moment of composition, overpowered by a feeling of glory to which he gives expression in rapturous and almost self-obscuring lines (592 ff.). Not until the moment of composition, some fourteen years after the event, does the full motive behind his blind upward climb and subsequent melancholy slackening strike home : and it strikes so hard that Wordsworth, for the first time in his narrative, gives to the unconditioned power revealed by the extinction of the immediate external motive (his desire to cross the Alps), as by the abyss of intervenient years, the explicit name *Imagination* :

> Imagination – here the Power so called
> Through sad incompetence of human speech,
> That awful Power rose from the mind's abyss
> Like an unfathered vapour that enwraps,
> At once, some lonely traveller. I was lost;
> Halted without an effort to break through;
> But to my conscious soul I now can say –
> 'I recognize thy glory' (592–99)

Thus Wordsworth's failure vis-à-vis Nature (or its failure vis-à-vis the Poet) is doubly redeemed. After descending, and passing through a gloomy strait (VI 621 ff.), he encounters a magnificent view. And crossing, one might say, through the gloomy gulf of time, his disappointment becomes retrospectively a prophetic instance of that blindness to the external world which is the tragic, pervasive, and necessary condition of the mature poet. His failure taught him gently what now (1804) literally *blinds* him; the growing independence of Imagination from the immediate external world.

I cannot miss my way, the poet exults in the opening verses of *The Prelude*. And he cannot, as long as he respects the guidance of Nature, which leads him along a gradual *via negativa*, to make his soul more than 'a mere pensioner/On outward forms' (VI 737). It is not easy, however, to 'follow Nature'. The path, in fact, becomes so circuitous that a poet follows Nature least when he thinks to follow her most. He must pass through the gloomy strait where the external image is lost yet suddenly revived with more than original immediacy. Thus a gentle breeze, in *Prelude* I, calls forth a tempest of verse, but a splendid evening wanes into silence. A magnificent hope, in *Prelude* VI, seems to die for lack of sensuous food, but years later the simple memory of failure calls up that hope in a magnificent tempest of verse. The poet is forced to discover the autonomy of his imagination, its independence from present joy, from strong outward stimuli – but this discovery, which means a transcendence of Nature, is brought on gradually, mercifully.

The poet does not sustain the encounter with Imagination. His direct cry is broken off, replaced by an impersonal construction, '– here the Power . . .', and it is not Imagination but his 'conscious soul' he addresses directly in the following lines. What, in any case, is a soul to do with its extreme recognition? It has glimpsed the height of its freedom. At the end of this passage Wordsworth returns to the idea that the soul is halted by the light of its discovery, as a traveler by a sudden bank of mist. But the intensifying simile this time suggests not only a divorce from but also, proleptically, a return to Nature on the part of the independent soul :

> Strong in herself and in beatitude
> That hides her, like the mighty flood of Nile
> Poured from his fount of Abyssinian clouds
> To fertilise the whole Egyptian plain (613–16)

III

We are now in a position to compare the structure of all the episodes. The first (1 1 ff.) falls roughly into three parts: the spontaneous 'tempest' of verse, the quietly active grove, and the splendid evening that ends too calmly. In the skating scene of book I, the splendid silence of a winter evening, set off by the clear strokes of a clock, increases to a tumult of reciprocal sounds, which yield in turn to a vision of a silently sustaining power. In the one case we go from Poetry to Nature, in the other from Nature to a more deeply mediated conception of Nature. Thus, at the beginning of his narrative, Wordsworth prefers to plunge into *medias res*, where the *res* is Poetry, or Nature only in so far as it has guided the poet to a height whence he must find his own way.

The major episode of book VI, the encounter with Imagination, may also be regarded as falling into three parts. Its first term is neither Nature nor Poetry. It is, rather, Imagination in embryo – muted yet strengthened by Nature's inadequacies. Though the poet's memory of Nature's past intimacy reaches its height, her presences are no longer intimate. Blankness and utter dark vacillate before his eyes, relieved only occasionally by sights of 'milder magnificence'. At first the vine-clad hills of Burgundy, the valley of the Saône, and later of the Rhône, lead him and his friend gently on; but soon the quiet river, the church spires and bells, disappear, and they enter the solitary precincts of the Alps. Nature now appears in turn excessive or null; sublimity and profound calm, known from earliest childhood, revolve in their intensity, are too awe-ful or too calm. A human response is scarcely possible in the face of such 'ungrateful' vicissitude.

Yet this is the very time of the active Imagination's birth-pangs. 'The poet's soul was with me', Wordsworth writes at the beginning of the book, and later notes, in his curiously matter-of-fact, yet absolutely unrevealing fashion, that dejection itself would often lead him on to pleasurable thoughts. Still deeper than such dejection, a 'stern mood, an under-thirst/Of vigour' (558 ff.) makes itself felt and produces a special sort of sadness; and now, in order to throw light on the nature of that sadness, the 'melancholy slackening' which ensues on the nature of the peasant's words, he tells the incident of his crossing the Alps.

The first part of the tryptich, then, illustrates a critical stage in the history of the poet's Imagination. The stern mood can only be Wordsworth's premonition of spiritual autonomy, of independence from the immediacy of sense experience, fostered in him by Nature since earliest childhood. We know with some precision how this mood manifests itself. In *Prelude* II 312 ff., it is described as 'an obscure sense/Of possible sublimity' for which the soul, remembering *how* it felt but not *what* it felt, continually aspires to find a new content. The element of obscurity, therefore, is inseparable from the soul's capacity of growth; it is obscurity that both feeds the soul and vexes it toward self-dependence. The divine yet natural pasturage becomes viewless; the soul cannot easily find the immediate external source from which it used to drink the visionary power; and, while dim memories of passionate commerce with external things drive it more than ever to the natural world, this world makes itself more than ever inscrutable. The travelers' separation from their guides, then that of the road from the stream (568 ff.), and finally their trouble with the peasant's words, that have to be 'translated', all subtly express the soul's desire for a world 'beyond'. Yet only when poet, brook, and road are once again 'fellow-travellers' (622), when Wordsworth holds on to Nature, does that reveal (a Proteus in the grasp of the hero) its prophecy.

With this we come to what was, originally, the second part of the adventure: the dislodgement of melancholy and the gloomy strait's 'Characters of the great Apocalypse' (617–40). In its temporal rather than narrative sequence, therefore, the episode has only two parts. The first term, the moment of natural immediacy, is omitted; we go straight to the second term, the inscrutability of an external image, which leads via the gloomy strait to an apocalyptic image. Yet, as if this pattern demanded a substitute third term, Wordsworth's tribute to

'Imagination' severs the original temporal sequence and fore-
stalls Nature's exhibition to the bodily eye with an ecstatic
excursus on the inner eye.

In the 1805 *Prelude* the transition from the poet narrating
the past, gazing like a traveler into the mind's abyss, to the poet
gripped by something rising unexpectedly from that abyss, is
still respected in cursory fashion (526); but the 1850 *Prelude*,
as if the poet labored under a 'strong confusion', solders past
and present so well that the circuitous series of events seems
immediately to evoke 'Imagination'. The apocalypse of the
gloomy strait loses, in any case, the character of a *terminal*
experience and appears as an anagogical device, now trans-
cended. For the Imagination, at the time of writing, is called
forth by the barely scrutable, not by the splendid image. This
(momentary) displacement of emphasis is the more effective
in that the style of lines 617 ff., and the very characters of the
apocalypse, suggest that the hiding places of power cannot be
localized in Nature.

Thus the three parts (henceforth vi-*a*, vi-*b*, and vi-*c*,)
trace the mind's growth toward independence from the immediate external world. The measure of that independence is
'Imagination', and to define what Wordsworth means by this
word is to add a sad incompetence of the interpreter to that
of the poet. But we see that the mind must pass through a
stage where it experiences Imagination as a power separate
from Nature, that the poet must come to think and feel by his
own choice or from the structure of his own mind.[6]

vi-*a* (557–91) shows the young poet still dependent on the
immediacy of the external world. Imagination secretly frus-
trates that dependence, yet its victory dooms more than the
external world. For its blindness toward Nature is accompanied by a blindness toward itself.

vi-*b* (592–616) gives an example of thought or feeling that
came from the poet's mind without immediate external excitement. There remains, of course, the memory of vi-*a*, and vi-*a*
tells of an experience with an external, though no longer
immediate, world. From the perspective of vi-*b*, however, that
world is not even external. The poet recognizes that the power

he has looked for in the world outside was really within and frustrating his search. The shock of recognition then feeds the very blindness toward the external world which produced that shock.

In vi-*c* (617–40) the landscape is once more an immediate external object of experience. The mind cannot separate in it what it most desired to see and what it sees bodily. It is a moment of apocalypse, in which the poet sees not as in a glass, darkly, but face to face. Thus, vi-*c* magnifies subtle details of vi-*a* and *seems* to actualize figurative details of vi-*b*.[7] The matter-of-fact interplay of quick and lingering movement, of up-and-down perplexities in the ascent (562–85) reappears in larger letters; while the interchanges of light and darkness, of cloud and cloudlessness, of rising like a vapor from the abyss and pouring like a flood from heaven have entered the landscape almost bodily. The gloomy strait also participates in this actualization. It is revealed as the secret middle term which leads from the barely scrutable presence of Nature to its resurrected image. The travelers who move freely with or against the terrain, hurrying upward, pacing downward, perplexed at the crossing, are now led narrowly by the pass as if it were their rediscovered guide.

IV

The Prelude, as a history of a poet's mind, foresees the time when the 'Characters of the great Apocalypse' will be intuited without the medium of Nature. The time approaches even as the poet writes and occasionally cuts across his narrative, the Imagination rising up, as in book vi, 'Before the eye and progress of my Song' (1805). This expression, so rich when taken literally yet so conventional when taken as a simple figure, Wordsworth replaced in the 1850 version, but did not lose sight of. It suggests that the Imagination forestalled Nature, so that the very 'eye' of the song, trained on a temporal sequence with the vision in the strait as its last term, was disrupted, obscured. The poet, in both versions, says that he was halted and could not or did not make any effort to 'break through'.

If this has an intent more specific than to convey abstractly the Imagination's power – if, in other words, the effect the Imagination has tells us something specific about the power behind that effect – then the poet was momentarily forced to deny Nature the magnificence of self-representation it had shown in the gloomy strait and to attribute that instead to Imagination, whose interposition (vi-*b*) proves it to be a power more independent of time and place than Nature, and so a better type 'Of first, and last, and midst, and without end' (640).

In vi-*b* something that happens during composition enters the poem as a new biographical event. Wordsworth has just described his disappointment (vi-*a*) and turns in anticipation to Nature's compensatory finale (vi-*c*). He is about to respect the original temporal sequence, 'the eye and progress' of his song. But as he looks forward, in the moment of composition, from blankness toward revelation, a new insight cuts him off from the latter. The original disappointment is seen not as a test, or as a prelude to magnificence, but as a revelation in itself. It suddenly reveals a power that worked against Nature in order to be recognized. The song's progress comes to a halt because the poet is led beyond Nature. Unless the temporal, which is also the natural, order be respected by the poet, his song, at least as narrative, must cease. Here Imagination, not Nature (1 96), defeats Poetry.

This conclusion may be checked by comparing the versions of 1805 and 1850. The latter replaces 'Before the eye and progress of my Song' with a more direct metaphorical transposition. Imagination is said to rise from the mind's abyss 'Like an unfathered vapour that enwraps,/At once, some lonely traveller'. The (literal) traveler of 1790 becomes the (mental) traveler at the moment of composition. And though one Shakespearean doublet has disappeared, another implicitly takes its place : does not Imagination rise from 'the dark backward and abysm of time' (*The Tempest*, 1 ii 50)? The result, in any case, is a disorientation of time added to that of way; an apocalyptic moment in which past and future overtake the present; and the poet, cut off from Nature by Imagination, is, in an absolute sense, lonely.

The last stage of book vi as a progress poem has been reached. The travelers of vi-*a* had already left behind their native land, the public rejoicing of France, rivers, hills, and spires; they have separated from their guide and, finally, from the unbridged mountain stream. Now Imagination separates the poet from all else, human companionship, the immediate scene, the remembered scene. The end of the natural *via negativa* is near. There is no more 'eye and progress': the invisible progress of vi-*a* reveals itself now as a progress independent of visible ends, engendered by the desire for an 'invisible world' – the substance of things hoped for, the evidence of things not seen. Wordsworth descants on the Pauline definition of faith :

> in such strength
> Of usurpation, when the light of sense
> Goes out, but with a flash that has revealed
> The invisible world, doth greatness make abode,
> There harbours; whether we be young or old,
> Our destiny, our being's heart and home,
> Is with infinitude, and only there;
> With hope it is, hope that can never die,
> Effort, and expectation, and desire,
> And something evermore about to be (599–608)

If there is any further possibility of progress for the enwrapped and rapt poet, it is that of song itself, no longer subordinate to the mimetic function, the experience faithfully traced to this height. The poet is a traveler in so far as he must respect Nature's past guidance and retrace his route. He did come, after all, to an important instance of bodily vision. The way is the song. But the song all the time strives to become the way. And when this happens, when the song seems to capture the initiative, in such supreme moments of poetry as vi-*b* or even vi-*c*, the way is lost. Nature's apocalypse shows 'Winds thwarting winds, bewildered and forlorn', destroys the concept of the linear path, and also severs finally the 'eye' from the 'progress'.[8]

In vi-*c*, however, Nature still stands over and against the poet; he is yet the observer, the eighteenth-century gentleman admiring new manifestations of the sublime, even if the 'lo!' or 'mark!' is suppressed. He moves haltingly, but he moves; and the style of the passage emphasizes continuities. Yet with the Imagination athwart there is no movement, no looking before and after. The song itself must be the way, though the way of a blinded man, who admits 'I was lost'. When he *speaks* once more to his conscious soul (598), he can only recognize that 'infinitude' is not at the end of the path but in a crossing and a losing of the way, by which a power transcending all single ways guides the traveler to itself.

The poet's desire to cross the Alps may already imply a wish to overcome Nature. Yet the stern mood of vi-*a* (Imagination not yet recognized as a power distinct from Nature) helps the poet to gain more than this – its own – end. It gains the poet's end *imperceptibly* in order to defeat the very idea of an end as the motive power. The travelers' *melancholy* slackening, when they think the end attained, proves it was more than a specific end (here the crossing of the Alps) which moved them. And in vi-*c* Nature itself affirms this lesson. The travelers find a vision which both clarifies the idea by which they were moved and destroys it as the idea of an end – specifically the idea of Nature as an end. It is, rather, the idea of something 'without end' and, specifically, *the idea of Nature itself teaching the travelers to transcend Nature*. The apocalypse is a picture of a self-thwarting march and countermarch of elements, a divine mockery of the concept of the Single Way. Nature seems to have guided the travelers to a point where they see the power which causes it to move and be moving. This power, when distinct from Nature (as in vi-*b*), is called Imagination. But, when thus distinct, when unmediated, it blinds speech and extinguishes the light of the senses. The unfathered vapor, as it shrouds the poet's eye, also shrouds the eye of his song, whose tenor is Nature guiding and fostering the power of song.

Wordsworth has discovered the hidden guide which moved him by means of Nature as Beatrice moves Dante by means of Vergil. It is not Nature as such but Nature indistinguishably blended with Imagination which compels the poet along a *via naturaliter negativa.* Yet, if vi-*b* prophesies against the world of sense experience, Wordsworth's affection and point of view remain unchanged. After a cloudburst of passionate verses he returns to the pedestrian attitude of ·1790, when the external world and not imagination appeared as his guide ('Our journey we renewed,/Led by the stream', etc.). For, with the exception of vi-*b*, Imagination never moves the poet directly, but always *sub specie naturae*. The childhood 'visitings of imaginative power' depicted in books i and xii also appeared in the guise or disguise of Nature. Wordsworth's journey as a poet can only continue with eyes, but the Imagination experienced as a power distinct from Nature opens his eyes by putting them out. Thus, Wordsworth does not adhere to Nature because of natural fact, but despite it and because of human and poetic fact. Imagination is not called an awe-ful power for nothing.

SOURCE : *Modern Philology*, LIX (Feb 1962) 214–24.

NOTES

Seven footnotes in the original text are here deleted, and two abbreviated.

1. See *Blake, Coleridge, Wordsworth, Lamb, etc., being Selections from the Remains of Henry Crabb Robinson,* ed. Edith J. Morley (Manchester, 1932) pp. 5 and 15.
2. Quotations, unless otherwise stated, are from the 1850 text and the 1926 edition. . . .
3. Emancipated – but through exile. See *Prelude,* I 14 and 16–18. . . .
4. *The Unmediated Vision* (New Haven, 1954) pp. 17–20.
5. Marginalia to Wordsworth's poems. Northrop Frye, *Selected Poetry and Prose of William Blake* (New York : Modern Library ed.) p. 455. I may venture the opinion that Wordsworth, at the beginning of *The Prelude,* goes back to Nature, not to increase his chances of sensation, but rather to emancipate his mind from immediate external excitements, the 'gross and violent stimulants' (1800 Preface) of the city he leaves behind him.

6. Cf. Preface to *Lyrical Ballads* (1802) : '[The Poet] has acquired a greater readiness and power in expressing . . . especially those thoughts and feelings which, by his own choice, or from the structure of his own mind, arise in him without immediate external excitement. . . .'

7. vi–*b* was composed after vi–*c*, so that while the transference of images goes *structurally* from vi-*b* to vi-*c*, *chronologically* the order is reversed.

8. Cf. *The Unmediated Vision*, pp. 129–32.

W. J. Harvey

VISION AND MEDIUM IN
THE PRELUDE (1966)

I do not wish to say that there is a single Wordsworthian style in *The Prelude*, any more than that there is a single Miltonic style in *Paradise Lost*. In both poets an apparent continuity and sameness in the medium masks an astonishing variety of styles. But granted this, I think we can fairly take *The Prelude*, I 1–54, as representative of staple Wordsworthian blank verse, of the poet in his middle-flight, writing the kind of poetry that must sustain him throughout his great work. It is a verse that must accommodate the prosaic but not lapse too obviously or for too long into mere prosiness. It must be supple and flexible enough to act, as it were, like a springboard from which the poet can launch into those climactic moments of emotional crisis or of heightened vision that demand an intensified response in his style. Without such flexibility these crises will seem isolated or contrived, will savour merely of the purple patch.

In one important sense, of course, this passage is untypical. It is the very opening of *The Prelude* and must therefore fulfil certain functions not demanded of other passages. The right note must be struck at the outset; hence, for example, the unusual number of Miltonic echoes. These should not surprise us since we know from other sources – notably from *The Recluse* fragment – that Wordsworth invited comparison with his predecessor. In this passage he is clearly concerned to avoid any kind of formal epic invocation, yet the submerged Miltonic echoes assert without presumption the dignity of his subject and look forward to that note of bardic dedication so often struck later in the poem. Such tact is necessary in a poem which is so personal, so essentially a voyage to the interior. The poet as poet must take up a position psychologically intimate with, yet aesthetically distant from, himself as man. This he must do without seeming pompously egocentric or clinically self-detached, and the Miltonic references – there but disguised – seem to me to help him achieve this difficult poise.

One echo, indeed, is hardly disguised; even the most casual reader must recognize in

> The earth is all before me : with a heart
> Joyous, nor scar'd at its own liberty,
> I look about, and should the guide I chuse
> Be nothing better than a wandering cloud,
> I cannot miss my way.

an allusion to Adam and Eve :

> The World was all before them, where to choose
> Thir place of rest, and Providence thir guide :
> They hand in hand with wandring steps and slow,
> Through Eden took their solitarie way.
>
> (*Paradise Lost*, XII 646–9)

Paradise Lost ends where *The Prelude* begins. Adam and Eve have lost their Paradise; Wordsworth is about to enter his Paradise regained. Their guide is Divine Providence; his is the providence of Nature, 'a wandering cloud . . . a twig or any floating thing'. This natural providence is, of course, given strong religious overtones. The note struck by the '*blessing* in this gentle breeze' is continued through 'miraculous gift . . . dedicate . . . consecrate : . . . the sweet breath of Heaven' to conclude in 'The holy life of music and of verse'. But though Nature restores to Wordsworth a paradise within him, happier far, he, too, suffers a fall from innocence to experience, from imagination to Godwinian rationalism. For Wordsworth, as for his parodist, Shelley, 'Hell is a city much like London' and so at the outset he celebrates his release :

> O welcome Messenger ! O welcome Friend !
> A captive greets thee, coming from a house

> Of bondage, from yon City's walls set free,
> A prison where he hath been long immured.

This again recalls a famous passage from *Paradise Lost* in which Satan in the Garden of Eden is described, the passage beginning

> As one who long in populous city pent
> Where Houses thick and Sewers annoy the air . . .
> (*Paradise Lost*, ix 444 ff.)

But it also invokes yet another Miltonic character; we may remember Samson's opening lines:

> A little onward lend thy guiding hand
> To these dark steps, a little further on;
> For yonder bank hath choice of Sun or shade,
> There I am wont to sit, where any chance
> Relieves me from my task of servile toil,
> Daily in the common prison else enjoyn'd me,
> Where I a prisoner chain'd, scarce freely draw
> The air imprison'd also, close and damp,
> Unwholsom draught : but here I feel amends,
> The breath of Heav'n fresh-blowing, pure and sweet,
> With day-spring born : here leave me to respire.
> (*Samson Agonistes*, 1–11)

Wordsworth is no longer a 'captive' in 'bondage'; he is already

> from yon City's walls set free
> A prison where he hath been long immured.

and, like Samson, he too feels 'the sweet breath of Heaven'. In *Samson Agonistes* we are, I think, entitled to feel 'the breath of Heav'n fresh-blowing' as a poetic anticipation of that other breath of Heaven which will revive Samson; under that divine inspiration he will change from patient to agent and will move forward to heroic action. So for Wordsworth the breath of nature portends that internal breeze of poetic inspiration; he, too, will move forward to his dedicated task, enjoying

                              the hope
            Of active days, of dignity and thought,
            Of prowess in an honourable field.

These Miltonic echoes on which I have so laboriously commented have far more than a purely local importance in *The
Prelude*, but let me return for the moment to their immediate
context. As I have said, one of their functions is to signal to us
that while this is not a poem cast in the traditional epic mould,
yet it is still a poem of epic seriousness, commanding responses
appropriate to that kind of verse. But, beyond this such echoes
play their part in contributing to the general density and
weight of Wordsworth's poetry. Wordsworth is frequently
austere; he is sometimes prosaic; but he is hardly ever thin.

Consider for a moment the sheer technical difficulties of
writing a very long poem in blank verse. It must, first of all,
have élan and impetus; it must carry us along. This implies
that local complexity must be subdued, if by complexity we
mean the sort of thing we find in Donne or Hopkins. We may
want to read slowly and reflectively but we also want to read
continuously; we do not want to stop and unravel or analyse
in depth; hence too much local richness of texture would soon
clog the overall movement. But too *little* local richness and we
shall sink; the motive for reading on will be lost; hence we wish
not only to feel carried forward but also to feel buoyed up. We
must have the reassurance of mass beneath momentum, the
feeling that if we *did* choose to stop and analyse the verse in
depth, then we would be amply rewarded. Dr Johnson
expressed the difficulty in his own characteristic way. 'If blank
verse be not tumid and gorgeous, it is crippled prose', he
wrote in the *Life of Somerville*, and amplified this in the *Life
of Akenside* :

> The exemption which blank verse affords from the necessity
> of closing the sense with the couplet betrays luxuriant and
> active minds into such self-indulgence, that they pile image
> upon image, ornament upon ornament, and are not easily
> persuaded to close the sense at all. Blank verse will there-

fore, I fear, be too often found in description exuberant, in argument loquacious, and in narration tiresome.

I think it fair to take Milton and Wordsworth, at their weakest, as representing the opposing dangers noted by Johnson; Milton tends to 'the tumid and gorgeous', Wordsworth to 'crippled prose'. But it is better to examine these poets at their best, to see how they combine mass and momentum, buoyancy and impetus, in such a way as to sail triumphantly through Johnson's Scylla and Charybdis.

One obvious way in which Milton enriches his verse is by his use of allusion and reference. These are nearly always functional, rarely sonorous ornaments; even if we are not always sufficiently erudite to appreciate how they extend his meaning we still feel that something is at work beneath the surface of his verse. This is a prop on which Wordsworth rarely leans though, I have suggested, the Miltonic echoes in his opening passage have something of the same status. Milton has a belated Elizabethan's taste for word-play and profuse rhetorical device. Again, Wordsworth is comparatively innocent of such artifice, though more felicitous and delicate than most people suppose. Thus in this passage, when he feels within himself

> A corresponding mild creative breeze,

his interior life both corresponds and co-responds with external nature. But what Wordsworth does share with Milton is something that I can only call a high level of semantic density. By this I do not mean primarily an exploitation of the connotations and overtones of words, though this is certainly part of it. I have more in mind the way in which Milton will often allow the root meaning of his words to lie side by side with the accretions of meaning they have historically acquired. Something of the same sort happens with Wordsworth and it is important to my argument that such diction, however abstract, generally retains something of its original physical signification. The most obvious instance in the present passage is *redundant* which certainly does not here mean 'unnecessary' nor even merely 'copious' or 'excessive' but in its context also carries the sense of an upsurging wave. But there are many other examples. *Vexing* has as part of its meaning 'to agitate physically', *tiresome* has the sense of 'physically fatiguing'; *enfranchisement* does not merely repeat *free* but narrows down the general sense of that word to 'release from confinement or servitude'. Even in that quintessentially Wordsworthian line,

> Trances of thought and mountings of the mind

I think it is possible that *trances* and *mountings* have for Wordsworth a greater physical emphasis than they do for us.

If these things help to create mass, what about momentum? How does the verse carry us forward? What we have to attend to here, I suspect, is not simply the rhythm but rather the poet's control of syntax. If Milton is complicated, Wordsworth is simple; if Milton propels us forward by the Latinate convolutions of his paragraphs then Wordsworth's sentences, even when they seem long, are usually analysable into a number of short clauses, fairly loosely linked. If Milton is mainly periodic, then Wordsworth is mainly linear in his structure. The danger of this style is that it may sometimes halt or limp; its virtue lies in its great flexibility. Let me illustrate from a passage which comes a little later in book I of *The Prelude*:

> Thus occupied in mind, I linger'd here
> Contented, nor rose up until the sun
> Had almost touch'd the horizon, bidding then
> A farewell to the City left behind,
> Even with the chance equipment of that hour
> I journey'd towards the vale that I had chosen.
>
> (95–100)

The apparent opposition here created points in fact to a deeper similarity between the poet and his landscape. The rising of the man and the setting of the sun have almost equal status; both seem equally *natural* events. Although, if we read it carefully, it is clear that 'bidding . . . farewell' belongs to the human traveller, the syntax is so fluid that the sense of the Sun 'bidding . . . farewell' to the city is also allowed into the passage, at least as a collateral possibility. The syntax thus enacts one of the great themes of the poem, the interaction of internal and external, of nature and the human mind. The mode of connection here is a common feature of Wordsworthian syntax; we have a number of clauses, each in themselves fairly simple, relating to a central verb. This is just one way of suggesting the unity and interdependence of things and it is done not by images, not by comparison of disparate attributes, but by making things share in a common activity. The emphasis on the verb conveys the essential dynamism of the process. Wordsworth tells us in *The Recluse* that

> My voice proclaims
> How exquisitely the individual Mind
> (And the progressive powers perhaps no less
> Of the whole species) to the external World
> Is fitted – and how exquisitely too –
> Theme this but little heard of among men –
> The external world is fitted to the Mind,
> And the creation (by no lower name
> Can it be called) which they with blended might
> Accomplish – this is our high argument.
>   (*The Recluse*, 834–43)

With this emphatic statement of his theme in mind, let us return to the opening passage of *The Prelude* to see how far our initial analysis is confirmed or needs extension. The most obvious mode of interconnection – that of Ruskin's 'pathetic fallacy' – is obviously there; the breeze 'seems half-conscious of the joy it gives'. But the simple bestowal of human attributes is complicated by the rest of the passage; the humanized breeze of the opening lines modulates into Wordsworth's sense of freedom – 'I breathe again' – reverts back to the literal 'sweet breath of Heaven' and finally turns into 'the corresponding mild creative breeze' which is 'felt within'. If Wordsworth bestows human attributes on external nature, then far more important is his transference of natural attributes to the human mind. This is no self-conscious, 'literary' example of the pathetic fallacy; it is rather a continuous process, a genuine communion of mind and nature. Indeed, it is the interior breeze that is most elaborated as it

> travelled gently on
> O'er things which it had made.

Notice the implications of that innocent word, *on* – how it implies a whole landscape of the mind across which the wind of inspiration travels.

De Quincey, quoting the lines:

> a gentle shock of mild surprise
> Has carried far into his heart the voice
> Of mountain torrents ...

once commented:

> This very expression 'far' by which space and its infinities are attributed to the human mind, and to its capacities of re-echoing the sublimities of nature, has always struck me as with a flash of sublime revelation.[1]

We have a less dramatic instance of precisely the same thing in these opening lines of *The Prelude*. When I speak of 'the landscape of the mind' I am converting into metaphor something that would for Wordsworth be very nearly literal truth. Ever since De Quincey, critics have commented on the way in which Wordsworth imparts an unusual palpability and solidity to the life of the mind, how there is a real configuration – a geography almost – in his description of his interior world. It is because of this that I stressed earlier the submerged physical significance of his apparently abstract diction. And it provides another reason for that relative austerity of texture that I mentioned earlier. Wordsworth hardly ever indulges in the minute, sensuous precision of a Tennyson, since this might lead us to think of nature as something merely external and objective; it would detract attention from

> The mind of Man,
> My haunt, and the main region of my song.
>
> *(The Recluse,* 812–13)

Wordsworth's account of his fall from innocence is partly in terms of a contrast between country and city, partly in terms of succumbing to Godwinian rationalism, partly in terms of frustrated revolutionary ideals. But in book xi he adds another reason :

> The state to which I now allude was one
> In which the eye was master of the heart,
> When that which is in every stage of life
> The most despotic of our senses gain'd
> Such strength in me as often held my mind
> In absolute dominion. (171–6)

Luxuriant description would therefore betray him to the despotism of his senses whereas his true talent is fulfilled only when, like the protagonist of *Samson Agonistes*, he moves from sight to insight. Just as Wordsworth endows his interior landscape with solidity, extension and contour, so conversely he tends to stress the basic geometry of external nature, to concentrate on the primary properties of mass and rough form, the essential configuration which underlies the accidents of scenic detail. This is no defect in him; he had a keen eye for significant detail which he chose to reserve for exceptional or climactic moments in the poem.

This austerity of texture, this distinctive blend of generality and solidity, means that there are relatively few striking or elaborate images in *The Prelude*. This again is from choice and not from deficiency : Wordsworth could, when he wished, establish a simile as detailed and controlled as anything in Milton or a metaphor as compressed and daring as anything in Donne. Some of the reasons for this austerity I have already suggested but the basic reason, I believe, is because he takes literally what most of us would take metaphorically. The result is a continuous pressure of unobtrusive analogy – analogy is not the right word but there is really no critical term

for what I mean. It is, if you like, a continuous traffic across
the boundaries separating the literal from the metaphorical.
If we were to think of this traffic as though it were *merely*
metaphorical, then we would have to say that Wordsworth
was content with clichés. But because of this continual imaginative pressure what might have been cliché turns into something fresh and individual.

What, for example, could be more trite than the idea of life
as a journey? Yet this is the controlling metaphor of the opening passage – perhaps, indeed, of *The Prelude* as a whole.
Wordsworth reinvigorates this commonplace in a number of
ways. First, and least successfully, by another of those epic
echoes; this time, surely, not of *Paradise Lost* but of the
Odyssey.

Wordsworth hopes that he :

> May quit the tiresome sea and dwell on shore,
> If not a settler on the soil, at least
> To drink wild water and to pluck green Herbs
> And gather fruits fresh from their native bough.

This *may* carry a further meaning in that the green herbs and
fresh fruits are perhaps emblems of the poem he wishes to
write; it is just possible that we may again recall Milton :

> Yet once more, O ye laurels, and once more
> Ye myrtles brown, with Ivy never-sear,
> I come to pluck your berries harsh and crude,
> And with forc'd fingers rude,
> Shatter your leaves before the mellowing year.
>
> <div align="right">(<i>Lycidas,</i> 1–5)</div>

Where Milton is compelled to violate the rhythm of the
seasons, Wordsworth will gather a natural harvest : he feels
himself *ripe* for his poem. But this is mere conjecture in the
margin of the poem; far more important is the way the metaphor is rooted in fact. Wordsworth is indeed beginning an
actual journey; if this had not been firmly established on the
literal level, metaphorical extension would have been impossible. This extension goes in three related directions. Words-

worth is to make a journey into his poem and a journey
forwards – and backwards – in time. In both senses we car₁ see
how firmly though unobtrusively he relates metaphor to literal
circumstance and how in both instances he assimilates himself
to Nature. For in both cases Nature will be his guide and it is
Nature which links the journey into poetry and the journey in
time to the third extension of the metaphor – the journey
across the interior landscape of his soul.

> Long months of ease and undisturb'd delight
> Are mine in prospect; whither shall I turn
> By road or pathway or through open field,
> Or shall a twig or any floating thing
> Upon the river, point me out my course?

One notices how easily, how naturally, the course of his life
stems from the course of the river. But the key-word in the
passage is *prospect*. The obvious sense is of course 'expectation
or a consideration of what the future holds for him' but it also
has the sense of 'an extensive or commanding view of the landscape'. Thus within the one word – and without any sense of
mere word-play – Wordsworth reconciles space and time,
relates the actual landscape to the interior landscape. Across
both of these he will make his journey and the result will be
his poem. *The Prelude* is very much a poem of discovery, of
exploration both of the self and of one's true poetic theme; the
metaphor of the journey is thus particularly appropriate.

To sum up, then, the argument so far; our analysis of
Wordsworthian blank verse has shown it to be apparently
simple and austere but actually of a surprising richness beneath
the surface. We have examined the function of various echoes,
the potency of certain words, the fluidity of the syntax and the
ramifications of the metaphor. Certain claims have been made
for the medium : that it combines buoyancy and impetus in a
way appropriate to a long poem, that it reflects or enacts the
interchange between Mind and Nature, and that it provides a
context in which moments of intensity may be related to the
ordinary world.

But a context for *what*, precisely? And in what ways does

the opening anticipate the rest of the poem? To answer these questions I must hurry you forward to book XI, the book entitled 'Imagination and Taste, how Impaired and Restored'. . . . It is a natural enough stopping point since here the poem completes one of its great imaginative sweeps, bringing us back to the precise point of time from which we started in book I. Most of the details of that opening passage are explicitly recalled; we have again the brook, the grove, the 'breezes and soft airs'. But we return with a difference for now we have behind us the whole weight of the poem, the whole story of Wordsworth's Fall. As he himself says :

> Long time hath Man's unhappiness and guilt
> Detain'd us; with what dismal sights beset
> For the outward view, and inwardly oppress'd
> With sorrow, disappointment, vexing thoughts,
> Confusion of opinion, zeal decay'd,
> And lastly, utter loss of hope itself,
> And things to hope for. (*The Prelude,* XI 1–7)

In this perspective certain features of the opening passage now become clearer. We now know what he meant by

> That burthen of my own unnatural self

and what seemed a slightly awkward allusion to the *Odyssey* is now expanded, clarified and made more relevant.

>   What avail'd,
> When Spells forbade the Voyager to land,
> The fragrance which did ever and anon
> Give notice of the Shore, from arbours breathed
> Of blessed sentiment and fearless love?
> What did such sweet remembrances avail,
> Perfidious then, as seem'd, what serv'd they then?
> My business was upon the barren sea,
> My errand was to sail to other coasts.
>   (*The Prelude,* XI 48–56)

We have been with Wordsworth on his spiritual Odyssey; we know now – as we did not in book I – what he means.

After this recollection of book 1, and after analysing his lapse from true communion with Nature in terms that I have already suggested, Wordsworth celebrates the restoration of Imagination with this general statement :

> There are in our existence spots of time,
> Which with distinct pre-eminence retain
> A vivifying Virtue, whence, depress'd
> By false opinion and contentious thought,
> Or aught of heavier or more deadly weight,
> In trivial occupations, and the round
> Of ordinary intercourse, our minds
> Are nourished and invisibly repair'd,
> A virtue by which pleasure is enhanced
> That penetrates, enables us to mount
> When high, more high, and lifts us up when fallen.
> This efficacious spirit chiefly lurks
> Among those passages of life in which
> We have had deepest feeling that the mind
> Is lord and master, and that outward sense
> Is but the obedient servant of her will.
> Such moments worthy of all gratitude,
> Are scattered everywhere, taking their date
> From our first childhood; in our childhood even
> Perhaps are most conspicuous. (*The Prelude,* xi 258–77)

It is a pity that Wordsworth's most detailed statement of this central theme should be in such relatively undistinguished verse. Something can be done for the passage, I suppose, if we put full stress on Wordsworth's geography of the mind and on the way in which he treats time in terms of space. The 'spots of time' with their 'distinct pre-eminence' then become not merely moments remembered but mountains standing out in the landscape of the imagination. And it is, of course, those imaginative peaks, so carefully described, so intensely recaptured, that we take away with us when we close *The Prelude.* We remember the boy birdnesting, the boy stealing the boat and rowing on the lake, we remember Wordsworth crossing the Alps, the hill with the beacon on its summit and the girl fighting the wind; above all we remember the ascent of Snowdon in the concluding Book. It is significant how often these imaginative peaks are associated with literal mountains in the poem; for this reason I have allowed the abstract phrase 'spots of time' greater concreteness and metaphorical weight than it will perhaps bear.

Though these passages are what most of us remember from *The Prelude* it would be quite wrong to take them in isolation from the rest of the poem. Mountains are only mountains because lowlands also exist; so these 'spots of time' have 'distinct pre-eminence' only because they stand out from the world of

> trivial occupations, and the round
> Of ordinary intercourse.

In this Wordsworth is true to the nature of all human experience. Although life is so various that any categories we may create to describe it will inevitably be too narrow and rigid or too broad and imprecise, we do surely feel a contrast between that large part of our experience which is mundane, prosaic, commonplace, and that small part which is intense, extreme or in some other way abnormally significant. We know, of course, in how many different ways these two kinds of experience can interact. Sometimes they seem to lie side by side within our split selves, so that while part of us is dazed by joy or grief another part of us continues evenly in its quotidian routine. Sometimes, again, it is only the perspective of memory which gives a moment its significance within the context of our mundane lives. Mundane context there must be if the moment is to have any significance at all and to discover that significance we have to relate these two kinds of experience. That is what Wordsworth is trying to do; his poetry is, above all, poetry of discovery and relation.

This process has been finely described by Professor Lindenberger and I gratefully abstract several sentences from his study of *The Prelude*. 'The visionary experiences recorded in the poem', he says, 'generally begin with a down-to-earth, often prosaic statement closely rooted in the world of ordinary perception. . . . From here on there is a steady probing inward.

... Throughout we are aware of a probing towards something, a forward movement broken at frequent intervals by shifts into new directions of thought. ... The probing, moreover, is constantly interrupted by qualifications and rhetorical backtracking. . . . In this recapturing the mind's struggle for expression of the inexpressible, Wordsworth stands apart from such visionaries as Boehme, or the Blake of the prophetic books, who set down their visions directly, without creating the rhetorical bridge from the observable world of the reader to the new world to be uncovered.'[2]

Rhetorical bridge there must be, and this is built – as I have tried to show – by Wordsworth's characteristic use of a blankverse flexible yet massive, austere yet richly potent. While there is a building up from common experience to those 'spots of time', these themselves vary in quality and in relation to our prosaic world. Some are indeed analogous to our own experience but some are extreme, remote from us by virtue of their intensity and inwardness. Some of them are mainly psychological and explicable in terms of their human origin, but some of them point to transcendental or mystical experience, to those moments when

> the light of sense
> Goes out in flashes that have shown to us
> The invisible world. (*The Prelude*, VI 534–6)

Precise categories are not possible; I believe that Wordsworth characteristically works in an area which points both ways, a shadowy region where psychological and metaphysical meet. Even in what seems to be predominantly psychological – the stolen boat episode, for example – there is some metaphysical shadowing. But the important thing is that both areas are united in that they issue from and return to some ordinary human experience. Wordsworth is, above all, interested in the consequences of such 'spots of time'; they are usually embodied in a context of moral reflection; how, he asks in effect, do these visionary moments diffuse themselves in the great general course of human life? No poet, I believe, has asked the question more strenuously; no poet can offer us a more satisfying answer.

We can better estimate the full measure of Wordsworth's achievement if we compare him with another poet much concerned with the same themes of time, of memory and of visionary experience. I think Mr Eliot's *Four Quartets* a very good poem, a great poem. And, of course, if we compare it with *The Prelude*, we must take account of differences of ambition, scale and amplitude. But granted this, do we not feel in the *Four Quartets* a certain narrowness and exclusiveness, a certain thinness in the texture of ordinary life? How easily, for example, is the London of Eliot's poem converted into symbol or used merely as a starting point of meditation; how various and vivacious by contrast is Wordsworth's description of London. Whatever moral Wordsworth educes from the city, whatever symbolic weight it carries, our primary impression is of a delighted and energetic rendering of London for its own sake. Again – to focus unfairly on a mere detail – consider one of Eliot's many attempts to define by negation the quality of his 'spots of time':

> The moments of happiness – not the sense of well-being,
> Fruition, fulfilment, security or affection,
> Or even a very good dinner, but the sudden illumina-
> tion ... (*The Dry Salvages,* part II)

Eliot, I think, knows what he is risking by that 'even a very good dinner'; nevertheless the poem teeters on the edge of the wrong kind of bathos. Eliot's concern for visionary experience has too narrow a base in the common world. The problem is, of course, more acute in Eliot's plays; in *The Cocktail Party*, for example, the saintly life of Celia is not *really* related to the humdrum worldliness of the Chamberlaynes. Wordsworth is so often accused of lacking dramatic imagination, yet I daresay that *The Borderers* is a more interesting play than any product of the so-called revival of poetic drama in the last thirty years. Modern poetry in general, so it seems to me, has purchased intensity and complexity at the expense of excluding that feeling for the dense, prosaic texture of life which even poets of the second rank – a Cowper or a Crabbe – could once encompass with assurance, and which in Wordsworth becomes the necessary context for his 'spots of time'. One of our hopes for poetry must be that in the last ten years the appetite of our poets for the ordinary bread-and-butter world of daily experience has begun once more to sharpen.

But in the end Wordsworth speaks not merely to modern poets, but to all of us. He is, as John Stuart Mill remarked, 'the poet of unpoetical natures'. What he enacts in *The Prelude* is, after all, common experience raised to an uncommon power. 'Only connect', says Margaret Schlegel in *Howard's End*, 'only connect the prose and the passion and both will be exalted.'

It is an imperative we cannot but obey. Yet, of course, we are generally too timid, too lazy or too clumsy in our efforts to connect. Hence we find in great art a discipline and a consolation precisely because it builds more perfectly 'the rainbow bridge that should connect the prose in us with the passion'.

The Prelude is indeed just such a 'rainbow bridge'. It arches towards transcendental realities; it ranges through the many-coloured spectrum of human life and it is rooted firm in the rich soil of common experience.

SOURCE : Adapted from *Poetic Vision in the World of Prose* (1966), Professor Harvey's Inaugural Lecture at the Queen's University, Belfast.

NOTES

Two footnotes in the original text are here deleted.

1. De Quincey, 'The Lake Poets : William Wordsworth', *Tait's Edinburgh Magazine*, VI (Feb 1839). This passage was omitted in Collected Editions of De Quincey's work.

2. H. Lindenberger, *On Wordsworth's Prelude* (Princeton, 1963) pp. 51–8.

Morse Peckham

A POST-ENLIGHTENMENT IMAGINATION* (1962)

Wordsworth is usually called a nature poet; but that is an error, and a particularly unfortunate one, for so to categorize him is to identify him with the nature poets of the eighteenth century, who selected from the natural world in order to confirm their conviction that by the activity of the imagination man derives value from nature through the imaginative perception of the meaningful order of the world. But Wordsworth saw in nature not merely the source of 'moods of calmness' but equally a source of emotional disturbance; and it was the interaction of the two which led to genius and the stimulation and growth of the poetic imagination. The mind was not merely reflective and imitative; it was not a mere mirror; it was a lamp. The capacity of the individual to profit from the order and disorder of the natural world was a function of the strength and health of his 'imagination'. Therefore the climax of *The Prelude* is called 'The Imagination and Taste, How Impaired and Restored'. Clearly, the old meaning of 'imagination' has been discarded for a new one.

The pre-Enlightenment meaning, for which Coleridge and Wordsworth used the word 'fancy', a lesser power of the mind, was the mental ability to create something unreal out of elements found in reality, like a unicorn or a chimera. It was regarded as a dangerous power, closely allied with madness. Shakespeare put in the same category the lunatic, the lover,

* Editor's title. This passage occurs in a chapter on 'Explorers', in a section on 'Alienated Vision', in *Beyond the Tragic Vision: The Quest for Identity in the Nineteenth Century*. It would have been misleading to adopt any of these titles for so brief an extract from a very comprehensive work.

and the poet. During the Enlightenment 'imagination' was not regarded with such suspicion. On the contrary, the poet's imaginative power allied him not with the madman but with the philosopher and the scientist. It was the power to see beyond the superficial confusion of phenomena to the laws of order and of cause which governed the world. The notion of Wordsworth and Coleridge was profoundly different. The one poet speaks of 'What we half create and half perceive', while the other insists that 'we receive but what we give'. But both statements are virtually the same, and to attempt to say what he meant Coleridge coined the word 'esemplastic', from Greek 'into' plus 'one' plus 'make'. The imagination now becomes radically creative. The forms with which it organizes the world are derived from within, not reasoned, or perceived, or intuited from the outer world.

The power of the new perception is that it can see both order and disorder in experience without claiming that one or the other is the true character of reality. This is the orientation Coleridge symbolizes in 'Kubla Khan', in which Kubla's paradisiacal garden includes both beauty and terror, both sun and ice. To Coleridge the imagination was the power to experience the reconciliation of opposites without emptying them of their contradictions and disparities. And Keats, learning from both Wordsworth and Coleridge, saw the poetic power as the power of 'negative capability', the power not to make up your mind in the face of logical contradictions but to maintain those contradictions. Such notions clearly make it possible for the poet to engage his mind with reality in all its contradictory and confusing concreteness; like Wordsworth, he felt that here is our home, not in some lost paradise or future heaven. To Wordsworth the imagination is an adaptive power, and his theme is how that imaginative power grows, how it is destroyed, and how it is restored. His subject is not nature but psychology.

. . . [Wordsworth] grew up, then, in a pre-Enlightenment culture, nor did his stay at Cambridge, sunk like Oxford in a mindless somnolence, make much difference. When, on a walking trip through France, he encountered the French Revolution in its initial joyous urgency, he experienced for the first time the full force of the Enlightenment in its apparently irresistible sweep toward triumph and the establishment of heaven on earth. Under the pretense of studying French he returned to the country where everything suddenly made sense; and there he embraced revolutionary republicanism and sentimental 'natural' love. Indeed, he became so solemn in his later years and his public image as laureate was so cleaned of his youthful radicalism by himself and his worshipers, that it came as a relief in 1916 to learn that he had had an illegitimate daughter.

In spite of his bliss, his uncles, who had charge of his patrimony, insisted that he return to England, and in 1793 he was horrified to learn that England and France were at war. All his new beliefs allied him with the French republican effort against his own country. But that emotional conflict was not to last long. The Revolution rapidly revealed its inescapable tendency toward terror and tyranny. Now the problems of the Enlightenment rose before him. Passionately he studied schemes of human regeneration, of social perfection – all the marvelous fantasies of the late Enlightenment. Inevitably he was led to logical contraries with which the reason could not deal. This shattered his faith that a solution to moral difficulties could be found in the study of the empirical world. The result was despair. He fled from London to a farm in southern England, where his sister joined him; and there he did a most interesting thing. For a year and a half he studied mathematics. Like Kant he found that only in mathematics could be found a perfect self-consistent order. That order was in the mind, not in reality. But whereas Kant, with his devotion to the technicalities of academic philosophy, buried deep and almost completely suppressed the emotional drives, in Wordsworth they were right at the surface.

Indeed, that was all he was really interested in. His devotion to mathematics can be seen as a turning away from reality and society in order to regain orientative equilibrium, in order again to release from the 'under-consciousness' the orientative drive, the imaginative power. He had had a sense of emotional vitality; it had disappeared; how was it to be recovered? With the aid of the emotional ambience of his sister Dorothy and of his inspiring and philosophically learned new friend, Coleridge, it was recovered; and once he had found it again, he reinforced it by recalling in his new tranquillity those exaltations and agonies of his childhood and youth which originally brought his imagination to life. And he wrote *The Prelude*, his interpretation of his experiences.

'There are', he said, 'in our existence spots of time,'

> passages of life in which
> We have had deepest feeling that the mind
> Is lord and master, and that outward sense
> Is but the obedient servant of her will.

Innumerable passages in this poem enable us to comprehend and experience the emotional vitality and force that must have lain behind the academic and abstract style of Kant. Yet because Wordsworth was an amateur philosopher and more interested in emotional vitality than correctness and impregnability of reasoning, Wordsworth said things that Kant would never have said. The mind, he was convinced, was exquisitely adapted to the outer world, and that world was equally adapted to the mind. Of the union of the two he speaks as of a wedding and a consummation, the offspring of which is creation. Yet in comparison to the mind, the world is passive, although a wise passiveness is necessary to prepare the mind for the consummation. That passiveness is necessary to free the mind from its superficial drives toward rational comprehension. Without that initial passiveness before nature, the mind does not wed; it seduces and rapes. Once the mind is released by contemplation and passiveness and tranquil restoration, the deeper forces begin to work and to appear in the guise of 'love and holy passion'. From the inviolate self issues forth the power to relate man to his world, and this act of relation is the act of the creation of value. We see intuitively, through unconscious powers, into the structure of order of which the visible universe is a symbol. Really it is not too distant a position from Kant's notion that the structural power of the mind is a guarantee that the world has structure, even though the mind cannot create a structure which corresponds to the structure of the world.

In the moments of revelation, then, the spots of time, the world is seen as a symbol of the self which underlies the conscious rational powers. But the world and the self have the same origin – the divine. The imagination closes the gap between man and the world, and the divine current, as it were, runs unhindered through the great triad of God, man, and nature. The results are exciting, or at least Wordsworth makes them so when we read him, for no author has succeeded so well in communicating the feeling of the aroused imagination 'when it sees into the life of things'. In such states the ordinary rational distinction between organic and inorganic life disappears. At that time there was no possible way to explain the origin of life, or at least the distinction between the organic and the inorganic; and the nature of life was a problem that Goethe and Coleridge, among others, wrestled with rather profitlessly. Wordsworth's simple assertion is more convincing, for he *feels* the life in rocks and stones, and he can make that feeling almost unbearably moving. We cannot believe it, yet it is irresistible. It is as if a poet of today could make us feel the life in atomic particles and the continuity of that life with our own, even though we know that we are not talking about levels of reality but levels of analysis, or different kinds of scientific constructs, made for different purposes. The hypothetical organicism of Kant has been metamorphosed into an experienced reality.

> Not Chaos, not
> The darkest pit of lowest Erebus,
> Nor aught of blinder vacancy, scooped out
> By help of dreams – can breed such fear and awe
> As fall upon us often when we look
> Into our Minds, into the Mind of man –
> My haunt, and the main region of my song.

It is the imagination that redeems the world; in the deepest recesses of the self is the source of value. In opening ourselves to beauty and to terror we release its power.

Few understood Wordsworth. The high tide of his vision receded after 1805 and he regressed to embracing more commonplace orientative drives, became Christian and timid. Yet he had gone far; several profoundly important notions were implanted firmly in the minds of his readers: the sacredness of the poet, who through the exercise of his imagination releases value (or indefinable 'truth') into the world and makes it available to the rest of us; and the necessity of engaging with this world, of finding our relation to this world, the world of the senses, of ordinary human experience, not of dreaming up fantasies of an unreal world to which we may escape, now in reality and in spirit after death. For though the world is a symbol, it is not only a symbol, not nothing but a symbol. There is no Platonizing reductivism in Wordsworth's vision. The imagination does not leap across to the divine beyond the world; it finds its path and its expression through the senses. The world does not vanish when we see a blinding radiance behind it. It becomes pellucidly beautiful as the divine glow shines through each particle of it. But Wordsworth was much misunderstood. His subjects, nature and simple and ordinary men, were confused with the imaginative power he used to look at them. His failure to publish *The Prelude* was, for English and American literature particularly, something of a disaster. The guidance – and the problem – which the next generation received came not from Wordsworth but from Goethe's *Faust*.

SOURCE : *Beyond the Tragic Vision: The Quest for Identity in the Nineteenth Century* (1962) pp. 112–18 – extract.

Robert Langbaum

THE EVOLUTION OF SOUL IN WORDSWORTH'S POETRY
(1967)

When Keats in a letter calls this world 'The vale of Soul-making', he comes close to Wordsworth's way of thinking. For Keats says that we come into the world as pure potentiality or 'Intelligence' and that we acquire a 'Soul' or 'sense of Identity' through 'Circumstances'. And it is the main purport of Wordsworth's poetry to show the spiritual significance of this world, to show that we evolve a soul or identity through experience and that the very process of evolution is what we mean by *soul*.

To understand the implications of Wordsworth's view and why it is distinctively modern, we have to go back to the psychological assertions that Wordsworth was both absorbing and answering – we have to go back to Locke and Locke's disciple Hartley. The best analogy to the challenge raised by Locke is the challenge raised in our time by computers. For Lockean man is like a computer in that everything inside him comes from outside, through sensation; so that Lockean man gives back only what has been 'programmed' into him. Even his choices are no evidence of free will; for once the idea of choice has entered his head, he must choose and he must choose between predetermined alternatives. 'A man that is walking,' says Locke, 'to whom it is proposed to give off walking, is not at liberty, whether he will determine himself to walk, or give off walking or not: he must necessarily prefer one or the other of them; walking or not walking.'[1] One would use the same line of reasoning to show that a computer, for all its ability to make choices, is not free.

Although Locke lays great emphasis on self-consciousness, in that he shows that the greatest part of mental life consists of reflections on our own ideas, his system does not, as Blake pointed out in 'There is No Natural Religion', allow for anything new to come into the world, since Locke's 'complex ideas' merely complicate a fixed number of sensations. Lockean self-consciousness is the sort we may well predict for the formidable computers of the future.

As computers become increasingly complex, as they become capable of making choices, learning and giving orders, we inevitably wonder at what point of complexity they can be considered human, as having a soul. Now in *The Prelude* Wordsworth was trying to answer some such question as this regarding Lockean man. If we consider that the human psyche is built up of sensations, then at what point do sensations add up to soul, or how do we jump from sensations to soul? We can understand Wordsworth's answer to Locke if we imagine him answering the question in regard to computers. His answer would be that computers will never be human until they are born and grow up.

If sensations turn into soul – into an ineffable quality that can never be accounted for by the sensations themselves – it is because the sensations reach an ever-changing mind that transforms them as a merely passive receiver, the sort of mind Locke likens to blank paper could not. No two succeeding sensations from the same object can be the same, because the later sensation reaches a mind already modified by the earlier sensation. Locke recognizes all this, but it remains for Wordsworth to draw the necessary conclusions in his poetry and for Coleridge to formulate them in his theory of the imagination. The necessary conclusions are summed up in the idea of interchange between man and nature – the idea that the mind modifies sensation as much as sensation modifies the mind.

It may be argued that computers, too, as they learn, offer a changing receiver to external data. This brings us to the second important point in Wordsworth's answer to Locke. Wordsworth portrays the mind as itself part of the nature it perceives; and it is this connection, sensed through what Wordsworth calls *joy*, that gives us confidence in the reality of ourselves and the external world. Dare one predict that no computer is likely to have this organic connection or to sense it through *joy*?

In *The Prelude*, Wordsworth tells us that his life began to the sound of the Derwent River that 'loved/To blend his murmurs with my nurse's song' and 'sent a voice/That flowed along my dreams', making

> ceaseless music that composed my thoughts
> To more than infant softness, giving me
> Amid the fretful dwellings of mankind
> A foretaste, a dim earnest, of the calm
> That Nature breathes among the hills and groves.
>
> (1 270–81; 1850)

There, in the best Lockean fashion, Wordsworth traces all his mature thoughts back to the sound of the river. But unlike Locke, Wordsworth presents the mind as an active principle. The nurse's song with which the river blends is a sign that the mind is analogous to the river; that is why the river's voice flows along the dreams of the growing Wordsworth. When we read that the river 'loved/To blend', we understand that the baby did not merely receive but loved the river's sound, reached out to it as a flower reaches out to the sun and air and rain it has the potentiality to receive. The blending and inter-change turn sensation into experience, an experience of joy that will in future years spread around the mature man's thoughts an affective tone – a tone objectified in 'the calm/That Nature breathes'. This tone, this atmosphere of the mind, sensed as at once inside and outside the mind, is what the mature man will call *soul*.

The river received on its 'smooth breast the shadow of those towers' of Cockermouth Castle (1 283). The reflection of the towers was perceived, we gather, at a somewhat later age than the sound of the river. Visual sensations are in Wordsworth more intellectual than sensations of sound. The composite experience of river and towers – which might be understood as an experience of female and male principles – stands behind the experiences of beauty and fear described in the rest of book I, which are composite experiences of natural and moral power.

In book II, the mature man's capacity for love is traced back to the contentment of the infant

> who sinks to sleep
> Rocked on his Mother's breast; who with his soul
> Drinks in the feelings of his Mother's eye !

Through his connection with his mother, he gains a sense of connection with nature, a connection portrayed through the imagery of flow and blending :

> No outcast he, bewildered and depressed :
> Along his infant veins are interfused
> The gravitation and the filial bond
> Of nature that connect him with the world.

The infant is from the start an active agent of perception who 'drinks in' feelings. Because he inhabits the loving universe circumscribed for him by his mother's 'Presence', he loves or reaches out to all that he beholds. That sense of 'Presence', the baby's first apprehension of Deity, is produced by the sympathetic relation of mind to universe which is, says Wordsworth, the 'Poetic spirit of our human life'. The mind is portrayed as a relation and a process – a process *growing* from feeling through power, sense, thought, into the one great Mind and between subject and object, in such a way that the parts flow one into the other and can hardly be discriminated.

> For, feeling has to him imparted power
> That through the growing faculties of sense
> Doth like an agent of the one great Mind
> Create, creator and receiver both,
> Working but in alliance with the works
> Which it beholds.

This poetic spirit, says Wordsworth, is in most people 'abated or suppressed' in later years. But in some few it remains 'Preeminent till death', and those few are, we gather, poets (II 235–65).

We have here an accounting for affect, for the value or 'glory' we find in the world, which seems to contradict the accounting in the 'Immortality Ode'. The accounting in *The Prelude* is the authentically Wordsworthian one, because it is naturalistic, psychological, and sensationalist. The Platonic idea of pre-existence is advanced in the 'Ode' – Wordsworth tells us in the Fenwick note to that poem – as a figure of speech, as a fanciful and traditional way of generalizing the pychological phenomenon revealed to him by his own life – that 'the Child is Father of the Man', that spirit is to be found in the primitive. 'I took hold of the notion of pre-existence', says Wordsworth, 'as having sufficient foundation in humanity for authorizing me to make for my purpose the best use of it I could as a Poet.' The Platonic idea is used with fine artistry in the 'Ode' as a counterpoint to the primitivist idea. It is the primitivist idea that takes over when in stanza ix Wordsworth gets down to the serious business of answering the question of the poem, the question posed by the adult's sense of loss. His answer is that nothing is lost. Even if we no longer experience the 'glory' we experienced in childhood, 'nature yet remembers'. Our souls, he concludes in a strikingly primitivist image, can in a moment travel backward

> And see the Children sport upon the shore,
> And hear the mighty waters rolling evermore.

Yet the Platonic idea is not lost sight of even here. It is so blended with the primitivist idea that we can see that its function all along has been to ennoble and spiritualize the primitivist idea. Thus the sea is the physical sea where all life began; but the sea is also immortal, through its very age ageless and transcendent :

> Hence in a season of calm weather
> Though inland far we be,
> Our Souls have sight of that immortal sea
> Which brought us hither.

Growing-up has been mainly compared to a journey of the sun across the sky; now it is compared to a journey inland from the sea. Wordsworth explains the adult's sense of loss by telling us that we come down from the sky and up from the sea, and by blending the two directions to evoke an original spiritual source that is unlocatable.

The blending goes even farther in the imagery through which Wordsworth tells us that the adult responds to the objects before him because he sees them through the lens of his memory of childhood experiences. Those 'first affections' and 'shadowy recollections', he says,

> Are yet the fountain light of all our day,
> Are yet a master light of all our seeing.

There is an inextricable blending here of light and water, the ideal and the primitive, Platonic metaphysics and Lockean psychology.

We find the same blending in two adjacent passages of *The Prelude*, book I. In the first, Wordsworth speaks of experiences that cannot be accounted for by the Lockean theory of memory and association he has been developing – experiences which would seem to require, to account for them, some Platonic theory of 'first-born affinities' (I 555), of archetypes, of innate ideas. He had such an experience when gazing over an expanse of sea,

> Of shining water, gathering as it seem'd,
> Through every hair-breadth of that field of light,
> New pleasure – (I 578–80)

new, because not deriving from association with earlier pleasures. Wordsworth evokes the transcendent quality of the experience by turning shining *water* into a *field* of light, by dissolving both water and land into light. But in the next passage, he says that he loves to travel backward down through the corridors of memory, from forms down through sensations,

to recover at the point where conscious memory fades out just
such a vision of light :

> Those recollected hours that have the charm
> Of visionary things, those lovely forms
> And sweet sensations that throw back our life,
> And almost make remotest infancy
> A visible scene, on which the sun is shining. (1 631–5)

We have only to recall Locke's description of the mind as a
dark closet penetrated by certain rays of light from the outside world,[2] we have only to recall this comparison, which is
even more revealing of Locke's outlook than his better known
comparison of the mind to white or blank paper, to understand the sense in which Wordsworth answers Locke. Yet it is
Locke who supplies the concepts of memory and association
through which Wordsworth can give psychological substantia-
tion to his experience of his own mind as light or music. And
it is important to note that the mind recognizes itself in an
external sensation, that Wordsworth arrives at his concept of
mind by tracing his life back to an original sensation – to 'A
visible scene, on which the sun is shining' or to the sound of
the Derwent River.

Much ink has been spilled over the question whether Wordsworth believed that his apprehension of spirit came from outside or inside, whether he was a Lockean empiricist or a
Platonic believer in innate ideas. The answer is that Wordsworth, when he is writing his best poetry, uses both doctrines
as possibilities, blending them in such a way as to evoke the
mystery he is talking about – the mystery of life, vitality,
organic connection. The case should teach us something about
the proper relation of ideas to poetry. And, indeed, Wordsworth himself pronounces on the subject in his first essay
'Upon Epitaphs', where he speaks of the antithetical ideas of
two Greek philosophers about the value of body in relation to
soul. In spite of their opposite ideas, says Wordsworth, modu-
lating from talk of thought to talk of feelings, 'Each of these

Sages was in sympathy with the best feelings of our Nature; feelings which, though they seem opposite to each other, have another and a finer connexion than that of contrast. – It is a connexion formed through the subtle progress by which, both in the natural and the moral world, qualities pass insensibly into their contraries, and things revolve upon each other.'[3]

The case also suggests why *The Prelude*, which Wordsworth wrote with his left hand or deepest artistic instinct while trying with his right hand or conscious will to write the long philosophical poem Coleridge had put him up to, why *The Prelude* is so much more successful than what we have of that long philosophical poem, *The Recluse*, of which *The Excursion* is Part Two. *The Prelude* is successful, and successful as an appropriately modern poem of ideas, just because Wordsworth did not consider that he was at that point writing a philosophical poem. In the passage I have quoted above, he is apologizing to Coleridge for not getting on with the philosophical poem but dwelling instead, out of 'an infirmity of love' for them, on 'days/Disowned by memory' (I 614–15) – by conscious memory, that is.

To understand what Wordsworth has achieved in *The Prelude*, we have only to read Coleridge's description, in his *Table Talk* for 21 July 1832, long after he himself had turned against Locke and Hartley, of the original plan of *The Recluse*.

The plan laid out, and, I believe, partly suggested by me, was, that Wordsworth should assume the station of a man in mental repose, one whose principles were made up, and so prepared to deliver upon authority a system of philosophy. He was to treat man as man, – a subject of eye, ear, touch, and taste, in contact with external nature, and informing the senses from the mind, and not compounding a mind out of the senses.

Aside from the fact that *The Prelude* portrays a mind in evolution not in repose, we precisely do not find there the doctrinaire anti-Lockean stand described by Coleridge.

Wordsworth no sooner tells us in *The Prelude*, book 1, how nature through 'extrinsic passion' or association first peopled

his 'mind with forms sublime or fair', than he speaks of other
pleasures

> Which, if I err not, surely must belong
> To those first-born affinities that fit
> Our new existence to existing things,
> And, in our dawn of being, constitute
> The bond of union between life and joy. (554–8)

Note the tentativeness of 'if I err not', and how even innate
affinities are traced back to a primitive origin which one may
still understand to be natural. Such blending evokes 'the bond
of union between life and joy' that is Wordsworth's answer to
the question at the heart of *The Prelude*, the question that no
simply rational account of life can answer. I mean the question, why live at all, why bother to get up in the morning? As
so often in Wordsworth's best lines, the answer is couched in
words that are general, even vague. Yet the 'Presence' evoked,
to use that other vague but potent Wordsworthian word, is
definite enough and the only answer to the question, 'Why
live?' We can infer that 'the bond of union between life and
joy' is the thing that will always distinguish human beings
from computers. We can also infer that the philosopher's
question, 'Why live?' can only be answered by the poet. For
the answer is that we take pleasure in the world we behold
because we are one with it. And it is only the poet who can
make pleasure and oneness real for us by just such blending
as Wordsworth employs.

F. R. Leavis and Donald Davie have shown, through an
analysis of Wordsworth's syntax, how he gives us poetry by
blurring the thought.[4] One can say even more specifically that
Wordsworth gives us poetry by being both Lockean and anti-
Lockean at the same time. For Wordsworth answers Locke by
using the Lockean concepts of memory and association. It is
only through memory, says Locke, that the mind has any
effectiveness, and he equates the self with the sum of conscious
memory ('whatever has the consciousness of present and past
actions, is the same person to whom they both belong'). But

Locke does not speak of memory as modifying the actions remembered; these actions remain fixed, like the data 'remembered' by a computer. It is in speaking of the accidental association of ideas that Locke recognizes a modifying and transforming process. Locke accounts for our irrational behavior and for affect – for what he calls our 'sympathies and antipathies' – by the connexion through *'chance* or *custom'* of ideas that have no correspondence in nature or logic. Through association, in other words, sensations and ideas are transformed into something other than they would be in themselves, with a value they would not have in themselves.

The difference between Locke and the romanticists is that Locke deplores the process of association as unamenable to reason;[5] whereas the romanticists glory in it because it shows the mind as creative and carries them over from sensation to value. It is significant that Wordsworth and Coleridge took their Locke by way of the eighteenth-century medical doctor, David Hartley, who builds his whole system on the theory of association that is in Locke only one proposition. From association, Hartley derives the affective responses of pleasure and pain which lead to Christian values and faith. Hartley must have seemed to Wordsworth and Coleridge to have transcendentalized Locke. In 'Religious Musings', Coleridge hails Hartley as 'of mortal kind/Wisest', because he is the first to establish value on a materialistic and therefore scientific basis – the 'first who marked the ideal tribes/Up the fine fibres through the sentient brain' (368–70). Hartley comes close to calling this world a vale of soul-making when he says: 'Some degree of spirituality is the necessary consequence of passing through life. The sensible pleasures and pains must be transferred by association more and more every day, upon things that afford neither sensible pleasure nor sensible pain in themselves, and so beget the intellectual pleasures and pains.'[6] In other words, we grow spiritually by conferring spirituality upon the world. The issue between the Locke-Hartley doctrine and the Platonic doctrine of pre-existence is whether we gain or lose spirituality by living.

Nevertheless, Hartley's system remains mechanical because

he does not recognize that the crucial element in Locke's
theory of association is this – that only in speaking of association does Locke allow for any unconscious mental process.
Wordsworth and Coleridge modify Hartley by dwelling on the
unconscious aspects of the associative process. Thus Coleridge,
in beginning to object to Hartley, says that 'Association
depends in a much greater degree on the recurrence of resemb-
ling states of feeling than on trains of ideas', and that 'Ideas
no more recall one another than the leaves in a tree, fluttering
in the breeze, propagate their motion one to another'. Wordsworth says much the same thing when, in *The Prelude*, book
II, he describes the delayed effect of epiphanies :

> the soul,
> Remembering how she felt, but what she felt
> Remembering not, retains an obscure sense
> Of possible sublimity, whereto
> With growing faculties she doth aspire
> With faculties still growing, feeling still
> That whatsoever point they gain, they yet
> Have something to pursue. (315–22)

Association takes place not through the ideas or manifest content of an experience but through the affective tone, which can
then be communicated to experiences with quite different
manifest contents. Wordsworth makes clear what is implied in
Coleridge's second statement – that this affective tone is a feeling of infinity which connects the individual mind with the
Great Mind and cannot be entirely accounted for by the
present, or even recollected, experience.

For Locke, we apprehend infinity as an idea of quantity –
the result of our understanding that we can count indefinitely
and can indefinitely add line segments to a given line segment.
The idea is inapplicable, in the same way, to quality : 'nobody
ever thinks of infinite sweetness, or infinite whiteness.' For
Wordsworth, instead, we apprehend infinity as a feeling
having to do with quality and organic wholeness – we cannot
add to an organism as to a line segment. For Locke, the idea

of infinity follows from our experience. For Wordsworth, we not only bring the feeling of infinity to later experiences through associated memory of earlier experiences, but the feeling somehow both rises out of and is anterior to even our primal experiences. The ambiguity is projected through the use of both memory and the fading-out of memory. Because the soul remembers not what but how she felt, we carry with us a feeling larger than anything we can remember of our primal experiences; and the soul grows, in this vale of soul-making, toward a feeling of wholeness that seems recollected though we cannot say from where. Locke refutes the theory of pre-existence by saying that if a man has no memory at all of his previous existence, if he has 'a consciousness that *cannot* reach beyond this new state', then he is not the same person who led the previous existence since 'personal identity [reaches] no further than consciousness reaches'.[7] Wordsworth's answer is to blur the line between remembering and forgetting, to introduce a notion of unconscious memory. By combining memory and association, Wordsworth sets the Lockean system in motion, infusing it with vitality, surrounding it with mystery, and carrying the mind back beyond conscious memory to the 'dawn of being' where it is undistinguishable from its first sensation.

Memory becomes in Wordsworth the instrument of the associative or transforming power. It is because we see with stereoscopic vision – as Roger Shattuck puts it in speaking, in *Proust's Binoculars*, of Proust's use of memory – it is because partly we see the tree before us and partly we see all the trees we have ever seen that we see from outside and inside and have not sensations but experiences.[8] That is the meaning of the crucial line in 'Tintern Abbey': 'The picture of the mind revives again.' Wordsworth sees the present landscape through his mental picture of the landscape five years earlier. Because he discovers continuity in the disparate pictures through a principle of growth, he becomes aware of the pattern of his life – he binds his apparently disparate days together. He may be said to evolve his soul in becoming aware that his soul evolves. Included in the present experience is Wordsworth's

sense that he will in future feed upon it, just as in the inter-
vening five years he has fed on his last visit to this place. The
experience includes, in other words, the consciousness of laying
up treasure – not in heaven but in the memory. It is the point
of 'Tintern Abbey', the 'Immortality Ode', and *The Prelude*
that this spiritual storehouse of memory *is* our soul.

In one of the earliest written passages of *The Prelude*, one
of those passages that must have helped Wordsworth find his
theme, the poet thanks nature, in a tone of religious solemnity,
for having from his 'first dawn/Of childhood' intertwined for
him 'The passions that build up our human soul' (1 405–7).[9]
The whole poem traces this building-up process, but the words
soul and *imagination* are used interchangeably and Wordsworth speaks more often of the building-up of imagination.
That is because the poet or man of imagination is being used
to epitomize a psychological process.

The poet, we are being told, is more spiritual than the rest
of us because he *remembers* more than we do – though his
remembering is often spoken of as a kind of forgetting: 'By
such forgetfulness the soul becomes,/Words cannot say how
beautiful' (*Recluse* 1 297–8). The poet filters a present experience back through memory and the unconscious river in his
veins – Wordsworth habitually speaks of thought as flowing in
and out of the veins – to the external river that was his first
sensation. That is why the poet can respond to the world and
see it symbolically. That is why seeing is better than faith – it
is revelation. 'Nor did he believe, – he *saw*', says Wordsworth
of the poetical Pedlar in *The Excursion* (1 232).

Wordsworth achieves his symbolic effects through a regres-
sion in the mind of the observer and in the object observed. He
makes the human figure seem to evolve out of and pass back
into the landscape – as in 'The Thorn' and the Lucy poems,
including 'Lucy Gray'. And he makes the landscape itself, in
his most striking effects, seem to evolve out of water. In
'Resolution and Independence', the old leech gatherer is seen
by a pool. He is so old that he seems to hang on to life by a
thread; and the observer understands this by carrying the old

man's existence back to the line between the inanimate and the animate. The observer sees the old man as like a huge stone that seems almost alive because you cannot imagine how it got where it is, or as like a sea beast that at first seems part of the rock on which it lies. He is – if you assimilate this poem, as Geoffrey Hartman has so beautifully done, to the recurrent imagery of *The Prelude* – like something left behind by the inland sea that once covered the landscape.[10] Because the old man is seen through the eye of unconscious racial memory, he is transformed into an archetype of human endurance capable of alleviating the observer's distress.

In one of the epiphanies or 'spots of time' of *The Prelude*, book XII, Wordsworth recalls how as a boy he fled in terror from a low place, where a murderer had been hanged, to a hill where he saw a pool and a girl approaching it, bearing a pitcher on her head, her garments blowing in the wind. Through the conjunction with water and wind, the girl turns for the boy into an archetypal figure who transforms the unpleasant experience into a pleasant one; so that in later years, when Wordsworth was courting Mary Hutchinson, he often returned with her to this place, finding in 'the naked pool and dreary crags' a 'spirit of pleasure and youth's golden gleam' (264, 266). Here and elsewhere in Wordsworth – the same female figure with a basket on her head is remembered through water imagery in 'The Two April Mornings' – water and memory, water as perhaps the counterpart of memory, turn the individual event into an archetype; and it is through archetypalization that turbulence and pain are turned into spiritual treasure, into the recognition of that surrounding aura of pleasurable tranquillity which is soul. 'How strange', says Wordsworth in speaking of soul-making,

> that all
> The terrors, pains, and early miseries,
> Regrets, vexations, lassitudes interfused
> Within my mind, should e'er have borne a part,
> And that a needful part in making up
> The calm existence that is mine when I
> Am worthy of myself ! (1 344–50)

The transformation of pain into pleasure is achieved through archetypalization and objectification. The terrifying boyhood experience of book XII passes into the landscape, making it a pleasant and spiritually rewarding place to return to. Wordsworth says that 'The sands of Westmoreland, the creeks and bays/Of Cumbria's rocky limits' can tell of his boyhood epiphanies; and that, conversely,

> The scenes which were a witness of that joy
> Remained in their substantial lineaments
> Depicted on the brain, (I 567–8, 599–601)

that he remembered those early experiences as places.

The pleasurable tranquillity that is soul exists outside us as well as inside; it exists in those places hallowed by significant experiences. Place, in Wordsworth, is the spatial projection of psyche, because it is the repository of memory.[11] We can understand the relation in Wordsworth between mind and nature, once we understand that Wordsworth evolves his soul or sense of identity as he identifies more and more such hallowed places. We can understand the relation in Wordsworth between the themes of memory and growing up, once we understand that for Wordsworth you advance in life, by travelling back again to the beginning, by reassessing your life, by binding your days together anew.

In Coleridge's periodical *The Friend*, Wordsworth answers a conservative attack on the belief in progress, by saying that in the progress of the species and the individual mind we must often move backward in order to move forward. Progress

neither is nor can be like that of a Roman road in a right line. It may be more justly compared to that of a river, which, both in its smaller reaches and larger turnings, is frequently forced back towards its fountains by objects which can not otherwise be eluded or overcome; yet with an accompanying impulse that will insure its advancement hereafter, it is either gaining strength every hour, or conquering in secret some difficulty, by a labor that contributes as effectually to further it in its course, as when it moves forward uninterrupted in a line.

And Coleridge in *The Friend* uses 'My Heart Leaps Up', the poem in which Wordsworth speaks of binding his days together, to support his idea that we must in growing up be able to correct the delusions of our childhood without repudiating the child who held them.

If men laugh at the falsehoods that were imposed on themselves during their childhood, it is because they are not good and wise enough to contemplate the past in the present, and so to produce by a virtuous and thoughtful sensibility that continuity in their self-consciousness, which nature has made the law of their animal life. Ingratitude, sensuality, and hardness of heart, all flow from this source. Men are ungrateful to others only when they have ceased to look back on their former selves with joy and tenderness. They exist in fragments. Annihilated as to the past, they are dead to the future, or seek for the proofs of it everywhere, only not (where alone they can be found) in themselves.[12]

The old Pedlar of *The Excursion* shows that he has bound his days together; for age has

> not tamed his eye; that, under brows
> Shaggy and grey, had meanings which it brought
> From years of youth; which, like a Being made
> Of many Beings, he had wondrous skill
> To blend with knowledge of the years to come,
> Human, or such as lie beyond the grave. (1 428–33)

Because 'like a Being made/Of many Beings', he possesses his past, he possesses the future too and seems to transcend time. The same is true of old Matthew in 'The Two April Mornings', who, in the moment when he was able to immerse himself completely in the stream of time by remembering and reconciling himself to his daughter's death, became for the young narrator immortal :

Mathew is in his grave, yet now,
Methinks, I see him stand,
As at that moment, with a bough
Of wilding in his hand.

In *The Prelude*'s climactic 'spot of time', the epiphany on
Mt Snowdon in book xiv, the whole world seems under
moonlight to be returned to water. The mist below is a silent
sea, the hills around static billows; and this illusory sea
stretches out into the real Atlantic. The optical illusion is sub-
stantiated when, through a rift in the mist, Wordsworth hears
the roar of inland waters. The movement from sight to sound
is always in Wordsworth a movement backward to the beginning of things, to sensation and the sentiment of Being; later,
in book xiv, Wordsworth says that he has in *The Prelude*
traced the stream of imagination back from 'light/And open
day' to 'the blind cavern whence is faintly heard/Its natal
murmur' (195-7). Wordsworth understands, therefore, that
he has had on Mt Snowdon an epiphany of pure imagination
or pure potentiality. He has beheld, in the moon over the
waters, 'the emblem of a mind' brooding over the abyss –
waiting, like God in the opening passage of *Paradise Lost*, to
bring forth the world. Wordsworth transcends even the beginning of things by moving back from sight to sound and then to
an inextricable blending of sight and sound :

the emblem of a mind
That feeds upon infinity, that broods
Over the dark abyss, intent to hear
Its voices issuing forth to silent light
In one continuous stream. (70-4)

'This', says Wordsworth, 'is the very spirit' with which
'higher' or imaginative 'minds' deal 'With the whole compass
of the universe' (90-3). Confronted with sensory experience,
the poetical man travels back *that far* in order to perceive it
imaginatively. He recreates the world in his imagination; so
that he can return to the scene before him, imposing upon it
the picture in his mind and thus finding there the surrounding

aura of calm that is his soul. Only by travelling back to the beginning can we achieve the 'repose/In moral judgments', which is a sign that we have bound our ideas up with our primitive sensations. In borrowing, to describe the repose or calm, words of Holy Scripture, in describing it as 'that peace/Which passeth understanding' (126–8), Wordsworth shows that he considers his naturalistic revelation to be not only the equivalent of the Platonic idea, but this time the equivalent of Christian revelation itself.

SOURCE : *PMLA,* LXXXII (May 1967) 265–72.

NOTES

Five footnotes in the original text are here deleted, and one is abbreviated.

1. John Locke, *Essay Concerning Human Understanding,* collated and annotated by A. C. Fraser, 2 vols (Oxford, 1894) book II, chap. xxi, par. 24.
2. Book II, chap. XI, par. 17.
3. Smith (ed.), *Wordsworth's Literary Criticism,* p. 84.
4. *Revaluation* (London, 1936) chap. 5; *Articulate Energy: An Inquiry into the Syntax of English Poetry* (London, 1955) pp. 106–16. . . .
5. Book II, chap. xxvii, par. 16; chap. xxxiii.
6. *Observations on Man,* in Two Parts, 6th ed. corrected and revised (London, 1834) prop. xiv, cor. viii.
7. Book II, chap. xvii, par. 6; chap. xxvii, par. 14.
8. New York, 1963, pp. 42–3. With the 'impressions' before him, says Wordsworth in *The Excursion,*

would he still compare
All his remembrances, thoughts, shapes and forms;
And, being still unsatisfied with aught
Of dimmer character, he thence attained
An active power to fasten images
Upon his brain; and on their pictured lines
Intensely brooded, even till they acquired
The liveliness of dreams. (1141–8).

9. See *Excursion*, II 1264–6, written at about the same time:
– So build we up the Being that we are;
Thus deeply drinking in the soul of things
We shall be wise perforce.

10. *The Unmediated Vision* (New Haven, 1954) pp. 33–4.

11. See Geoffrey Hartman's subtle analysis of Wordsworth's sense of place throughout *Wordsworth's Poetry, 1787–1814* (New Haven and London, 1964).

12. S. T. Coleridge, *The Complete Works*, ed. W. G. T. Shedd, 7 vols. (New York, 1884) II : Wordsworth's 'Reply to Mathetes' in Introduction, Second Section, p. 362 (see also p. 373); General Introduction, Essay v, p. 46.

W. J. Harvey

RETROSPECT AND PROSPECT

The Prelude urges on us, in a particularly acute form, the problem of what part meaning plays in poetry. Some Victorians clearly thought that Wordsworth's poetry was valuable for the ideas it expresses; the poet was primarily a great sage and teacher. For other Victorians, such as Mill and Arnold, Wordsworth's poetry was valuable not so much for its philosophical 'content' but rather as a refreshment and education of the emotions. Arnold, in declaring that the philosophy was an illusion, is the ancestor of some influential modern critics, including T. S. Eliot and William Empson, who have been much concerned with the way in which a poem can 'mean' anything at all.

It is only within the last thirty years that *The Prelude* has been the true subject of literary criticism, has been considered as a properly aesthetic artefact. This may have been due, in part, to the manifold interests of its 'content' which led to an emphasis on the biographical and philosophical approaches. But it was also in part due to a real uncertainty as to what kind of poem *The Prelude* essentially is. On the one hand it clearly emerges out of a mingled poetic tradition, part of which is the descriptive-cum-meditative poem of the eighteenth century (such as Thomson's *The Seasons*) and part of which is a mutation of the great epic tradition. On the other hand it is a strikingly original poem. In its central themes and modes of organisation, moreover, it seems to anticipate the novel rather than other poems, to be more akin to the work of George Eliot and Hardy, Lawrence and Joyce, Proust and Thomas Mann. It raises large questions about texture (Wordsworth's diction and imagery, his control of syntax and rhythm) and about structure (particularly the complicated control of time and memory, the relation of past to present). And it is complicated by its binary nature. The 1805 version is in thirteen books, the 1850 version is in fourteen books – how important is this structural alteration? Or, given that this is very much an *organic* poem, a poem of continuity and growth, why should any of its books begin or end where it does? Is this an arbitrary or a functional structure? Some simple, obvious, but basic questions have hardly yet been adequately explored.

What future criticism must surely stress is that while this is a poem rooted in the past, a culmination of many traditions of thought and culture, it is at the same time the first great *modern* poem. I emphasise this because I find that for many readers *The Prelude* is a cumbrous and curiously remote poem, somehow irrelevant to our own complicated and largely urban society. This is not a new reaction; when Arnold wrote

> And Wordsworth's eyes avert their ken
> From half of human fate

it was not, I think, that he meant that Wordsworth is a facile optimist, blind to the darker aspects of evil and suffering, or that Wordsworth's idea of nature was invalidated by evolutionary theories and by Tennyson's 'nature, red in tooth and claw'. If that is what Arnold did mean, then he had simply not read his Wordsworth properly. But he also meant, I think, that Wordsworth's poetry is somehow too pastoral, belonging to a world of childhood and innocence, a world remote from modern industrial civilisation with its complicated and conflicting ideologies and doubts. But this, too, is a misconception which stems, I suspect, from a limited view of Wordsworthian nature as meaning mountains and rivers, dales and lakes, peasants and village idiots, daffodils and rainbows. It cannot be stressed too strongly that Wordsworth is essentially concerned with *human* nature, with aspects of consciousness and being that are still relevant to our modern interests and predicaments. So I wish to isolate here, however briefly and schematically, some of those features of *The Prelude* which make it a modern poem, which anticipate the interests and tensions of our own society and culture.

The Prelude presents, among other things, the poet in quest of his identity. Although poets and moralists have for centuries urged man to 'know himself', it had always been in relation to pre-established moral or metaphysical principles. Identity in the Wordsworthian sense is a new theme for such detailed treatment in a non-dramatic poem. As orthodoxies have crumbled, and certainties dissolved, it has become more and more imperative for the artist to seek a point of stability within himself, to establish a principle of continuity within change. Wordsworth saw this paradox in Nature; he knew

> The immeasurable height
> Of woods decaying, never to be decay'd,
> The stationary blasts of waterfalls,

and took them to be

> The types and symbols of Eternity,
> Of first, and last, and midst, and without end.

But at the same time, *The Prelude* was his attempt to establish the same connections within himself, to bridge

> · The vacancy between me and those days,
> Which yet have such self-presence in my mind
> That sometimes, when I think of them, I seem
> Two consciousnesses, conscious of myself
> And of some other being.

It is a theme which has obsessed the modern imagination, replacing the quest of Everyman or of Bunyan's pilgrim; thus the lines I have just quoted strike to the heart of a great deal of existentialist philosophy. And in so far as *The Prelude* is concerned with 'the growth of a *poet's* mind' it foreshadows all those modern works, both of poetry and of fiction, which might be lumped together under the common title of 'A Portrait of the Artist as a Young Man'.

Because of this, *The Prelude* is characteristically modern in another way; it is a self-reflexive poem. By this I mean a poem

which has as part of its subject the writing of the poem itself,
the effort to master and to articulate experience, the struggle
to communicate, and the assertion of poetry as a value and as
a form of knowledge in its own right. It is there in the other
Romantic poets – one thinks of Coleridge's 'Dejection' or of
Keats's Odes – but *The Prelude* is surely the true ancestor of
all those subsequent works of art which, so to speak, coil back
upon themselves. The line includes *In Memoriam*, *The Wreck
of the Deutschland*, *Four Quartets*, much of the poetry of
Yeats and Wallace Stevens. In French literature one thinks of
Proust, of Gide, of Valéry. It is really a universal modern
theme, though with the increasing alienation of the artist the
stresses and strains have increased. Wordsworth could still just
rely on relatively enfeebled but surviving traditions of rhetoric;
he did not have to undergo, like Eliot, 'the intolerable wrestle/
with words and meanings' – at least not to the extent that the
struggle to articulate so exhausts the poet as to constrict the
area of his possible subject-matter. Nevertheless, *The Prelude*
points in that direction; having written it Wordsworth could
have said, in the words of *Ash Wednesday*:

> Consequently I rejoice, having to construct something
> Upon which to rejoice.

Both the beginning and the end of this double quest – the
voyage of self-discovery and the effort to articulate experience
– are perhaps those 'spots of time', those moments of intense
visionary experience, which form the poetic peaks of *The
Prelude* and of which Wordsworth wrote so movingly:

> So feeling comes in aid
> Of feeling, and diversity of strength
> Attends us, if but once we have been strong.
> Oh ! mystery of Man, from what a depth
> Proceed thy honours ! I am lost, but see
> In simple childhood something of the base
> On which thy greatness stands, but this I feel,
> That from thyself it is that thou must give,
> Else never canst receive. The days gone by

> Come back upon me from the dawn almost
> Of life : the hiding-places of my power
> Seem open; I approach, and then they close;
> I see by glimpses now; when age comes on,
> May scarcely see at all, and I would give
> While yet we may, as far as words can give,
> A substance and a life to what I feel :
> I would enshrine the spirit of the past
> For future restoration.

Again, one has only to recall Hopkins's concern with inscape, Joyce's concern with his epiphanies, Eliot's concern with his moments of reality, to see the modern relevance of *The Prelude*. Since I have argued the case elsewhere, I would only add here that Wordsworth seems to me to have been more successful than most in satisfactorily relating these visionary experiences to the full range and body of human experience.

For body and range there are in *The Prelude*; it is by no means so convoluted and introverted a poem as my account of it so far may have suggested. It is also outward-looking; it embraces the variety and solidity of social existence. The world of *The Prelude* is not just the world of the mind communing with Nature; it is also the world of the university, the metropolis and the arena of power and politics. Wordsworth's city is, in one aspect, distinctively modern; it is the city seen as inferno. One thinks of the Paris of Baudelaire or the London of *The Waste Land*. Yet while this is the main stress it is not the only one; Wordsworth's vision is more balanced and comprehensive. He also evokes the variety and vivacity of city life; it contains, but is more than, Hell; in this Wordsworth's London is perhaps more akin to the Dublin of James Joyce than to any other. As to politics, his anguished swing from revolutionary idealism to the despair produced by the tyranny that followed – nowhere could we find a more prophetic paradigm of the states of mind of so many modern liberals. Wordsworth knew upon his pulses that process whereby utopian ideology is corrupted and corroded by the appetite for power. He knew how weak a defence reason might be in the political jungle; hence his growing conservatism and his praise in the

1850 version of the 'genius of Burke'. Beyond even this, underlying his change of political heart, Wordsworth knew the in-
adequacy of the reason – abstracted as a faculty from the whole
human psyche – to deal with experience :

> Thus I fared,
> Dragging all passions, notions, shapes of faith,
> Like culprits to the bar, suspiciously
> Calling the mind to establish in plain day
> Her titles and her honours, now believing,
> Now disbelieving, endlessly perplex'd
> With impulse, motive, right and wrong, the ground
> Of moral obligation, what the rule
> And what the sanction, till, demanding *proof*,
> And seeking it in everything, I lost
> All feeling of conviction, and, in fine,
> Sick, wearied out with contrarieties,
> Yielded up moral questions in despair.

In this description of mental crisis, one notices the climactic
force of 'Sick, wearied out with contrarieties'. For underlying
every aspect of the poem is the Wordsworthian variant of the
perennial and universal problem of the One and the Many, the
tension between the single experiencing mind and the multiplicity of what is experienced. The basic values asserted by
Wordsworth are those of unity, integrity, wholeness. Unity of
the mind with itself, of the present self with the plurality of all
one's past selves – this is what dictates his quest for identity.
Unity of the mind with Nature he had already expressed in
some famous lines of 'Tintern Abbey' :

> And I have felt
> A presence that disturbs me with the joy
> Of elevated thoughts; a sense sublime
> Of something far more deeply interfused,
> Whose dwelling is the light of setting suns,
> And the round ocean and the living air,

And the blue sky, and in the mind of man
A motion and a spirit, that impels
All thinking things, all objects of all thought,
And rolls through all things.

This experience he extends in *The Prelude,* in a passage which
meditates upon the transfiguring effect of moonlight on the
landscape around Mount Snowdon :

                    it appear'd to me
The perfect image of a mighty Mind,
Of one that feeds upon infinity,
That is exalted by an underpresence,
The sense of God, or whatso'er is dim
Or vast in its own being, above all
One function of such a mind had Nature there
Exhibited by putting forth, and that
With circumstance most awful and sublime,
That domination which she oftentimes
Exerts upon the outward face of things,
So moulds them, and endues, abstracts, combines,
Or by abrupt and unhabitual influence
Doth make one object to impress itself
Upon all others, and pervade them so
That even the grossest minds must see and hear
And cannot chuse but feel. The Power which these
Acknowledge when thus moved, which Nature thus
Thrusts forth upon the senses, is the express
Resemblance, in the fulness of its strength
Made visible, a genuine counterpart
And Brother of the glorious faculty
Which higher minds bear with them as their own.
That is the very spirit in which they deal
With all the objects of the universe;
They from their native selves can send abroad
Like transformation, for themselves create
A like existence, and, when'er it is
Created for them, catch it by an instinct;
Them the enduring and the transient both
Serve to exalt; they build up greatest things
From least suggestions, ever on the watch,

> Willing to work and to be wrought upon,
> They need not extraordinary calls
> To rouze them, in a world of life they live,
> By sensible impressions not enthrall'd,
> But quicken'd, rouz'd, and made thereby more fit
> To hold communion with the invisible world.

The creative force thus manifested in Nature has its dim analogies in all of us, even in 'the grossest minds'. But Wordsworth is mainly concerned to stress the corresponding creative force in the 'higher' mind of the poet, concerned as he is with the reconciliation of opposites ('the enduring and the transient'), himself caught up in the reciprocity of this process ('willing to work and to be wrought upon'). One result of this process is, of course, *The Prelude* itself; in seeking to articulate, order and interpret his own experience Wordsworth creates an aesthetic counterpart to that sense of unity-beneath-diversity which he knew to be part of every aspect of our lives, something which must be enduringly relevant to us because it is inherent in the very way in which we are able to experience anything at all.

SELECT BIBLIOGRAPHY

Books and essays discussed in the introduction are not listed.

BOOKS

Joseph Warren Beach, *The Concept of Nature in Nineteenth-Century English Poetry* (Macmillan, 1936). Like Beatty's book, an important discussion of Wordsworth's eighteenth-century dimension.

H. W. Garrod, *Wordsworth: Lectures and Essays,* 2nd ed. (Oxford, 1927). Less valuable now, than it was in its time, for its contribution to knowledge about the composition of *The Prelude*, and Wordsworth's Godwinist phase. But it remains important as a work of rare sympathy.

Jonathan Wordsworth, *The Music of Humanity* (Nelson, 1969). This study of 'The Ruined Cottage' is inevitably a study of *The Prelude*'s origins. It sees Wordsworth as a tragic artist, with deep insight into 'emotions not his own'.

F. M. Todd, *Politics and the Poet* (Methuen, 1957). An important study of a vital area of Wordsworth's intellectual life. Todd documents Wordsworth's so-called 'apostasy' and argues that much of the change was made under the tutelage of his poetic faith.

Mary Moorman, *William Wordsworth: A Biography,* 2 vols. (Clarendon Press, 1957–65; O.U.P. paperback, 1968). The writing of *The Prelude* is naturally a part of Wordsworth's biography, and Mrs Moorman's books are massively illuminating, both in data and commentary – and a beautiful biography.

CHAPTERS AND ESSAYS

Newton P. Stallknecht, 'Wordsworth and the Quality of Man'.

Josephine Miles, 'Wordsworth and the Mind's Excursive Power'. Both in *Major English Romantic Poets: A Symposium in Reappraisal*, ed. C. D. Thorpe, C. Baker and B. Weaver (Carbondale, Ill., 1957). Stallknecht discusses Wordsworth as a source of democratic feeling, linking his influence with Haldane, Bergson, Pascal, Santayana, Schweitzer, White-head, Alexander and Sartre. Josephine Miles writes of the philosophical suppleness of Wordsworth's blank verse and diction.

Colin Clarke, 'Landscape in the Poetry of Wordsworth', *Durham University Journal*, n.s., XI (Mar 1950).

John F. Danby, 'The "Nature" of Wordsworth', *Cambridge Journal,* VII (Apr 1954). Both of these pursue the way Wordsworth took 'nature poetry' into new dimensions, after Akenside. Professor Danby's essay, which appears also in his influential book *The Simple Wordsworth* (Routledge, 1960), contains excellent readings of 'There was a boy' and 'Simplon Pass'.

Edwin Morgan, 'A Prelude to *The Prelude*', *Essays in Criticism,* V (Oct 1955). Notable readings of the 'dedication' in book IV and the love of shepherds passage in book VIII.

F. R. Leavis, 'Wordsworth', *Revaluation* (Chatto & Windus, 1936).

H. Lindenberger, 'The Reception of *The Prelude*', *Bulletin of the New York Public Library,* LXIV (Apr 1960).

Zera S. Fink, 'Wordsworth and the English Republican Tradition', *Journal of English and Germanic Philology,* XLVII (1948). Explains Wordsworth's attraction to the Girondin cause by his, and their, attraction to Milton, Sydney, Harrington.

Basil Willey, 'Postscript on Wordsworth and the Locke Trad-ition', in *The Seventeenth Century Background* (Chatto & Windus, 1934), and ' "Nature" in Wordsworth', in *The Eighteenth Century Background* (Chatto & Windus, 1940) – both in Peregrine Books; and 'A note on Stoicism' and

'Naturam Sequere', in *The English Moralists* (Chatto & Windus, 1964; Methuen, 1965).

Stephen C. Gill, 'Wordsworth's "Never Failing Principle of Joy" ', *Journal of English Literary History*, XXXIV (June 1967). Asks, very pertinently, whether it was.

S. G. Dunn, 'A Note on Wordsworth's Metaphysical System', English Association, *Essays and Studies*, XVIII (1932). Studies Wordsworth's faith in 'the life of things' from its *Lyrical Ballads* origins, through *The Prelude* to *The Excursion*, and constructs with great authority the unwritten argument of the entire *Recluse*.

M. H. Abrams, '*The Prelude* as a Portrait of the Artist', and Jonathan Wordsworth, 'The Climbing of Snowdon', in the latter's *Bicentenary Wordsworth Studies* (Ithaca, N.Y., and London : Cornell U.P., 1970). Abrams discusses, with reference to Proust, Augustine, Mill and others, the originality of Wordsworth's form, and 'the power of his evangel'. Jonathan Wordsworth continues brilliantly the debate begun by Hartman's essay on the *via naturaliter negativa*.

BIBLIOGRAPHIES

The simplest approach is to consult J. V. Logan, *Wordworthian Criticism: A Guide and Bibliography* (Ohio State University, 1947), followed by E. F. Henley and D. H. Stam, *Wordsworthian Criticism 1945–1964: An Annotated Bibliography* (New York Public Library, 1965). For later work, consult the continuing bibliography 'The Romantic Movement' in the *Philological Quarterly* until 1965 and in *English Language Notes* from September 1965 onwards. There is an excellent discussion of modern trends in criticism, until 1964, in the critical bibliographies of Geoffrey Hartman's *Wordsworth's Poetry: 1787–1814*. It is well worth consulting the Wordsworth entry by Ernest Bernbaum and J. V. Logan in the revised edition of T. M. Raysor's *English Romantic Poets: A Review of Research* (M.L.A., 1956) for evaluative comments and orientation.

NOTES ON CONTRIBUTORS

WALTER BAGEHOT (1826–77). Economist, journalist, constitutionalist. His book *The English Constitution* (1867) is the classic interpretation, much studied by modern parliamentarians. Co-editor, with Hutton, of *The National Review*.

JONATHAN BISHOP is Professor of English at Cornell University, and the author of *Emerson on the Soul* (1964), a discriminating retrieval of the psychological Emerson.

COLIN CLARKE is Reader in English in the School of English and American Studies at the University of East Anglia, and author of *River of Dissolution: D. H. Lawrence and English Romanticism* (1969).

SAMUEL TAYLOR COLERIDGE (1772–1834). 'The rapt One, of the godlike forehead' (Wordsworth).

HELEN DARBISHIRE, who died in 1961, was a great editor, notably of De Quincey's criticism, Milton's poems, the *Paradise Lost* MSS., and, pre-eminently, of Wordsworth : the *Poems in Two Volumes*, the *Poetical Works*, the *Journals of Dorothy Wordsworth*, and *The Prelude*.

GEOFFREY H. HARTMAN is Professor of English and Comparative Literature at Yale. His other works are *The Unmediated Vision: An Interpretation of Wordsworth, Hopkins, Rilke and Valéry* (1954), *André Malraux* (1960), and *Beyond Formalism: Literary Essays* (1970). *Wordsworth's Poetry, 1787–1814* (1964) won the Christian Gauss Award in 1965.

W. J. HARVEY was Professor of English at the Queen's University, Belfast, until his death in 1967. Author of *The Art of George Eliot* (1961) and *Character and the Novel* (1965). He was a co-editor, with F. W. Bateson, of *Essays in Criticism*.

RICHARD HOLT HUTTON (1826–97), theologian and man of letters, was joint editor of the *Spectator* and of the *National Review*. The author of a biography of Newman, *Cardinal Newman* (1891), and of *Essays, Theological and Literary* (1871), Hutton had the most scientific mind among the nineteenth-century critics.

CHARLES LAMB (1775–1834), 'the frolic and the gentle'. Clerk, essayist, poet, schoolfriend of Coleridge, and of Wordsworth from 1797. The best-loved man of his age, and the best critic of the nineteenth century.

ROBERT LANGBAUM is Professor of English and American Literature at the University of Virginia, and author of *The Poetry of Experience* (1957), *The Gayety of Vision: A Study of Isak Dinesen's Art* (1964), and *The Modern Spirit* (1970).

ÉMILE LEGOUIS (1861–1937) was Professor of English at the Sorbonne, and co-author, with Louis Cazamian, of *A History of English Literature* (1924).

ELLEN DOUGLASS LEYBURN is Professor of English at Agnes Scott College, Georgia. Her *Satiric Allegory: Mirror of Man* (1956) is a study of five modes of allegory in literature from Aesop to Orwell, and especially the two Samuel Butlers and Swift.

JAMES R. MACGILLIVRAY is Professor of English at the University of Toronto. He is a Wordsworth scholar of repute, and the author of *John Keats: A Bibliography and Reference Guide* (1949).

WALTER HORATIO PATER (1839–94), critic. An associate of the 'Pre-Raphaelites' who practised, in his essays on the Renaissance (1873) and his *Appreciations* (1889), a highly expressionistic style of criticism.

MORSE PECKHAM is Professor of English at the University of South Carolina, and author of *Beyond the Tragic Vision: The Quest for Identity in the Nineteenth Century* (1962), *Victorian Revolutionaries* (1970), and three essays on the theory of Romanticism.

HENRY CRABB ROBINSON (1775–1867). Diarist and traveller. Special correspondent of *The Times* during the Napoleonic Wars. He met almost everybody of literary consequence in early nineteenth-century Europe and was a notable go-between for the literatures of England and Germany.

INDEX

Akenside, Mark 24

Arnold, Matthew 14, 25, 182, 237–8; 'Memorial Verses' 17, 25; *Essays in Criticism* 20

Bagehot, Walter; 'Hartley Coleridge' 55–7

Baudelaire, Charles 241

Beatty, Arthur 19, 22, 24, 29n

Beaumont, Sir George and Lady 40, 41, 42, 45, 47

Beaupuy, Michel 18

Beddoes, T. L. 15

Bentham, Jeremy 23

Berkeley, George 132n, 159

Bishop, J. 26; 'Wordsworth and the "Spots of Time" ' 26, 134–54

Blake, William 94, 95, 175, 183, 209, 219

Boehme, Jakob 22, 23, 209

Borderers, The 37n, 101, 210

Bosanquet, Bernard 170

'Boy of Windermere, The' 64, 136–8

Bradley, A. C. 19, 20, 22, 25, 27; 'Wordsworth' 19, 72n; 'The Long Poem in the Age of Wordsworth' 26; *English Poetry and German*

Philosophy in the Age of Wordsworth 29n

British Quarterly 13, 14

Brooke, Stopford A. 20, 29n

Browning, Robert 12

Bunyan, John 239

Burke, Edmund 73, 242

Butler, Bishop 20

Byron, Lord 14, 22, 59

Carlyle, Thomas; *Sartor Resartus* 13

Carter, John 51, 51n

Chase, Thomas 12

Chateaubriand, F. R. 66, 76

Chaucer 177–8

Clark, Lord 159

Clarke, C. C. 24, 25; 'Nature's Education of Man' 22; *Romantic Paradox* 24, 155–74

Clough, A. H. 14

Coleridge, S. T. 23, 25, 41, 42, 55, 58, 61, 94, 104, 110–12, 147, 182, 215–16, 240; *The Prelude* addressed to 15, 81–3, 100, 105, 108–9, 111; and 'The Recluse' 20, 35, 50–1n, 100–1, 105; and *Lyrical Ballads* 103; 'To William Wordsworth' 15, 43–5; extracts from

Coleridge, S. T.—*cont.*
    letters 37–9, 47–9; *Table
    Talk* 49–50, 225; *Osorio*
    101; *Biographia Literaria*
    114–15n, 116; 'Kubla Khan'
    213; 'Religious Musings'
    227; *The Friend* 228,
    232–3; on Imagination
    212–13, 219
Condillac, Étienne de 23
Cookson, Elizabeth 51
Cooper, Thomas 12, 28n
Cottle, Joseph 101
Cowper, William 211
Crabbe, George 211

Danby, J. F. 25
Darbishire, H. 15, 19, 20,
    36, 99; 'Wordsworth's
    Prelude' 81–98
Davie, Donald 226
Day, Thomas; *Sandford and
    Merton* 110
De Quincey, Thomas 39,
    109, 112, 202
'Descriptive Sketches' 24
de Selincourt, E. 15, 28n,
    81, 82, 99, 157, 159
de Vere, Aubrey 51
'Discharged Soldier, The'
    37n, 90, 136–9, 147,
    155–8
Donne, John 198, 203

Eclectic Review 13, 45, 46n
Edinburgh Review 28n, 46,
    46n
Eliot, George 237
Eliot, T. S. 25, 237, 241;

The Cocktail Party 210;
    Four Quartets 210, 240;
    Ash Wednesday 240; *The
    Waste Land* 241
Empson, W. 19, 237; 'Sense
    in *The Prelude*' 19, 123,
    132n
Erdman, David 110, 115n
'Essay upon Epitaphs' 224–5
'Evening Walk, An' 24
Everett, Barbara 15
Examiner, The 12
Excursion, The 11, 15, 16, 20,
    23, 24, 28n, 35, 37n, 45–8,
    49–50, 55, 159–60, 162, 233,
    236n; 'Prospectus' 37,
    94–5, 173; 'Preface' 113;
    see also 'The Ruined
    Cottage' *and* THE PEDLAR
    and THE SOLITARY
Existentialism 23, 239

Fancy 39, 212
Ferry, David; *The Limits of
    Mortality* 19, 27
Finch, John Alban 36n
Forster, E. M. 211
'Fragment of a Gothic Tale'
    167
French Revolution 72–6,
    141–4, 183, 214

Gainsborough, Thomas 66
Gallie, W. B.; 'Is *The Prelude*
    a Philosophical Poem?' 21
Gautier, Théophile 66
Gentleman's Magazine 12, 14
Gide, André 240

Godwin, William 110, 196, 203

Goethe, J. W. von 12, 61, 216; *Dichtung und Wahrheit* 13; *Faust* 70, 217

Graham's Magazine 11

Gray, Thomas; 'Elegy' 117

Hardy, Thomas 237

Hartley, David 21, 22, 23, 218, 225, 228; *Observations on Man* 227

Hartman, G. 19, 231; 'Wordsworth and the *Via Naturaliter Negativa*' 25, 175–94; *Wordsworth's Poetry 1787–1814* 25, 28, 236n

Harvey, W. J. 26; 'Vision and Medium in *The Prelude*' 195–211; 'Retrospect and Prospect' 237–44

Havens, R. D. 19; *The Mind of a Poet* 21, 29n, 147, 154n

Hazlitt, Walter 12

Hegel, G. W. F. 23, 92, 95

Heidegger, M. 23

Hirsch, E. D.; *Wordsworth and Schelling* 23

Hobbes, Thomas 167

'Home at Grasmere' *see* 'The Recluse'

Homer 204, 206

Hopkins, G. M. 198, 240, 241

Hugo, Victor 66

Husserl, Edmund 23

Hutchinson, Sara 47, 81

Hutton, R. H. 17; 'The Genius of Wordsworth' 58–65

'I wandered lonely' 71

Imagination 116, 119, 149–51, 168, 182, 184–93, 207, 213, 215–17, 230

Jeffrey, Lord 15

Johnson, Dr Samuel 87, 159, 198–9

Jones, H. J. F.; *The Egotistical Sublime* 19, 27

Jones, Robert 149–50

Joyce, James 237, 241

Kant, Immanuel 23, 214–16

Keats, John 16, 213, 218, 240; 'St Agnes' Eve' 67

Kierkegaard, S. 23

Klopstock, F. G. 104

Kroeber, Karl; *Romantic Narrative Art* 26

Lamb, Charles 15, 46n, 48, 49

Landor, W. S. 48, 149

Langbaum, Robert; *The Poetry of Experience* 24; 'The Evolution of Soul in Wordsworth's Poetry' 218–36

Lawrence, D. H. 237

Leavis, F. R. 226

Legouis, Émile; *La Jeunesse de William Wordsworth* 18, 73–8, 149; *William Wordsworth and Annette Vallon* 18, 28n

Lenin, V. I. 23

Leyburn, E. D. 19; 'Recurrent Words in *The Prelude*' 20, 116–33

Lindenberger, H.; *On Wordsworth's Prelude* 26, 208–9
'Lines left upon a seat in a yew-tree' 77
Locke, John 22, 23, 219–20, 223–8; *Essay Concerning Human Understanding* 218, 224, 229
Louis XVI 142
Louvet de Courbay, Jean Baptiste 142–3
Lowell, J. R. 14, 28n
Lucretius 48
'Lucy Gray' 230
Lyrical Ballads 39, 100, 101, 103, 118–19, 182, 194n; *see also individual entries*

Macaulay, Lord 11, 26
MacGillivray, J. R. 16, 36, 40n; 'The Three Forms of *The Prelude*' 99–115
Mann, Thomas 237
Manuscripts 81–2, 88; B 28n, 35, 37n, 102, 161–2; JJ 105, 115n; M 112; U 105, 109; V 106, 109, 168–9; W 109, 111, 147, 154n; Alfoxden Note Book 164
Marx, Karl, 23
Miles, Josephine 24, 29n, 116
Mill, J. S. 12, 14; *Auto-biography* 17, 237
Milton, John 16, 38, 50, 60, 87, 181, 198–200, 203–4; *Paradise Lost* 167, 177, 195–7, 234; *Samson Agonistes* 197, 203

Montgomery, James 15, 46n
Moorman, Mary 36, 37n
Morley, John 25, 29n

New English Dictionary 88, 89, 123, 126–8
Nietzsche, F. 23
North American Review 12

'Ode, Intimations of Immortality' 71, 222, 230
'Ode to Duty' 23
'Old Cumberland Beggar, The' 77

Pantheism 21, 93, 175
Pater, Walter 16, 19; *Appreciations* 66–72
Peckham, Morse; *Beyond the Tragic Vision*, 16; 'A Post-Enlightenment Imagination' 212–17
PEDLAR, THE (*The Excursion*) 102, 103, 108, 158, 160–4, 230, 233, 235n; *for* 'The Pedlar' *see* 'The Ruined Cottage'
Peter Bell 92
Petrarch 13
Plato 125
Platonism 23, 217, 222–4, 227, 235
Poe, Edgar Allan 12
Poems in Two Volumes, The 15
Poole, Thomas 38
Pope, Alexander 55, 117–18
Pottle, F. A. 117
Potts, Abbie F.; *Wordsworth's Prelude: A Study of its Literary Form* 26, 27

Pre-Raphaelitism 14
Price, Bonamy 159
Prospective Review 13, 14
Proust, Marcel 229, 237, 240

Rader, Melvyn 19, 22, 29n
Read, Sir Herbert; *Wordsworth* 18; *The True Voice of Feeling* 23
'Recluse, The' (the uncompleted project) 35–6, 37–42, 45, 47–9, 51, 75, 81, 100–1, 105, 108, 113, 225; ('Home at Grasmere', published as *The Recluse*) 35, 39, 40n, 170, 173, 195, 201, 230
Reed, Mark; *Wordsworth: The Chronology of the Early Years* 36n
Rembrandt van Rijn 56
'Resolution and Independence' 67, 69, 170, 230–1
Reynolds, Joshua 66
Rilke, R. M. 19
Robespierre, Maximilien 142, 144
Robinson, H. Crabb 14, 28n, 49; *Diary* 45–6
Rousseau, J.–J. 66
'Ruined Cottage, The' 28n, 35, 49, 101–4, 108, 114, 155, 158–64, 171, 172
Ruskin, John 12, 28n, 201

'Salisbury Plain' 101
Saul, L. S. 148, 154n
Schelling, F. W. J. von 21, 23

Scott, Sir Walter 45
Sénancour, Étienne Pivert de 66
Shakespeare, William 39, 71, 87, 190, 212
Sharp, Richard 38, 39n, 40
Shattuck, Roger 229
Shelley, P. B. 14, 59, 66, 68, 196
Sheppard E. 148, 154n
'Simplon Pass' 149–52, 183–93
Smith, Nowell C.; *Wordsworth's Literary Criticism* 132n
'Snowdon' 89, 111, 141, 147, 234–5, 243–4
Snyder, T. R. 148, 154n
SOLITARY, THE (*The Excursion*) 87
Southcote, Joanna 22
Spenser, Edmund 181
Spinoza, Baruch de 23, 115n
Stallknecht, N. P. 19, 22; *Strange Seas of Thought* 23, 29n
Stephen, Leslie 17; 'Wordsworth's Ethics' 20, 29n
Stevens, Wallace 240
Stewart, J. A. 23
Swedenborg, Emanuel 22
Swinburne, A. C. 17, 19; *Miscellanies* 20

'Tables Turned, The' 25
Tait's Magazine 13
Taylor, Rev. William 143–4
Tennyson, Lord 15, 62, 202, 238; *In Memoriam* 11, 240
Thomson, James 24, 237
'Thorn, The' 230

'Tintern Abbey' 16, 23,
    56–7, 94, 103, 104, 108,
    114, 164–5, 229–30, 242
Tobin, James 37
'Two April Mornings, The'
    71, 231, 233

Valéry, Paul 240
Vallon, Annette 18, 141
Vermeer, Jan 159

Walsh, G. 101, 114n
Wedgwood, Thomas 110–11
Whitehead, A. N. 20, 29n
Willey, Basil 22, 134
Wordsworth, Christopher
    (Bishop of Lincoln,
    nephew of W.W.); *Memoirs*

of William Wordsworth 12,
    114n, 148
Wordsworth, Dora (daughter
    of W.W.) 49
Wordsworth, Dorothy (sister
    of W.W.) 47, 49, 81, 82,
    102, 215; *Journal* 101, 104,
    109
Wordsworth, Gordon 81
Wordsworth, John (brother of
    W.W.) 41, 42
Wordsworth, Jonathan;
    Bicentenary Wordsworth Studies
    36n
Wordsworth, Mary (wife of
    W.W.) 100, 231
Wrangham, Francis 109

Yeats, W. B. 240